AF538261

Where Angels Tread

Stanley Durland

Indian Stream Republic, Ltd.

Arlington, Massachusetts

First printing, 1998
Printed in the United States of America

Library of Congress Catalog Card Number 97-76955
Durland, Stanley Warren
Where Angels Tread by Stanley Durland

ISBN 0-9661118-0-X

Dedication

For Tanya

Contents

Preface

The two books in this collection -- *Angels We Have Heard on High* and *The Content of Consciousness* -- present a definitive account of Twentieth Century angels and their human listening posts. It is based on the private papers of Ruth Ebright Finley, the famous *Joan* of Stewart Edward White's *The Unobstructed Universe*, and its pages present the work of that illustrious pair who in my opinion were the finest, most dedicated, and most reliable mediums of all time -- Mrs. Finley herself and her colleague and collaborator, Elizabeth Calvert White, known to the multitude who love her simply as Betty.

This volume also sees itself as siding with Balaam's angel, shown on the cover, in a war between two worlds. World No. 1, the world of standard science, was created by Einstein and his fellow cosmologists. It is not a nice world. It contains neither God nor Heaven, and it has made every second professor an atheist and every second atheist a cynic.

Marshaling its forces against Einstein's world is the world of little children. It is a nice world, and there are angels in it. It is the world of young innocents for whom stars are peepholes into Heaven; whose instincts tell them that children like themselves are immortal, that God is in His Heaven and all's right with His world. The children are right. They are always right, and we are always wrong.

This volume presents an unusual account of this second world. Read on and you will become something of an expert on contemporary angels. To say that the biographies in Book I are unusual is to understate the case. They would be incredible except for the simple fact that they are true accounts. These character sketches include both the people who produced the material for this volume as well as the angels who trained them. It is indeed a definitive account of angels at work in the Twentieth Century. You will not want to miss it.

The material for Book II was found as a sheaf of sitting notes in the personal papers left by Mrs. Finley when she died. Never before published, it was intended as a sequel to White's book, for which Mrs. Finley was the medium, and which was a World War II best seller. Now that this its sequel is in print after a wait of half a century, perhaps it can still serve its original purpose.

There is much left to be said on how this material fits into the mainstream of modern thought, but I have not troubled the reader with it for now. So just relax and enjoy yourself. Perhaps your personal angel will be looking over your shoulder. I know mine will.

Stanley Durland
1998

Acknowledgments

First of all I would like to express my gratitude to William and Margaret Dague for the sense of vision that prompted them to donate the private papers of their aunt, Ruth Finley, to her alma mater, the University of Akron, thereby rescuing a national treasure from obscurity, and to their generosity in making those papers available for this study; next, I would like to express my deep indebtedness to my faithful colleague, E.W. (Bill) Dykes, retired architect of Canton, Ohio, an indefatigable psychic researcher, for his patient effort in preparing the papers for archival, and not incidentally for discovering among them the sitting notes for *The Content of Consciousness*, which is what this book is all about; then to Kenneth C. Cramer, retired Dartmouth College archivist, for his generosity in sharing with me the records concerning Richard Nelville Hall, Dartmouth celebrity, World War I hero, and consort of angels; also to my wife, Tanya, who suffered through many a vacant stare when I could think of nothing but THE BOOK, and whose forbearance contributed materially to its execution; to Alfred North Whitehead, for various borrowings, attributed and not attributed; to Martin Gardner, vigorous and charming foe of psychic research, for his defense, in *The Whys of a Philosophical Scrivener*, of William James's "transmission theory" of immortality, not to mention the decades during which he kept me royally entertained with his column in Scientific American; to Martin Ebon, staunch proponent of psychic research, for various unattributed borrowings from *They Knew the Unknown* (The World Publishing Co., 1971); to Douglas T. Ross of SofTech, for teaching me to think in terms of successive layers of abstraction; to Laura D. Weeks for pointing out the presence in Steiner's Theosophical colony in Switzerland of the Russian symbolist poet Andrei Bely; to Michael Servetus, 16th Century Spanish theologian, heretic and martyr, who dared to challenge Church doctrine in an age when it was as much as a man's life was worth (it cost him his), and to the members of the Wednesday morning Men's Breakfast at Grace Chapel in Lexington, Massachusetts, who have listened to my own unbridled heresies with Amazing Grace; and finally to Richard Hall himself, arch soldier of the spirit, whose lively prompting rescued *The Content of Consciousness* from oblivion, and who has never been more alive than since that dark night in 1915 when, at the front line in France, nearing the top of Hartmanns-Weilerkopf on a mission of mercy, he encountered the enemy shell through whose ghastly embrace he was ushered into eternity, and by virtue of which he was recruited for a species of war work beyond his wildest imaginings; and to his associates, that band of intrepid angels, whose work has added in ways unfathomable to the richness of the materials underlying this book, and whom I cannot hope ever in this world to repay, so hopelessly in their debt am I.

I would like to thank Harvard University's Houghton Library and also Bay James for permission to use the photograph of William James and of his Cambridge, Massachusetts, library. Thanks also to

Simon & Schuster for permission to use excerpts from the writing of Theodore Roosevelt. Thanks also to AFS Intercultural Programs, Inc., for the courtesy of using excerpts from *Friends of France*, and to their archivist, Eleanora Golobic, whose diligence led to the unearthing of the original photographs of Richard Hall taken in France during World War I. A special thanks in absentia to Gustave Doré for his absolutely marvelous rendition of the angel that prompted Balaam's donkey to acquire the knack of human speech at a critical juncture in her career as beast of burden. My special thanks to Laura D. Weeks for reading the entire manuscript, including a projected third book that ended up on the cutting room floor, but for which one has hopes for the future; and to Jana Durland Howland for the sagacity to suggest putting the angel book ahead of the model, thus saving generations of readers from falling asleep before they get to the really good stuff.

Many are the errors now corrected owing to the gracious attention of these and other reviewers. The errors remaining are of course my own.

Stanley Durland

Picture Credits

PICTURE CREDITS

Cover : Angel from "Balaam and his Donkey" by Gustave Doré. "Balaam got up in the morning, saddled his donkey and went with the princes of Moab. But God was very angry when he went, and the angel of the Lord stood in the road to oppose him." Numbers 22: 21-22. Old Testament, New International Version. From *ANGELS: 100 Engravings by Gustave Doré,* by Dan Malan. (Malan Classical Enterprises, St. Louis, 1996.)

PHOTOGRAPHS

1. Ruth Ebright Finley as a young woman. Courtesy of William E. and Margaret B. Dague.
2. Ruth Ebright Finley, 1929. Courtesy of William E. and Margaret B. Dague.
3. Surgeon General L.S. Ebright. *The Army and Navy Magazine,* Vol. III, No. 13, September 16, 1893, page 8. Courtesy of William E. and Margaret B. Dague.
4. Robert Emmet Finley as a young man. Courtesy of William E. and Margaret B. Dague.
5. William James. By permission of the Houghton Library, Harvard University, and Bay James. Houghton Library citation "WJ and Mrs. Montgomery Sears: pfMS Am 1092".
6. Richard Nelville Hall. Courtesy of Louis Hall and E.W. Dykes.
7. The library of William James at 95 Irving Street, Cambridge, Massachusetts. By permission of the Houghton Library, Harvard University, and Bay James. Houghton Library citation "Library at 95 Irving St.: Am 1092".
8. Dr. Leonidas S. Ebright, father of Mary Ebright Dague and Ruth Ebright Finley. Courtesy of William E. and Margaret B. Dague.
9. Mrs. Leonora Piper. By permission of the Houghton Library, Harvard University, and Bay James. Houghton Library citation "WJ and Mrs. Piper: pfMS Am 1094, box 1". An account of

James's considerable study of Mrs. Piper is presented starting on page 491 of *The Jameses* by R.W.B. Lewis.

10. William James participating in a seance with a Mrs. Walden. By permission of the Houghton Library, Harvard University, and Bay James. Houghton Library citation "WJ and Mrs. Walden: pfMS Am 1092".
11. Richard Nelville Hall in Mollau, Alsace, 1915. From the album of A. Piatt Andrew, founder of the American Field Service, in which Hall served. Courtesy of AFS Intercultural Programs, Inc.
12. Richard Nelville hall and his ambulance. (Hall's machine is on the left.) Place and date are uncertain. But there exists a photograph of Hall taken with a group of American Field Service drivers, and it shows him wearing the same uniform and leather puttees. The latter photograph was taken in July, 1915, at St. Maurice sur Moselle, Alsace. This gives a probable place and date for the ambulance photograph shown. Courtesy of AFS Intercultural Programs, Inc.
13. The remains of Hall's ambulance after it was struck by a German shell. The photograph was taken near the dressing station at Thomannsplatz on Hartmanns-Weilerkopf, Alsace, December 25, 1915, the day Hall was killed. Courtesy of AFS Intercultural Programs, Inc.
14. Stewart Edward White. Courtesy of E.W. Dykes.
15. Betty (Elizabeth Calvert White). Courtesy of E.W. Dykes.
16. Note from Stewart Edward White. Courtesy of E.W. Dykes.
17. Betty and her dogs. Courtesy of E.W. Dykes.
18. Betty White with her sewing. Courtesy of E.W. Dykes.
19. Stewart Edward White. Courtesy of E.W. Dykes.
20. Ruth Ebright Finley when quite young. Courtesy of William E. and Margaret B. Dague.
21. Ruth and Emmet Finley, Hastings-on-Hudson, June, 1922. Courtesy of William E. and Margaret B. Dague.
22. (from left) William Ebright Dague, Ruth Finley, Emmet Finley, and Margaret Beazley Dague. The end of the Dagues' honeymoon, September, 1948. At the Finleys' home in Hempstead, Long

Island, New York. Courtesy of E.W. Dykes, from a photograph provided by William E. and Margaret B. Dague.

23. Ruth E. Finley. Courtesy of William E. and Margaret B. Dague.
24. (from left) William E. Dague as a young boy with Julia B. Ebright, Ruth Finley's mother. Courtesy of William E. and Margaret B. Dague.
25. The marriage of Margaret Cameron and Max Kilvert. June 12, 1929. Courtesy of William E. and Margaret B. Dague.
26. Emmet Finley. Courtesy of William E. and Margaret B. Dague.
27. E.W. Dykes. Courtesy of E.W. Dykes.

Book I. Angels We Have Heard On High

Chapter 1. Angel Voices

THE material on which this collection is based is so unusual that it calls for an explanation. It is material produced by psychic mediums, and it is undoubtedly the finest of its kind, certainly in the Twentieth Century, possibly the finest of all time. None of it has been published before. It has been sitting in the long-neglected private papers of author Stewart Edward White's favorite medium. These papers -- university archives now -- enable us to examine the work of not just one but three super mediums whose combined efforts have given us a unique insight into the secrets of the ages. *Where Angels Tread* details those secrets and presents also an unexpected bonus: a model of human consciousness constructed by angels, until now unpublished and unknown.

The undeniable accomplishments of these exquisitely talented mediums are best seen when contrasted to the failed ambitions of Theosophy, that precursor of the New Age described by Peter Washington in *Madame Blavatsky's Baboon*. Theosophy's leaders claimed mediumistic access to a Hidden Brotherhood of Masters and thus to an esoteric knowledge constituting the Secrets of the Ages. These claims appear to have been grossly inflated. Yet Theosophy reflected faithfully the spirit of the times and it attracted a wide audience, including many intellectual leaders. These included Oscar Wilde, W.B. Yeats, George Bernard Shaw, Frank Lloyd Wright, Katherine Mansfield, Aldous Huxley, and even the great Russian symbolist poet Andrei Bely (pseudonym of Boris Bugaev), who together with his wife Asia Turgenev joined Steiner's Theosophical colony in Switzerland. As for the Masters themselves, they were said to be secluded in a hidden monastery, God knows where; the search for them attracted many adventurers and it took them, now to Egypt, now to Tibet.

No one ever found the Masters. Madame Blavatsky -- Russian aristocrat, native of Dnepropetrovsk in the Ukraine, naturalized American citizen, a compulsive adventurer but immensely able, and finally, founder of the Theosophical Society -- Madame Blavatsky, as I say, claimed direct access to them in the seance room, but her mediumistic shenanigans, when publicly exposed, have undermined this claim. A pity, really. Her lifetime accomplishments were monumental, including as they did the reintroduction in the West of Eastern religious ideas. And her notions of a Hidden Brotherhood and an Esoteric Knowledge, while misplaced, were in essence right on the mark.

Madame Blavatsky's activities had a curious positive effect. They provided an effective smoke screen for related work that could only be accomplished outside the glare of public scrutiny. Thus while Theosophy was crusading in vain in the East, private Western mediums back home were, under their very noses as it were, establishing undeniable contact with a real-life counterpart of the Hidden Brotherhood. These mediums were few in number and they were a private lot, a sharp contrast to the bombast and pretentiousness of the others. The only one known to the public was Margaret Cameron, popular World War I author, whose automatic pencil produced *The Seven Purposes.* Tucked within this book are "The Twelve Lessons," a Twentieth Century re-statement of New Testament teaching, clothed in elevated language that touches the soul of the reader, and constituting a message direct from the Hidden Brotherhood if ever there was one. The book stands alone; Cameron produced no sequel.

Do good things come in threes? As was said, they do so here. There were then two others involved in this work, all friends, each considering that their combined efforts were of a piece.

Thus we have Betty White, wife of author Stewart Edward White, whose accomplishments were chronicled by her husband, but whose identity was not disclosed until after her death. While the gurus of alternative religion were propounding vain formulas for personal advancement, Betty embarked on the ancient practice of Christian mysticism under the tutelage of the Masters themselves, succeeding so spectacularly that her accomplishments rival those of the legendary Brother Lawrence, whose sense of the Presence of God was as acute in the Monastery kitchen as in the chapel. Betty's enraptured admirers suggested creating a cult based on her accomplishments; after all, wasn't everyone else doing so? But she would have none of it.

The final member of this triad of world-class performers also successfully preserved her anonymity while she lived. This was "Joan," the medium used by White to talk with Betty after her death, and his collaborator for *The Unobstructed Universe*, his World War II best seller. Joan was a well-known East Coast newspaperwoman and feminist named Ruth Finley. When she died she left papers disclosing a voluminous correspondence with White as well as a prize every archivist is dying to uncover. That prize is a mass of sitting notes with the deceased White in which is embodied the culmination of the work of these three super mediums: in short, a model of human consciousness intended as a sequel to *The Unobstructed Universe.*

These are the facts of the case. While the Theosophists were distracted in India and Tibet, the Hidden Masters were busy back home leaving a legacy any pilgrim worth his salt would give his (or her) life to uncover. The model is the one described in this book. The secret papers on which it is based have now been preserved in a university archive. The rest of this remarkable spiritual odyssey is available in the published works of the authors given above.

You will meet a lot of angels in this book. One of the most interesting is "Stephen," the communicator of *Our Unseen Guest* written by Ruth Finley and her husband immediately after World War I. He is identified in the Finley archives as Richard Hall, Dartmouth graduate and volunteer ambulance driver before he was killed by a German shell and thus ushered into angelhood. His identity has remained a secret until now.

You will also meet the archangel who masterminded the model, as well as two previous "divulgences," as she quaintly calls revelation, and discover that archangelhood does nothing to diminish the warmth and whimsy of human personality writ large. Once a Scotswoman from before the time of Shakespeare, she has left her imprint everywhere in these pages.

Ruth Finley's work as a medium is epochal beyond what mere words can describe. She was the official "receiving station" for a group of Invisibles whose work was intertwined with the world wars of this century, and whose philosophy was designed to explain those wars and ease mankind's entry into the next century and beyond. It is this group that I have called the real-life counterpart of the Hidden Brotherhood of Masters.

Three major "divulgences" (their word -- "revelations", as I have said, would have been more appropriate) were produced by this team, the Invisibles first preparing the text and subsequently dictating it to medium Finley. The first was *Our Unseen Guest.* In it the basic philosophy of the Invisible team was expounded -- a philosophy of consciousness in evolution. The second divulgence was published as *The Unobstructed Universe.* It is a description of the physics of the world inhabited by the Invisibles, dictated to Ruth Finley by Betty White, the recently deceased wife of White.

The third divulgence, which they named *The Content of Consciousness*, provides the material for *A Model of the Soul.* It was intended as the culmination of the three divulgences, but unfortunately has not been published until now. It is distinguished by a gestation period both arduous and long. The earliest mention of it in the archival correspondence was shortly after the publication of *Our Unseen Guest* in 1920. "Stephen," who dictated *Our Unseen Guest*, began at that time giving material for *The Content of Consciousness* to the Finleys, Ruth in trance as the "receiving" station, her husband Emmet taking notes in long hand. But Emmet Finley grew weary of the task and refused to continue it. After Betty White died in 1939 there was renewed talk about the new book, Betty promising her husband that when the time was ripe, this third divulgence would be given.

After White's death in 1946 the interest heated up and an effective working team was put together. Its members were as follows: White dictating; Ruth Finley, medium, receiving; and taking notes, Emmet Finley and Harwood White, brother of the author, who had come East expressly for this purpose.

I say, "taking notes." Understanding the notes states the case better. Actually, the bulk of the sessions was tape recorded and transcribed prior to a subsequent sitting, Emmet Finley and Harwood White arguing heatedly over their meaning. The sessions were so lively, one wonders how they remained together long enough to finish the work. But remain together they did. The team so constituted worked together for several weeks in the spring of 1947. When they had finished, the sitting notes of their sessions contained sufficient material for *The Content of Consciousness.*

What happened after that nobody knows, except that the book disappeared from view. The correspondence mentions Emmet Finley's opinion that the divulgence was incomplete. He died in 1950 with the book unpublished. No manuscript survives. Harwood White died in 1954 after a two-year illness. Ruth Finley died in 1955. In her papers one finds only the original sitting notes and a few unusable sketches made by Emmet Finley as illustrations. These materials have been gathering dust now for nearly half a century. In prying out their secrets one has the feeling of opening an ancient tomb and discovering treasure.

Of the three divulgences, Emmet Finley considered *The Content of Consciousness* the best of the lot. It is certainly an eye opener. It consists of a computerizable model of a living, breathing human being -- body, mind and soul. The body and mind we have always taken for granted. But the soul -- well, the model of the soul has compartments for this and that, data paths, data storage, apparatus for thinking, apparatus for feeling, apparatus for aspiring, and parts that survive the death of the body and ensure the immortality of the mind and the living soul. Not *pretend* parts, mind you; *real* parts. Every part of the model exists as a real thing -- palpable, pulsating, living, and as physically real as the book you now hold in your hands.

The Invisibles who put the model together are architects of civilizations. They think it important that we recapture the belief, anciently honored, in our own individual immortality. When a new civilization arises out of the ashes of a dying one, it does so on the basis of a re-discovered belief in individual human immortality. That is what they teach. They say further that we are at that point again -- an old civilization dying, a new one in its birth pangs. How unsettled things will get before this process is finished, this tale does not tell. But a renewed belief in our own individual immortality is essential to the stability we need to guide us through.

It is to the rebirth of that ancient faith in ourselves and our God that this volume is addressed.

Chapter 2. "The Gang"

HERE you will find intimate portraits of some of "the gang" -- that tiny group of individuals that left us The Content of Consciousness and the books that led up to it. In Book II I talk about heavy themes, like models of the human mind and soul. But in the remainder of Book I you can relax and enjoy the people. You will find them fascinating. As to what follows, at least you have been warned.

This book is based on the Ruth Ebright Finley archives at the University of Akron in Akron, Ohio. They were donated to the University by William E. Dague, nephew of Mrs. Finley. Mrs. Finley's papers were prepared for archival by E.W. Dykes, retired architect of Canton, Ohio, and former member of the executive board of Spiritual Frontiers Fellowship International, founded in Chicago in 1955 (Arthur Ford was one of the founders) and now located at P.O. Box 7868, Philadelphia, PA, 19104-7868. Mr. Dykes spent a number of years examining Mrs. Finley's papers in preparation for their archival. In his introduction to the archival material, which is reproduced in part below, he describes the remarkable group known to each other as "the gang" that participated in its formation. -- the author.

The Finley Papers

by E.W. Dykes

This narrative is written as background in the explanation of the secret "other life" of a very remarkable lady, Ruth Ebright Finley. There may come a time when mankind realizes that ". . . life is but prophecy, there is no death." Then Ruth Finley may receive her just due. The narrative is pieced together in small part from the two esoteric books for which she played a major role. Largely the narrative comes from the numerous letters and other evidence now located in the archives.

In circumstances which will later be described, Ruth was astonished to find she was quite capable of psychic reception. The two books which resulted were, first, *Our Unseen Guest*, published in 1920 under the pseudonym of "Darby and Joan" (Emmet and Ruth Finley). The second book was *The Unobstructed Universe*, published in 1940 under the authorship of Stewart Edward White.

Ruth, in trance, received the material used as the basis for both books. Ruth and Emmet together wrote *Our Unseen Guest*. The Finleys were active not only in the reception of the material which became *The Unobstructed Universe*, but also in the writing of it, Mr. White calling on them for much help in its editing. The two books were instrumental in bringing a belief in the survival of personality into the lives of numerous people. Many grateful readers wrote letters of appreciation about *Our Unseen Guest* in care of the publisher without ever knowing to whom they were writing other than to her pseudonym, "Joan". Most letters written in response to *The Unobstructed Universe* were written to Stewart Edward White and copies or excerpts of a number of those letters are in the files also. The point is that, on this side of "the line," Ruth Finley was the most important person in both of these books.

Ruth and Emmet were determined not to have their true identities known as receiver and author of these books and for quite understandable reasons. They were in the early years of their outstanding journalistic and business careers and believed -- as most of us would -- that identification with anything as insubstantial as psychic communication would be the kiss of death for their careers.

They were very successful in protecting their anonymity in connection with their psychic work. Actually it did not come to light until three years following Ruth's death, which will be explained later. Her passing was some thirty five years after *Our Unseen Guest* was published.

Ruth was born September 25th, 1884, into a well-known and socially prominent family who lived at 678 Market Street, Akron, Ohio. Her father was Leonidas Strickland Ebright, M.D., for twelve years the postmaster of Akron, for several years a representative to the Ohio House, and he was also a highly respected surgeon. With the title Surgeon General, Dr. Ebright was on the staff of William McKinley who was governor of Ohio before his term as President. These days such a combination of activities for a surgeon would raise questions but apparently not then. Ruth's mother was born Julia Ann Bissell. She was quite active in society and civic affairs. She had been in Oberlin College's first graduating class in which females were included.

Records of Ruth's early years are quite skimpy. A fair guess would be that she was a precocious child. Following in her mother's footsteps she enrolled at Oberlin in the fall of 1902. Through a circumstance which today we would regard as absolutely ludicrous she withdrew when the term was over. On a rainy day she accepted the offer of a male student to walk from one classroom building to another under the protection of his umbrella. This act of "indiscretion" was noted by a college official; Ruth was called on the carpet and reprimanded. Ruth's independent nature rebelled and she left Oberlin to enroll at old Buchtel College which later became the University of Akron. While at Oberlin Ruth attended a lecture by Sherwood Eddy who, at that time, was World Secretary for the YMCA. Dr. Eddy will play a part in the mystery of a "happening" in which Ruth herself will reveal her connection with the psychically received books.

Ruth Finley appeared in *Who's Who* in the 1930-31 issue because of her authorship of two books (certainly not the two referred to earlier) and because of her extensive career in journalism. Her husband, Emmet, is also included in that volume and it is a rarity for both husband and wife to be in *Who's Who*. Ruth was all the more remarkable because of the two lives she led and in her ability to draw a line between them. The two books she wrote under her own name were *Old Patchwork Quilts and the Women Who Made Them* (1929), followed in 1931 by *The Lady of Godey's*.

Her "other life" was of perhaps greater importance, according to how one looks at such things. During the thirty-five year period in which she was also known as "Joan," perhaps fewer than twenty people knew that Ruth was "Joan" and all of them were sworn to secrecy. It was a secret remarkably well kept. This reviewer can identify only fourteen for sure who knew of her psychic gift.

The events that led to her becoming "Joan" began during the evening of December 7th, 1916. Ruth, in what seemed to be a harmless experiment, would soon realize that she was a "receiving station." In these days she would have been called a medium or a channeler but she preferred "receiving station."

For this narrative it is not feasible to enter into a full scale discussion of the many difficulties which exist in the transfer of information from another dimension through a human "station." Errors do occur, primarily because of the problems to be overcome, and this is one of the reasons for the generally low status of "channeling." This writer has studied many and is convinced that the material in the two books for which Ruth was the receiving station is of top quality.

Earlier statements regarding the Finleys' attitude toward being connected with psychic communication might well raise the question: Then why did they enter into such a process and why did they continue it for so many years? The answer is simple. They entered into it believing only in its temporary entertainment value. Through what happened that first evening they were driven to experiment further. In that continuation they became convinced that 1), it was indeed coming from the "beyond" and 2), the message contained reasonable and apparently important information. They received information sufficiently evidential and verifiable to know that the reception was quite clear, and after a short while there was no alternative which made sense to them other than belief.

Back now to early events which shaped Ruth's life. Apparently Ruth felt no need for a degree because within just months of graduation she left Buchtel College and began work as a cub reporter for the Akron Beacon Journal. Her talent for investigative writing was apparent and it was not long before she had a by-line, well before any of the male members of the staff had done so. A key factor was in her obtaining an interview with Mrs. Thomas Edison who had always shunned interviews. The interview account was picked up by the wire services and Ruth was on her way.

In a few years she moved to the Cleveland Press and there she was the editor of the women's page. In those days there were relatively few women in the work force and her assignment was to report on various work activities in which women were engaged. She explained to her editor she thought the best way to go at it would be for her to work in such jobs for a short period and then to report on the basis of actual experience. It was a good idea, of course, and one of her early assignments was to investigate women who worked as live-in maids, usually for the well-to-do. She obtained such a position and after a short while her lady employer asked her why she had no male callers, saying that her previous maids always had male friends who called. Ruth suspected that her household employer was suspicious so she called her editor and asked if he could supply her with a date. When he suggested Emmet she had to ask which one he was. Upon the identification she was not impressed but then replied , "Oh I suppose he will do." Little did she know. When the editor asked Finley to meet Ruth at the home of her employer, Emmet asked, "Can't you get someone else?" Between that night and their marriage they missed only three days of not seeing each other and those three were rainy days. They were married in Ruth's family home in Akron on August 24, 1910.

Each progressed in their various work assignments and by the time they had their first psychic experience, Ruth had become the Scripps-Howard fiction editor. Finley had left the Press to become secretary of the Street Railway Commission. After two years he moved back to the Press as city editor. According to the early pages of their book, *Our Unseen Guest*, they took their evening meals at a boarding house within walking distance of their apartment. During their dinner on the evening of December 7th, 1916, a fierce storm blew in off Lake Erie and they decided to wait it out. They were alone in the reception room casting about for something to do when one spied a Ouija board in the corner. They had heard of the board but had never seen one. As a lark, they decided to try it. What else was there to do?

For some ten minutes or so nothing happened and they were about to give it up when the planchette began a slow movement. It spelled, "QUALITY OF CONSCIOUSNESS" and then repeated it. They each accused the other of moving the planchette. Neither could suggest why the other would come up with such a meaningless phrase. So they tried again. Then the planchette spelled out, "FOR YOU TWO I HAVE A MESSAGE, A REVELATION. COMMUNICATION IS SO SLOW, SO DIFFICULT, THAT I CAN DO LITTLE MORE THAN GIVE YOU THE SUGGESTION. BUT IF YOU WILL REASON ALONG THE LINES I POINT OUT YOU CAN REACH THE TRUTH."

"What truth?"

"IN AS FAR AS IT IS GIVEN YOU TO UNDERSTAND, THAT ULTIMATE TRUTH -- THE WHY, THE WHENCE, THE WHITHER WHICH MEN HAVE LONGED TO KNOW SINCE KNOWLEDGE WAS."

Feeling a bit silly addressing the empty air, Emmet asked, "Who are you?" At that point the planchette spelled out the full name, RICHARD NELVILLE HALL. In the book the name is not given and "Stephen" was substituted at his own request. Hall did not wish to bring any embarrassment to his family which very likely it would have done. That same evening he told them of his enlistment in the volunteer ambulance corps to serve in France and gave the details of his death which had occurred very early Christmas morning, 1915. On one of his missions to pick up the wounded, a German shell scored a direct hit on his vehicle, killing him instantly. All of these details proved out when the Finleys investigated his claims. They were contained in a book published during the war about the volunteer ambulance corps.

Here is a further word about mediums, about channelled information and about what appears to be a continuing intensive effort from "the other side" to help us gain accurate information of what to expect when our turn comes to cross that "line." The universe is a marvelous mechanism which relies on energy, perhaps in all its many and varied manifestations. Posit that the soul is a manifestation of energy. Energy is in vibration and its rate of vibration is called its frequency. Souls gain in frequency according to how well and far they have advanced in what seems to be an unending path toward perfection and supremacy. "Stephen" advised that his and Ruth's personal frequencies were very close to being the same, a positive factor for clear communication.

This is speculation. Suppose that you were on that "other side," that you were in charge of a team of souls poised to bring communications which would clarify the tasks of mankind and would explain away some of the many misconceptions about survival of personality, as well as bringing evidence for such survival. Your job over there would be to survey the living and the susceptibility of possible candidates to receive clearly and you must be able "to arrange" the conditions which would bring those "candidates" to accept the tasks which would be required. You have material for three books to be communicated and likely will require three teams for its accomplishment. What factors would you look for in living persons which would be best suited to bring about optimum results? The prime need, of course, would be the ability to receive. That would be known to a leader on the other side. Would it not be also of high priority to have persons whose writing skills would suit the task? Would it not be of high priority to have people whose financial conditions were such that money would not be a concern? Would it not be a good idea that these persons would be childless so that family matters would be less confusing? Still further, you would want your "teams" to have good reputations personally and in their work lives. We now take up the things which will show us how it all worked out.

The three books are to be those that will complement each other but also will have definite value when considered alone. Your books are already well outlined on that side ready to be transmitted. Your receiving persons or teams are to be attracted to the work, to be convinced somehow that their work is important to mankind and that they will endeavor to bring the overall task to completion.

The three books which the Invisibles later claimed to be a "triad" are *The Seven Purposes*, *Our Unseen Guest*, and *The Unobstructed Universe*. Around 1917 or so Margaret Cameron, who was an author and playwright, the wife of Harrison Cass Lewis, found to her astonishment that she could perform what is called "automatic writing." What circumstance led her to do it is not known here. In the course of her receptions there would be numerous instances of what may be called "evidential" material, carrying evidence of things known or unknown to the writer but which would yield to proof. Margaret's complete book, *The Seven Purposes*, was published in 1918. The Finleys published theirs in 1920. It would be 1940 before everything was in place to complete *The Unobstructed Universe*.

In 1919, Elizabeth Grant ("Betty") White, the wife of Stewart Edward White, a famous author, would find herself to be psychic in a similar way as did Ruth Finley. Betty was soon convinced that there was something there and she would then undergo intensive training by those whom she called "invisibles." By the time of her death in 1939, she had become capable of visiting at will that other side of life in her etheric body (as in the near-death experience) and returning with full knowledge of much of that "terrain."

We have to assume that the Whites and the Finleys acting separately, somehow found Margaret Cameron after her book appeared in 1919 under her own name. By 1920 the Finleys had moved to the New York City area. Through correspondence (we are still theorizing), they could have exchanged information with each other, compared their experiences and established friendships. Whatever way it happened, a strong bond was forged between them which was extended to include John and Lucy Gavit who lived in New York City and are presumed to be friends of Margaret. Each of the Gavits was psychically sensitive. By 1922 the group had become the Lewises (Margaret Cameron and husband Harrison Lewis), the Finleys, the Whites and the Gavits. They had become well enough acquainted to set up an experimental meeting. The group came together in Margaret's household in New York City. The New York meeting, which lasted about a month, was to attempt to bring physical manifestations of powers from the other side. The results were very encouraging and the whole set of events is described in an appendix to Stewart White' first frankly psychic book, *The Betty Book*, published in 1937. After that, when one was writing to another of the group, they often referred to the whole group as "the gang."

Going back now to our discussion of what qualities the individual performers on this side of the line should have to be most effective, we find that all three married couples were childless, all three had writing talents and all three were well able to handle these added tasks without financial concerns. As a matter of fact, White was wealthy, Margaret was either wealthy or very well-to-do in her own right and had married well. Certainly the Finleys were well able to sustain themselves. In addition all four persons who did the receiving or the writing or both were then in Who's Who in America or would later be so listed. In terms of integrity their credentials were impeccable. Planned from "the other side" such results would be expected. Your reviewer contends that chance played no part in this.

The Finleys, the Whites, Margaret Cameron and the Gavits were in rather constant touch with each other over the years. With respect to psychic awareness, the Whites broke their long public silence in 1937 with *The Betty Book*, the record of Betty's training by "invisibles." White, who had been a very successful author of adventure stories and attracted a very large following, disappointed many of them with this switch into books on the psychic. On the other hand many others were attracted to this obviously serious book and soon Mr. White was working on a second one, *Across the Unknown*, also based on Betty's experiences and a very good book. Due to an unsuccessful experiment with radium, Betty was taken ill with cancer and passed away on Easter Sunday April 5th, 1939.

The second book about Betty's experiences was almost ready for publishing when Betty "graduated" but Mr. White withheld final approval in order to add the very poignant chapter in which he related his experience which occurred just minutes following Betty's passing. The archived records include the letter he sent to his friends containing essentially what was in that chapter.

About six months following Betty's passing, Stewart White went to New York City to meet with his publisher to complete the details on *Across the Unknown*. On his third day there he was at the Finleys for dinner and chatter and Ruth felt the urge to go into trance for a reception. Betty introduced herself and what followed was a series of proofs by Betty that she was who she claimed to be. These bits of evidential material, mostly inconsequential in themselves, were things known to Stewart but not to Ruth or Emmet. The importance of their friendship then became evident. Betty told them they were to do another book working together, one that would be interesting to scientists as well as to the public. White extended his stay until forty sessions had been held, enough for Betty to complete the notes for the book, *The Unobstructed Universe.* This book received a fantastic public reception. It went through twenty-seven printings in hardback, tens of thousands in soft cover by E.P. Dutton and the most recent printing by Ariel Press. The importance of *The Unobstructed Universe* to these archives, of course, is that Ruth was the key figure in its reception, even though the note taking and the arranging of the facts for publishing carry the name of the author as Stewart Edward White. Many, many readers became believers through reading it, including this narrative writer.

During the interim between *Our Unseen Guest* and *The Unobstructed universe*, "Stephen" returned through Ruth to begin another book which was to be called *The Content of Consciousness.* It did not proceed rapidly until after Stewart White made his transition on September 18th, 1946. Within a few months, White, speaking now from the other side, took over from Stephen to extend the work that Stephen had begun. Stewart's brother, Harwood, joined with the Finleys as a conceiving station in this reception. Again, an explanation is necessary for persons who may not be familiar with psychic receptions. The medium is in trance and has to be told what took place, and therefore does little insofar as clearing up matters which need extensive explanation. For *Our Unseen Guest*, Darby served as the "conceiving station", raising the necessary questions to clear up difficult concepts. For *The Unobstructed Universe*, both Stewart White and Emmet served this function. Stewart's brother, Harwood White, aided Emmet as a conceiving station in *The Content of Consciousness.*

The Content of Consciousness was not to be completed. Emmet began to have physical problems and although receptions were completed before his death he did not bring the notes to a point of completion. The sitting notes on the book have a forty-four page gap, unfortunate because the book showed great promise of interest to the field of psychology.

Emmet passed away in December of 1950. Very little is in these records to indicate what Ruth did in the nearly five years before her passing in September of 1955. This writer is aware that at least once in that period she visited the Harwood Whites in Santa Barbara. One day before her 71st birthday death ended the fine career of the talented Ruth Finley, great journalist and great psychic medium. Well, not quite; Ruth would play an encore.

The mystery of how the public would become aware of the true identity of "Joan" will now be cleared up. There was a great clairvoyant by the name of Arthur Ford. In trance, he influenced the lives of many people by reporting evidential information from their loved ones in spirit. Harry Houdini was the most remarkable magician of his era. He was skeptical of psychics and, at his death, left a sum of $10,000 to be paid to anyone who would break the code which he would attempt to deliver from the invisible world. Awarding of the prize was vested in a committee of Houdini's friends. It was a complicated code involving his wife and their relationships on stage. Ford decided to make a try for the code. Houdini made his presence known to Ford and gave the code. There was a great outcry from much of the press and from skeptics everywhere. The reaction: *It is fraud. Communication is impossible. It just could not be.* Mrs. Houdini wrote to Ford as follows, "*Regardless of any statements made to the contrary, I wish to declare that the message, in its entirety, and in the agreed upon sequence given to me by Arthur Ford, is the correct message prearranged between Mr. Houdini and myself.*" Mrs. Houdini never backed off from her statement but the committee was adamant and refused to pay the reward. That is by way of introduction of Arthur Ford, indicating he was quite capable of clear reception. It also reveals skepticism at its worst. So far as the committee was concerned, there could never be a winner.

In about 1956, Ford was giving a reading for Sherwood Eddy who, since his speaking at Oberlin, had friends who had convinced him that he should look into the evidence for psychic communication. During the reading, one claiming to be "Ruth Finley" spoke to him (through Ford of course), identified herself as the "Joan" of *Our Unseen Guest* and *The Unobstructed Universe*, then told Eddy about hearing him speak at Oberlin and gave some of the details. This information is contained on page 106 of Ford's Book, *Nothing So Strange*.

Lovina May Knight of Akron was the daughter of a college friend of Ruth's. When she read the reference in *Nothing So Strange* she was astonished because Ruth had visited with them several times over the years and had never told her old friend about her psychic gifts. Miss Knight wrote an article under the title of "Who Was Joan?" which was published in the Journal of Spiritual Frontiers Fellowship and which finally cleared up the mystery of Ruth's secret identity.

Our Unseen Guest was well received but the number of books published by Harper & Brothers is not known. An additional publishing of 5,000 copies was made in 1945 by Borden Press of Los Angeles and the last of those was sold in about 1991.

As the collator of this narrative, I believe the three books, sometimes referred to as a "triad," to be of very considerable importance. Not only do they give much evidence for survival that is not otherwise explainable but they also bring what we may call theories as to how survival happens.

This narrative will be completed with bibliographical sketches of persons who were major participants in Ruth's "other life" but who are not treated in other parts of this book.

Author's note: The Whites and Mrs. Finley's husband Emmet get their own chapters so don't show up in the list below.

Margaret Cameron Kilvert

Margaret Cameron was born in Ottawa, Illinois, December 21st, 1867, and died February 4th, 1947, in Winter Park, Florida. She was educated largely in private schools in Santa Barbara. As a young lady Miss Cameron was a leading socialite in San Francisco. She was a gifted pianist. She became a writer of plays in the humorous vein, including *The Cat and the Canary*, and was quite well known in the first quarter of this century. In 1903 she married Harrison Cass Lewis and they lived in New York City. Mr. Lewis died in 1926 and in 1929 Margaret married Maxwell Alexander Kilvert. How she became aware of automatic writing is not clear but she did so and attracted the attention, probably through her husband, of a number of very influential men who met frequently with her to ask questions and to watch the writing which often foretold with amazing accuracy the events of World War I then raging in Europe. She had to have a very big table and used wallpaper as her "tablet." Sometimes the letters would be a foot high and on occasion the writing would be upside down and backwards, a feat which Margaret could not otherwise perform. These communications became the basis of her book, *The Seven Purposes,* in which her invisible communicators said that Germany would be defeated and that another war was already brewing that would be much worse. At the time of that writing, World War I was not over and in fact Germany appeared to be winning. *The Seven Purposes* was published by Harpers in October of 1918. Margaret followed it with the publication in 1919 of an extract from that book called *Twelve Lessons from The Seven Purposes.* There are hints but no details in the archives that suggest that Margaret had healing talents. In the numerous letters to Ruth by Margaret it is quite clear that Margaret deeply loved Ruth as a dear friend.

Mr. and Mrs. John Palmer Gavit (Jack and Lucy)

The Gavits were intimate friends of Margaret and of the Finleys, not mentioned by name in the books although occasionally they show up there. They are found frequently by name in the correspondence. They were part of "the gang" mentioned in *The Betty Book* appendix where they were called "The Gaines." Jack was psychic although the nature of his ability was not made clear. Lucy Lamont Gavit, wife of John, was psychic and worked with the Finleys at times. Lucy was a sister to Thomas W. Lamont, well known in publishing and financial circles. The Gavits had a daughter, Martha (Marty) who was married to Thurston Adams. She was psychic. She passed away at age thirty and was followed in death by her mother less than three weeks later. Both Lucy and Marty appear in readings shortly after their passing. The Gavits also had a son, Joe, who died at an early age and he occasionally appears in the readings. Gavit was into numerous activities in the publishing field. The various letters by him, or which mention his name, make it clear that he was very much interested in the Finley work. Lucy Gavit, after her passing and through Ruth, gave Jack instructions on some mundane matters.

Adele Halman

Mrs. Adele Halman of San Francisco was a cultured lady who was quite religious and very psychic. After Betty's passing, from time to time she communicated information through Adele for Stewart who would go to her San Francisco home when Betty issued a call. Betty had ways of identifying herself and Stewart never accepted any message without such evidence. Mrs. Halman was an excellent station and much evidential material came through her.

All in all, the gang added a great chapter to the paranormal work in this century.

Chapter 3. Biography of a Heavenly Messenger

IN Cleveland night had fallen, and from off Lake Erie an unexpected December storm dumped rain and sleet onto a surprised and dreary city. The onset of the storm found journalists Ruth and Emmet Finley at a boarding house near their apartment, eating their evening meal. It was a convenient arrangement most of the time for the married couple; both were busy professionals, and there were no children.

Convenient, that is, during good weather. On the occasion in question the weather was not good. Supper was over, and they wanted to go home. But home was several blocks away, blocks consisting that night of wind-swept streets, while rain pelted the windows of the boarding house in which, as the reader will have surmised, the couple was trapped.

What to do?

The Finleys sought haven in a deserted sitting room. A Ouija board lay beckoning on the table, but what of it? There was hardly a couple in Cleveland less likely to use one than this hard-nosed pair of reporters, he a trained lawyer, amateur philosopher, and holder of a Phi Beta Kappa key, she a "liberated," cynical woman of the world; both, however, regular church goers, probably Episcopalian.

Yet use it they did, and the results changed the course of their lives. The date is important; it was December 7, 1916.

We will return to the Ouija board, and the Finleys' fateful rendezvous with its animator, after reviewing certain relevant events of the war that transpired the previous year.

* * *

LONDON, Dec. 24. -- The fighting around Hartmanns-Weilerkopf, which is the chief incident in recent news from the western front, has not yet reached a decision, but all the reports indicate that the four days' losses on both sides have been so severe that some kind of a lull is almost inevitable . . . The enemy's artillery fire has been lively at certain points, especially in the Vosges.

The above is from the New York Times, Saturday, December 25, 1915 -- the disputed ground lying in the Alsace territory of France. Page one on the following day, Sunday, December 26, 1915, has this follow-up story, under the headline, "Dartmouth Recruit in Alsace is Killed":

PARIS, Dec. 25. - Richard Melville Hall of Ann Arbor, Mich., a volunteer driver attached to that section of the American Ambulance operating with the French army in Alsace, was killed Christmas Eve in the performance of his duty. The news was received by telephone today by the American Ambulance Committee.

Mr. Hall, who was 21 years old, was the son of Professor H.G. Hall of the University of Michigan. He was one of a group of Dartmouth College recruits who entered the ambulance service last June, and when he met his death he was driving a Dartmouth College field ambulance. A military funeral will be held at the front tomorrow afternoon . . .

The details of the young man's death have not been ascertained, except that he was driving, or standing near, his car when it was struck by a German shell and demolished."

Further details were shortly forthcoming. They were printed in the book, *Friends of France*, to which we now turn. The chapter in question was printed as a tribute and memorial to Hall, the first

American in that branch of service to die. It starts with a poem by Emery Pottle.

FRIENDS OF FRANCE

You were driving a hearse in the hell-black night,
With Death and a boy for your load.

O dump him down in that yawning shed,
A man at his head and feet;
Take off his ticket, his clothes, his kit,
And give him his winding-sheet.

It's just another *poilu* that's dead;
You've hauled them every day
Till your soul has ceased to wonder and weep
At war's wild, wanton play.

He died in the winter dark, alone,
In a stinking ambulance,
With God knows what upon his lips --
But on his heart was France![1]

And then Richard Hall's story.

CHRISTMAS EVE, 1915

In one of the most beautiful countries in the world, the Alsatian Valley of the Thur runs to where the Vosges abruptly end in the great flat plain of the Rhine. In turn a small valley descends into that of the Thur. At the head of this valley lies the small village of Mollau where is billeted the Section Sanitaire Americaine No. 3. It has been through months of laborious, patient, never-ceasing trips from the valley to the mountain-tops and back, up the broadened mule-paths, rutted and worn by a thousand wheels and the hoofs of mules, horses, and oxen, by hobnailed boots and by the cars of the American Ambulance (for no other Section is equipped with cars and men for such service), up from the small Alsatian towns, leaving the main valley road to grind through a few fields of ever-increasing grade on into the forest, sometimes pushed, sometimes pulled, always blocked on the steepest slopes by huge army wagons deserted where they stuck, rasping cartloads of trench torpedoes on one side, crum-

---

1. *Friends of France*, Houghton Mifflin, 1916. Page 138.

bling the edge of the ravine on the other, -- day and night -- night and day -- in snow and rain -- and, far worse, fog -- months of foul and days of fair, -- up with the interminable caravans of *ravitaillement*, supplies with which to sustain or blast the human body (we go down with the human body once blasted), up past small armies of Alsatian peasants of three generations (rather two -- octogenarians and children), forever repairing, forever fighting the wear and tear of all that passes, -- up at last to the little log huts and rudely made *postes de secours* at the mouth of the trench "bowels," -- a silent little world of tethered mules, shrouded carts and hooded figures, lightless by night, under the great pines where is a crude garage usually filled with grenades into which one may back at one's own discretion.

Day after day, night after night, wounded or no wounded, the little ambulances plied with their solitary drivers. Few men in ordinary autos or in ordinary senses travel such roads by choice, but all that is impossible is explained by a simple *C'est la guerre.* Why else blindly force and scrape one's way past a creaking truck of shells testing twenty horses, two abreast, steaming in their own cloud of sweaty vapor, thick as a Fundy fog? Taking perforce the outside, the ravine side, the ambulance passes. More horses and wagons ahead in the dark, another blinding moment or two, harnesses clash and rattle, side bolts and lanterns are wiped from the car. It passes again; *C'est la guerre.* Why else descend endless slopes with every brake afire, with three or four human bodies as they should not be, for cargo, where a broken drive-shaft leaves but one instantaneous twist of the wheel for salvation, a thrust straight into the bank, smashing the car, but saving its precious load? *C'est la guerre.*

The men in time grow tired as do the machines. A week before Christmas they rested quietly in their villages -- a week of sun and splendid moon, spent tuning up their motors and gears and jogging about afoot after all their "rolling." A lull in the fighting, and after three weeks of solid rain, nature smiles. The Section had been ordered to leave shortly, and it was only held for a long-expected attack which would bring them all together for once on the mountains in a last great effort with the Chasseurs Alpins and the mountains they both loved.

On December 21st the mountain spoke and all the cars rolled upwards to the *poste* of Hartmannsweiler-kopf, -- taken and retaken a score of times, -- a bare, brown, blunt, shell-ploughed top where before the forest stood, up elbowing, buffeting, and tacking their way through battalions of men and beasts, up by one pass and down by another unmountable (for there is no going back against the tide of what was battle-bound). From one mountain slope to another roared all the lungs of war. For five days and five nights -- scraps of days, the shortest of the year, nights interminable -- the air was shredded with shrieking shells -- intermittent lulls for slaughter in attack after the bombardment, then again the roar of the counter-attack.

All this time, as in all the past months, Richard Nelville Hall calmly drove his car up the winding, shell-swept artery of the mountain of war, -- past crazed mules, broken-down artillery carts, swearing drivers, stricken horses, wounded stragglers still able to hobble, -- past long convoys of *Boche* prisoners, silent, descending in twos, guarded by a handful of men, -- past all the *personnel* of war, great and small (for there is but one road, one road on which to travel, one road for the enemy to shell), -- past *abris*, bombproofs, subterranean huts, to arrive at the *postes de secours*, where silent men moved mysteriously in the mist under the great trees, where the cars were loaded with an every-ready supply of still more quiet figures (though some made sounds), mere bundles in blankets. Hall saw to it that those quiet bundles were carefully and rapidly installed, -- right side up, for instance, -- for it is dark and the *brancardiers* are dull folks, deadened by the dead they carry; then rolled down into the valley below, where little towns bear stolidly their daily burden of shells wantonly thrown from somewhere in Bocheland over the mountain to somewhere in France -- the bleeding bodies in the car a mere corpuscle in the full crimson stream, the ever-rolling tide from the trenches to the hospital, of the blood of life and the blood of death. Once there, his wounded unloaded, Dick Hall filled his gasoline tank and calmly rolled again on his way. Two of his comrades had been wounded the day before, but Dick Hall never faltered. He slept where and when he could, in his car, at the *poste*, on the floor of our temporary kitchen at Moosch -- dry blankets --

wet blankets -- blankets of mud -- blankets of blood; contagion was pedantry -- microbes a myth.

At midnight Christmas Eve, he left the valley to get his load of wounded for the last time. Alone, ahead of him, two hours of lonely driving up the mountain. Perhaps he was thinking of other Christmas Eves, perhaps of his distant home, and of those who were thinking of him.

. . .

Matter, the next American to pass, found him by the roadside halfway up the mountain. His face was calm and his hands still in position to grasp the wheel. Matter, and Jennings, who came a little later, bore him tenderly back in Matter's car to Moosch, where his brother, Louis Hall, learned what had happened.

A shell had struck his car and killed him instantly, painlessly. A chance shell in a thousand had struck him at his post, in the morning of his youth.

. . .

Up on the mountain fog was hanging over Hartmann's Christmas morning, as if Heaven wished certain things obscured. The trees were sodden with dripping rain. Weather, sight, sound, and smell did their all to sicken mankind, when news was brought to us that Dick Hall had fallen on the Field of Honor. No man said, "Merry Christmas," that day. No man could have mouthed it. With the fog forever closing in, with the mountain shaken by a double bombardment as never before, we sat all day in the little log hut by the stove thinking first of Dick Hall, then of Louis Hall, his brother, down in the valley. . . .

Gentlemen at home, you who tremble with concern at overrun putts, who bristle at your partner's play at auction, who grow hoarse at football games, know that among you was one who played for greater goals -- the lives of other men. There in the small hours of Christmas morning, where mountain fought mountain, on the hard-bitten pass under the pines of the Vosgian steeps, there fell a very modest and valiant gentleman.

. . .

Dick Hall, we who knew you, worked with you, played with you, ate with you, slept with you, we who took pleasure in your company, in your modesty, in your gentle manners, in your devotion and in your youth -- we still pass that spot, and we salute. Our breath comes quicker, our eyes grow dimmer, we grip the wheel a little tighter -- we pass -- better and stronger men.

Richard Hall was buried with honors of war in the Valley of Saint-Amarin, in the part of Alsace which once more belongs to France. His grave, in a crowded military cemetery, is next that of a French officer who fell the same morning. It bears the brief inscription, "Richard Hall, an American who died for France." Simple mountain people in the only part of Germany where foreign soldiers are to-day brought to the grave many wreaths of native flowers and Christmas greens. The funeral service was held in a little Protestant chapel, five miles down the valley. At the conclusion of the service Hall's citation was read and the Cross of War pinned on the coffin. On the way to the cemetery sixteen soldiers, belonging to a battalion on leave from the trenches, marched in file on each side with arms reversed. The *medecin chef* spoke as follows: --

"Comrades: --

"We are here to offer our last, supreme homage of gratitude and affection, beside this freshly dug grave, to this young man -- I might well say, this boy -- who fell yesterday, for France, on the slopes of Hartmannsweilerkopf. . .

"To the dear ones whom he has left in his own land, in Michigan, to his grief-stricken parents, to his older brother who displays here among us such stoicism in his grief, our respect and our expressions of sorrow are the most sincere and heartfelt.

"Driver Richard Hall, you are to be laid to rest here, in the shadow of the tri-colored flag, beside all these brave fellows, whose gallantry you have emulated. You are justly entitled to make one of their consecrated battalion! Your body alone, gloriously mutilated, disappears; your soul has ascended to God; your memory remains in our hearts -- imperishable! -- Frenchmen do not forget!

"Driver Richard Hall -- farewell!" [2]

We pick up the thread of the story at this point as told in Richard Hall's own words. For this account we are indebted to the Richard Hall of the Cleveland Ouija board. The Finleys have left us this account in two versions; the book, *Our Unseen Guest*, which they published under the pseudonyms "Darby & Joan," and an earlier version, *The Master Key*, unpublished but left in manuscript form in Ruth Finley's papers.

It is the finest account we have of the history of a man just prior to, and just after, his own physical death. On December 7, 1916, the Finleys had never heard of Richard Hall, and thus knew nothing of the stories about him which I have related above. All they knew at that point was that they had a very lively Ouija board by the tail, and it insisted on telling its story.

Here is what Richard Hall of the Ouija board had to add to the published accounts of his death.

"Millions . . . have already fallen. And the suffering and the wounds! . . .

---

2. *Friends of France*, Houghton Mifflin, 1916. Pages 139-147. The chapter was written by Waldo Peirce, a fellow member of Section 3, Hall's section, of The American Ambulance. The Harvard University archives say he was from Bangor, Maine, and was granted his bachelor's degree in 1908.

"There was a mist in the air -- half mist, half smoke from the battle that had been raging for days up and down the mountain . . . A call came . . . . The dark was of a blackness that could be felt, and it was cold. . . . I am not ashamed to say that I was afraid . . . . All day we had been under fire. . . I hummed a tune under my breath for company and to keep my courage up. Several shells burst ahead of me. . . . I went on . . . . I was singing when the shell that sent me into eternity, as I now know it, hit. . . .

"I went out, out, out, out -- beyond all comprehension, all consciousness of sunshine and dusty road and blood-stained grass. I can find no words to tell you the horror of sudden death. It is the one great tragedy. When thought returned, I was as one lost in a familiar yet wholly strange world. Aimlessly I wandered, seeking I knew not what, dazed, mystified. I did not know I was, as you say and as I used to say, dead.

"When death comes naturally there are always those here to meet the voyagers. But there was no one to meet me, no one to explain that I had graduated into a new plane of consciousness.

"At last one came, a woman, a very sweet woman whose service here has done much to alleviate the shock of battle-field graduation, and took me by the -- shall I say, hand? -- and led me to a -- may I say, quiet woodland spot? -- where after a time I learned the hope, the reality of the triumphant blessing I had achieved.

"And so I have chosen my work here, and with that work I go on -- the comforting of those who come to us suddenly out of the shock of battle. I meet them, poor frightened soldier-boys, and teach them the truth -- the simplicity of their own immortality." [3]

So began the story which Richard Nelville Hall, Dartmouth '15, spelled out to Emmet and Ruth Finley that stormy night of December 7, 1916. He had not

---

3. *Our Unseen Guest.* Harper & Brothers, 1920, with *The Master Key.*

yet been "dead" a year. What did he want? Why had he come back in so startling a fashion?

"The world is ready for the truth . . ." he said. "Never before, since man's own scientific knowledge has been developed to a point enabling him to understand the revelation now planned, has it been possible for the higher degrees of consciousness here to communicate with correspondingly high degrees on your side. Such communication is possible now because, owing to the vast slaughter of the war, so much of consciousness still close to earth is on my plane. As a result our potentiality here for the purpose of communication is strengthened, while earth's collected consciousness, strained by the upheaval of a world war, is rendered unusually sensitive.

"Listen! The time is ripe. The world is waiting for a reasonable peg on which to hang its faith." [4]

A man who had been a well-known professor -- the Finleys do not identify him but we will presently -- also spoke through the board. Richard had balked at giving unnecessary details as to the manner of his death.

"Richard's revelation is its own best test," the professor spelled out. "Its reasonableness, my dear sir, in the light of earth's already acquired knowledge, is its best proof."

"If I should appear to your physical eye," the professor added, "if I sat down and talked to your physical ear, you would call me an hallucination." [5]

To which Richard added:

"If I told you facts, dates, names, and places you did not know, and subsequently you ascertained their truth, you would have tested nothing. You would say you had learned them long ago and forgotten

---

4. *Our Unseen Guest*, Harper & Brothers.

5. *Our Unseen Guest*, Harper & Brothers.

them. If they concerned events happening as I spoke, you would say you received them telepathically from unknown, yet definite, earth personalities. As for prophecy, we here, rightly apprehended, are not soothsayers."[6]

Nevertheless Richard did permit the Finleys to verify his identity.

"I was decorated by France," he wrote out the evening of January 15, 1917. "You can find my record in . . . ." (Name not disclosed by the Finleys). "A book -- I cannot quite tell the name -- recently published, and to be had at any bookstore." [7]

Within days the Finleys had found the book. It was *Friends of France*. The reader is already familiar with the account it gave of Richard's life and death. The Finleys suppressed the name of the book in their published work, but you can find it in Ruth Finley's papers.

Richard Hall & Company

In the published version of *Our Unseen Guest* the Finley's do not identify the professor. Yet they devote an entire chapter (as have we) to the proofs of his identity. Why go to so much trouble and yet not give his name?

For the simple reason that the name was too illustrious to be believable. The professor was in fact William James, Harvard professor and America's foremost philosopher and psychologist. When *Our Unseen Guest* was published, the Finleys were not party to

---

6. *Our Unseen Guest*, Harper & Brothers.

7. *Our Unseen Guest*, Harper & Brothers.

our superior hindsight. How could such an eminently intelligent, respectable, professional couple possible believe that Ruth Finley was a world-class medium? Yet it is true. Her work on *Our Unseen Guest*, *The Unobstructed Universe* and *The Content of Consciousness* entitles us to believe whatever her Ouija board said as to the identity of the Professor. And the identification is unequivocal. The clinching testimony is Ruth Finley's trance description of the James's house at 95 Irving Street, Cambridge, Massachusetts, a stone's throw from Harvard. James's widow saw the sitting notes and wrote that they suggest an intimacy with the details of the house that was most convincing to her -- this despite the fact that neither of the Finleys had ever seen it.

And with Richard and Professor James positively identified, we have every justification for accepting the identity of the others that gathered around that inspired Ouija board. And what a select company they were! A fitting group to bring a philosophy whose merit cannot be too highly estimated.

Pity the identities were suppressed! Yet I give them now, just as Emmet Finley originally wrote the account. The excerpt is from the manuscript entitled *The Master Key*, Anne's[8] preferred title for the book eventually published as *Our Unseen Guest.*

Among our guests has been old Imannuel Kant, professor of metaphysics some generations ago at Koenigsberg University, Germany, who in this life helped to ground modern science, who served also as a sort of town clock for his fellow citizens. On the dot of four -- never by the fraction of a second earlier, never later -- he stepped from home for his afternoon stroll, and 'tis said that when the dis-

8. See chapter on Angels and Archangels.

tinguished and methodical professor appeared the worthies of Koenigsberg were accustomed to set their watches.

Kant, Joan and I, not forgetting the Ouija board, have discussed matters of lofty philosophic note, but for the most part, Stephen assures us, "through an interpreter". Kant it would appear still prefers his native tongue. And still is he methodical, insisting, for example, at one stage of Stephen's message: "It is essential to the further progress of this revelation that you, my good friends, understand thoroughly the nature of matter. This understanding is integral to mastery of true philosophy's whole."

And there has been Prof. William James, Harvard's great psychologist, who, if we are to believe the newspapers, communicates from time to time with every man and woman who owns a Ouija board, aspires to automatic writing or boasts trance proclivities. Prof. James has been very helpful to Joan and me -- and considerate always of our dull comprehension though he objects to my taking notes with a lead pencil and says it was his rule to encourage pupils at Harvard in the use of fountain-pens.

Then there has been Thomas Chatterton, England's boy poet of the eighteenth century, who when poetry didn't pay drank arsenic in a greater amount than the human system can imbibe and still retain any semblance of being a system at all. Chatterton died, in truth sadly, and left a bit of imperishable poetry behind. Seemingly, however, he left not all he was capable of. For Joan and me he has spelled out -- quickly, tunefully -- verse of perfect meter, happy rhyme and, we think, of rare literary value.

Keats, too, has come -- John Keats, another of England's unfortunate, but glorious youths. 1 He has given us poetry less wistful than the "Ode to A Nightingale". We wonder if the world will find it less beautiful.

And last there has been whimsical Anne o' Perth, who in this life appears to have carved out no monument of verse or high thought; yet has she now a store of charming allegories. These she has been pleased to share with Joan and me.

Whimsical Anne o' Perth, in repartee so keen! The quaintest of Scotch dialect is hers. Indeed, she asserts positively that she is Joan's great-grandmother, many times removed and wholly Scotch, the one whose features, family tradition says, are reproduced in the dear contour of Joan's face.

I name this company -- lightly, yet withal respectfully, appreciatively -- as a commentary on my subconscious mind and Joan's. Of what vigorous subconscious selves we are possessed! From this personality they shift in a trice to that, assume a third, achieve a fourth. The limit of their mutations even yet appears quite beyond our conscious guessings.

Sometimes in seeking to estimate our just portion of it all Joan and I are chagrined that egotism could prompt us to consider Stephen and his company as creations of our own minds. For this Stephen, this Kant of the Ouija board, these excellent spellers of an illuminative philosophy and verse have such deeper insights, such keener judgments than Joan and I heretofore have had reason to believe within our bounds of capability.[9]

At this point the reader is invited to re-explore *Our Unseen Guest* for the contributions of these individuals to that fascinating volume.

Hall established the foundation of the philosophy that underlies all subsequent work of the gang. It is so extensive that its treatment is beyond the scope of this book. Readers impatient for details can find them in *Our Unseen Guest* and in Stewart Edward White's *The Unobstructed Universe*.

---

9. *The Master Key*, pages 12-14

Chapter 4. Two Professors

AMONG that lively group of Invisibles who met regularly in the Finleys' drawing room, there were two who had left their mark on the history of human thought. I refer to Immanuel Kant and William James. The former was a regular visitor in the early years, and one supposes that he contributed materially to the philosophy published as *Our Unseen Guest*. The latter -- James -- was also an early visitor, but also persisted into the period of the third divulgence. One suspects, therefore, that he is a contributor to the model of the immortal psyche that is described in the *Content of Consciousness* sittings. While here, James published a defense of immortality that included his transmission theory -- that the brain transmits its thoughts to an immortal self, thereby preserving them. We will take the view that the *Content of Consciousness* model is an implementation of that theory.

It was Kant's view during the *Our Unseen Guest* discussions that we need to understand matter from his point of view in order properly to apprehend the philosophy being presented. Some of this material was published in *Our Unseen Guest*. But large portions exist only in the original unpublished manuscript entitled *The Master Key*. The text below, from that manuscript, is how Emmet Finley originally reported it.

It was in an early stage of our Ouija board adventures that the late lamented Kant told Joan and me understanding of the true nature of matter was essential to understanding of reality's whole. Therefore, when at length matter was announced by Stephen as the topic of extended discussion, we were not surprised that he should call the old German metaphysician into the conversation.

Methodically he who Stephen on his ghostly honor asserted was Immanuel Kant -- dust, as the saying goes, these many years -- spelled on our Ouija board these words: "Guten Abend."

When Joan and I confessed to rather slender German, Kant redivivus equalled our frankness by confessing to slender English. And so it was arranged that the great thinker should convey his thought to Stephen and Stephen then should convey the same to Joan and me. In such fashion Kant said: --

"It is a very great satisfaction to me to know that in the long ago as earth counts years I made myself heard among men. As a living voice I am recorded as having had the knowledge that matter wholly aside from appearance has a quality that is in and of itself. This quality I called 'ding-an-sich'.

"Tonight I, speaking to you through our mutual friend, Stephen _____, say to you that the ding-an-sich, which my earth degree of reason told me existed, is consciousness, the same consciousness that is the thing-in-itself of yourself.

"My contribution as a living voice to the scientific and metaphysical thought of earth I, a voice stilled yet speaking, would now confirm by saying to man, be he scientist or metaphysician: 'Turn your attribute of reason in on yourself and recognize that which you find. For I tell you that even as consciousness is the only reality of which man can be sure, so, too, is it the only reality of all that is or was or ever will be. Consciousness, the height of which as it is manifested on earth is man's self of self, is.

"And so I, joining in with the glorious little company that has talked to you and welded of eternal metal the master key, offer the gift of pluralistic monism to the groping yet ever seeking minds of men.

"I, Immanuel Kant, who gave all that I could when I was with you, now offer the supremacy of my giving after I have passed away from you."[1]

There followed a heated discussion, too long to repeat here, between Richard Hall and Emmett Finley on the meaning of these things. Hall maintained that as an observer he had it all over Finley. "We who are here see matter . . . in its component parts. Therefore, in comprehension of consciousness as the one and only reality, matter presents to us no difficulty."

"Men imagine that what they call matter is a fundamental, he continued. "Yet could they but see matter as it really is, they would immediately perceive that the thing they had been calling matter is in reality an attribute of a fundamental. That fundamental is consciousness, consciousness in degrees. Matter, as you know matter, is the form attribute of certain degrees of consciousness."

Finally, then, the tripod spelled:

"Kant would have you forget his ding-an-sich. He would have you say simply: Consciousness is; all consciousness has form." [2]

Of the two professors, William James looms the larger in the American consciousness. We need a brief reminder as to why this is so. He came from a family that was by any measure outstanding, and had been so for three generations -- the founder of the dynasty an eminently successful businessman; his best-known son a theologian and father of three individuals each of whom left a mark on their times:

---

1. *The Master Key*, pages 120-121

2. *The Master Key*, page 130

William James, America's most prominent psychologist and philosopher; Henry James, his generations's most famous novelist; and their sister Alice, gifted in her own right. A very competitive family, but this did not prevent the three from being exceptionally close all their lives.

We know James as a Harvard professor at the turn of the century. From his home at 95 Irving street near Harvard Square in Cambridge, he sallied forth to defend the things of the spirit from what he perceived as threats from materialist philosophers.

Thus we have from his pen such classics as *The Will to Believe*, *Human Immortality* (mentioned above), *A Pluralistic Universe*, and *The Varieties of Religious Experience*. These volumes were in addition to his ground breaking treatise on psychology. Upon his death the New York Times called him America's foremost philosophical writer, exponent of pragmatism, and virtual founder of the modern school of psychology.

With all his prominence in "respectable" fields, yet did James toy with fields more arcane. There seemed to be no field of inquiry that he rejected, and if the American physicist, Richard Feynman, invented the technique of a summary over histories to describe quantum phenomena, surely James used the same technique to capture the full reality of phenomena of the mind. Thus he was interested in psychic research, and we need to ask ourselves why. The Times deplored this interest, noting however that this side of the versatile genius had made probably the strongest impression upon the common mind. James liked the work of the British Society for Psychical Research and helped found a Boston chapter, of which he was principal researcher. When

Dr. Richard Hodgson, the English psychical researcher, died, James talked to him through the Boston medium, Mrs. Piper. Yet he was not a total convert; he entertained doubts as to whether such phenomena were decisively proved, doubts even that immortality was a proven fact. One sees James as the perpetual outsider, looking in, envious of those on the inside while he himself remained without. It was so in *The Varieties*. He chronicled all the mystical Christian experiences he could find, declaring them genuine, valid, and the quintessence of religion; but in his own life, he confessed to never having had such an experience himself. In this ambivalence we are reminded of Kant, who was alternately attracted and repelled by Swedenborg, and of Freud, who had a similar relationship with Jung.

James was exposed to these ideas at an early age. His father, Henry James Sr., father not only of William the philosopher, but of Henry James Jr., the most important American novelist of his time, was a Swedenborgian theologian, who spent a lifetime trying vainly to interpret Swedenborg's ideas to his own satisfaction, and getting himself booted out of the orthodox Swedenborgian church for his pains. The James household bubbled with the ferment of ideas. If there was a prominent thinker of the period, he was likely to be an intimate. Thus we see Emerson frequently there, and the father of Louisa May Alcott, and many another thinker of the period, as guests, a possibility arising not only from Henry James the senior's undeniable talent but also the social position he inherited from his outstanding father, along with a share in the millions he left his heirs.

Now why is the name Swedenborg important here? Simply because he was the pathfinder for the thought incorporated in the three divulgences reported in this book. His reports introduce us to the "modern" view of immortality, heaven and hell, and salvation. These were in his view first-hand reports of an investigator who had been "there" -- a tribute to his extraordinary psychic powers. Swedenborg reported that immortality is a fact of nature rather than something imposed as though from without by one's theology; that heaven and hell, while quite real, are more nearly akin to states of mind, and as such are wholly self-created and present in the here and now prior to the death of the physical body; and that all judgment, while again quite real, is self-judgment, and all punishment self-imposed.

Swedenborg was an eighteenth-century man. The Stockholm fire that he sensed clairvoyantly, and for which he is best known in the popular mind, occurred in 1759. Kant "dealt" with him, in *Dreams of a Ghost Seer*, in 1766, the "ghost" being Swedenborg himself.

Like William James, Swedenborg was a genius in his own right. He was a scientist, an authority on metallurgy; was offered (but declined) the chair in mathematics at Uppsala University; and engaged in a bewildering variety of intellectual pursuits, such as analyzing currencies, exploring the decimal system, examining alcohol production and consumption and inventing practical machinery. With all this he was socially prominent and a confidant of the Swedish royal family.

But here we see the paths of Swedenborg and James diverge. Swedenborg was the pathfinder and fully convinced of the authenticity of his findings. James was the wistful follower; full conviction always eluded him. Yet as psychic historians we know something of James's career as it developed after he died; and it may be that in his association with the divulgences group he found finally the serenity and conviction that eluded him during his lifetime. I am about to present this evidence. The reader is left to judge whether it is convincing.

There is a side of James not always noted in brief reports of his life, and it has to do with his mental stability. It was not as robust as one likes to think is consonant with the reputation of such a great man. One ordinarily looks to his younger sister Alice for this James characteristic. She was a brilliant individual, a political radical, but a lifelong invalid, victim of emotional and psychosomatic maladies that pursued her relentlessly as long as she lived.

From these propensities James himself was not wholly immune. He was himself as a young man invalided by bouts of depression for years on end. He finished his medical studies with difficulty because of them, surprising himself by passing the final examination while under this cloud.

We known these things from his own pen. There was a time in his his youth, then, that he was stricken with a terror that fastened itself on him and remained for months, just as it had on his sister. The brilliance of his ground-breaking tome on psychology was not altogether accidental; in part it was an account of a personal exploration into the pathology of the human mind.

But to return to happier reports. James defended the notion of immortality while here, and even anticipated the ideas concerning consciousness described above by Kant. "There is but one indefectibly certain truth . . ." he wrote, "the truth that the present phenomenon of consciousness exists."[3]

James's contributions to the notions of human immortality were greater after his death than before. The best records of this -- the sitting notes for *Our Unseen Guest* -- have unfortunately not survived. But Emmett Finley's initial report -- the manuscript for *The Master Key* -- has, and to this we now turn. The identification of James is unequivocal in the manuscript. It was suppressed prior to publication for reasons to which we are not privy. As to his contributions to *The Content of Consciousness*, he made but few personal appearances at the sittings, but he was there, and I think that is enough. Together with his transmission theory, and his prominence in the sittings on which *Our Unseen Guest* are based, we are entitled to assume that he is one of the authors of the model presented in this book.

Now for the record of his contributions to the first and third divulgences.

During his lifetime here James searched persistently for proof of life after death. He never found it. One gathers that he had been barking up the wrong tree. Here is how he put his post mortem view to the Finleys.

"If, my dear sir and madam, it were possible for me to appear to your physical eye, if I sat down and spoke to your physical ear, you would call me an hallucination. Richard's revelation must be its own test. Its reasonableness in the light of earth's already acquired knowledge is its best, its only proof. And, my dear sir, such is public opinion's

3. *The Will to Believe*, Dover, 1956. Pages 14-15.

present lack of understanding concerning those phenomena your world calls psychic that you would do well to withhold your name from any record it pleases you to make of these conversations." [4]

James died in 1910. The view presented above is how he saw things towards the end of World War I. *Pay attention to the philosophy*, he is saying. *Forget the evidential, you won't believe it anyway.*

In the *Content of Consciousness* model one sees free will defined in a a sort of abstract way, yet again so meticulously that a programmer can implement it on a computer. This was one of James's big themes in the sittings with the Finleys on which *Our Unseen Guest* and *The Master Key* are based. It was James's view that mankind is the free will degree of consciousness. Emmet devoted an entire chapter in *Our Unseen Guest* to the subject.

And the subject was not without its share of humor. *Get James's psychology*, said the Professor. *Read the definition of the will. Let's see if a dead man can improve on it.*

Easier said than done. Emmet didn't know where he had put the book. Nor did Ruth. James did, however. *Look behind Moliere.* And there it was.

Could a dead James correct the work of the live one? Not really. Instead, he approved of it! Then he went on with considerable elaboration, all of it fascinating. You can read the full report in Chapter 29 of *Our Unseen Guest.* [5] It is essential background for the use of the model.

But not always did the transcendent James approve of the life's work of the James that had been.

---

4. *The Master Key*, page 15

5. Page 275

The Finleys had been discussing James's *A Pluralistic Universe*, which Ruth, heeding a behind-the-scenes cue from Richard, had purchased at a bargain counter. Emmet was struck by the phrase "pluralistic monism," and was thanking James for it. But the tripod would have none of it.

"This is James talking," it spelled. "You have robbed the beggar. The phrase 'pluralistic monism' is not mine. It is your own."

His idea in life, James explained, was instead "pluralistic idealism". He was influenced unduly, he said, by materialism and its ally, the wizardry of science. He wanted to counter these thoughts and return a measure of emphasis to the spiritual side of man's nature. And so he overreacted and missed the truth by that much.

"I came so near the absolute truth," he said plaintively. "That I should have missed it by a hair is odd, my dear sir, very odd." [6]

In *The Master Key* James is identified by name. In *Our Unseen Guest*, Emmet Finley maintained the fiction that he was "The Professor," whose widow was named "Helen." (James's wife was in fact Alice Howe Gibbens James.) In lieu of calling him by his real name, Emmet substituted an entire chapter devoted to establishing his identity.

The principal evidence consisted in a description of James's home at 95 Irving Street in Cambridge, Massachusetts, provided by Ruth Finley while in trance. The Finleys provided a transcript of this sitting to James's widow, who asserted that it was a remarkably accurate reading. It was a home neither of the Finleys had ever seen.

---

6. *The Master Key*, page 84; Our Unseen Guest, page 205

Of the details provided by the entranced Ruth, that of James's library may be mentioned. The description was not letter perfect, but close enough for Mrs. James. She liked in particular the reference to a smoking lamp, for Professor James used his old student lamp, an oil burning one, in preference to an electric one, and the student lamp frequently smoked, to his considerable annoyance.

Interested readers can see a photograph of the study in question after page 554 in R.W.B. Lewis's *The Jameses.* [7] It was in this study, not long after the Jameses had taken up residence at Irving street, that they had held a seance with Mrs. Leonora Piper, with the English psychic researcher F.W.H. Myers, and also Richard Hodgson, secretary of the American Society for Psychical Research, present. [8] After Hodgson's death, James would try to contact him through Mrs. Piper.

During his investigations into psychic phenomena, James had never established to his satisfaction proof of communication with the dead, despite his apparently successful conversation with the late Dr. Hodgson. Yet Emmet Finley reports that in this endeavor he finally succeeded. James referred to a promise to his wife via a different medium to bring her an unequivocal message, saying finally, "Put it over, by George! put it over." [9] Mrs. James, in correspondence with the Finleys, confirms this: that several years prior to the Finley sittings, a medium

---

7. Farrar, Straus and Giroux, New York, 1991

8. *The Jameses* by R.W.B. Lewis, Farrar, Straus and Giroux, New York, 1991, page 491

9. *Our Unseen Guest*, page 199

had given her a script purportedly from her husband, saying that he would in time reach her through an unknown psychic.

Although James's activity as a direct speaker fades after these encounters, he remained a member of the divulgence team. He was present for the spectacular sittings recorded in the appendix of Stewart Edward White's *The Betty Book*; but the only text reported was his observation that the subconscious is to the Beta what the conscious is to the physical. [10]

I am not aware that James did any of the talking for the second divulgence. (*The Unobstructed Universe*) That one was dominated by the brilliant performance of White's wife, Betty. But of course it was not really her material. It had been carefully thought out, and even its presentation put into an orderly, step-by-step pattern. [11] Had James participated in this? It is only a conjecture. Betty frequently consulted her co-workers, but except for Anne, Richard Hall, and Ruth Finley's father, the doctor, White does not name them.

Nor does James do any talking during the Third Divulgence sittings. Nevertheless he is indicated as being present; we have the sitting notes to attest to this.

He was present, for instance, on June 2, 1947, during a discussion of the use of the AOC triangle in normal life, White saying, for instance, that during sleep the triangle tips and the "C" apex goes towards the top.

---

10. Page 250

11. *The Unobstructed Universe*, page 55

"If it went completely to the top," he noted, "you would have complete anesthesia."

Or if the triangle rotated the other way (clockwise), it would be for mediumistic communication, he continued. [12]

James is again present at the June 16, 1947, session. [13] The subject is a rather technical discussion of planes of the mind and types of attention, for which the reader is referred to the description of the model elsewhere in these pages.

How much of this material may be due to James is again wholly a matter of conjecture. With parts of it we may assume he was quite happy, particularly with the incorporation of the human will in the model, and especially with the elevation of the transcendent part of the mind to a level of equality with the subconscious -- certainly in line with his efforts to counter the drift towards pure materialism in his lifetime.

But a detailed discussion of these matters is best left to the specialist in the history of ideas.

---

12. *The Content of Consciousness* sitting notes. The June 2, 1947, sitting is recorded on sheets 212-216

13. *The Content of Consciousness* sitting notes, sheets 281-290

Chapter 5. Ruth Ebright Finley

OF the remaining members of the *Content of Consciousness* team, Ruth Finley's life bears some description. We have introduced her as author, feminist, and newspaperwoman. What does that really mean?

She was born September 25, 1884, in Akron, Ohio, to Leonidas S. and Julia (Bissell) Ebright. The early details of her life were collected by Barbara Brackman in a biographical sketch for Quilters Newsletter Magazine.[1] Her father was a surgeon; of him there will be more to tell later in this story. When Ruth was a child, she would copy medical case histories for him. From her mother, Julia Bissell, she inherited Connecticut roots. There were two state governors in the family tree, which had colonial forebears dating back to the 1600's.

This family background is doubly important to Ruth's life as a medium. Her spirit teacher and control, Anne o' Perth, claimed that between herself and Ruth Finley a blood relationship existed. In the character sketch of Anne given later in this book, there will be tantalizing details of Anne's background: who she was, where she was from.

Ruth attended Oberlin College for a semester, then switched to Buchtel College. Brackman writes that she left, without graduating, to travel and write in the western United States. Upon her return she became a journalist, working first for the Akron *Beacon-Journal*, later for the *Press* in Cleveland.

---

1. November/December, 1988. Leman Publications, Wheatridge, Colorado.

We have an account of her early career written in her own hand. It is a brief sketch -- 13 double-spaced typewritten pages -- of a projected autobiography, never finished, never published, that Betty, herself at that date an Invisible, "commanded" her to write. We can date the writing somewhere between 1944 and 1950.

Turning to Ruth Finley's personal account, then.

If I were reader instead of writer of this psychic "case history" I should want to know, before spending any more time on the detailed record of the -- shall we say, "patient?" -- just how reliable such an autobiography might be considered; what sort of reputation she had.

Under the very peculiar circumstances of being both writer and "patient", it is a great satisfaction to me to be able to state that for a good many years the practical world at large has considered me entirely reliable; accorded me a reputation of authority on mundane subjects; and that I can offer unimpeachable and easily verified evidence of this fact.

At the moment as I write not twenty people can possible know that Joan the psychic and Ruth E. Finley, listed as "editor, author" in *Who's Who in America* since 1930, are one and the same. I am the wife of Emmet Finley, also in *Who's Who*, and we are one of the comparatively few married couples both appearing in that roll of honorable workers every one of whom must win the right to inclusion on his own.

I won the hard way over a period of twenty-four work years: first as a cub reporter walking the streets of Akron gathering society tidbits about the then budding rubber millionaires for six dollars a week, for the self-satisfaction of seeing what I wrote in print, and in the hopeful determination of one day attaining a by-line.

I got my by-line -- the right to sign my stories -- rather quickly. To be honest -- and according to the Invisibles I must be what doubtless will prove to be painfully honest -- this step was not wholly due to my own ability. I could write and I am a born newspaper woman; that is, wholly aside from a faculty for expressing myself on paper, I have what is known in the journalistic world as a "nose for news." It is as special a gift as a singing voice or being able to paint. You have it -- or you haven't it. Also, like all talent, its endowment is in degrees. The degree of my own . . . (here the copy trails off).

I was, as I said, born with it. But I was young and exceedingly naive. Frankly, my early by-line was due in no small measure to the family name I wore. My father, Dr. Leonidas Strickland Ebright -- "Strickland Ebright" -- was himself news, and had been from Civil War days on into World War I, in Ohio, especially in the northern counties still known as the Western Reserve. Frequently "spot" news. My mother, born Bissell -- she was not of the carpet-sweeper branch, but it is all the same root -- was also of the mentality, disposition and temperament to make news. The combination -- Ebright plus Bissell -- was just too good locally, in Akron, for any up and coming editor to keep off his pages. So the by-line, "By Ruth Bissel Ebright," came easily.

But its coming easily made my work harder. First I had to live up to it. It made me double responsible for every word printed under it. Secondly, fellow reporters also dreaming of by-lines somewhat resented it. I was younger, much greener, and the only girl on the *Beacon-Journal* staff. The men had been sort of big-brotherly kind to me before. Now they were not unkind, but they certainly let me prove that I could go places on my own. Even my city editor stopped throwing me tidbits. Within six months I realized that if I were ever going to get beyond describing Mrs. X's teas or the gowns Mrs. Firestone wore to the Charity Ball, it would not be my city editor but myself who gave me the assignment. Which I proceeded to do forthwith.

This was back in 1906 when Thomas A. Edison was at the height of his wizardry. His second wife, whom he married in 1886, was the daughter of Lewis Miller, financial source of supply and co-founder of Chautauqua with Bishop John H. Vincent and one of Akron's most beloved elder citizens. Mrs. Edison frequently came home on visits but she had so persistently refused to be interviewed that all the papers finally had agreed to leave her large and unusually devoted family in peace. I knew this; her comings and goings were taboo even in the society columns, mine as well as those of my rivals.

However, Mina Miller Edison was a *really* nice person and a thoroughly human one. When I explained it to her she instantly understood why an interview with Thomas Edison's wife could mean a leg-up for me.

She was *really* nice because while she could see no sense in being personally publicized because of her famous husband, she was perfectly willing in an emergency to give somebody else a boost. Between the two of us we cooked up a not too innocuous little yarn about Mr. Edison; and as soon as she was on her train where reporters from the other papers couldn't pester her, I sailed into my office with it -- just in time for that day's Home Edition!

Ruth Finley's personal account of her career ends abruptly at this point. But we can piece it together from *Who's Who*, her New York Times obituary, and the sketch by Brackman.

Her subsequent career as a newspaperwoman and feminist is given in some detail in *Who's Who in America*. The 1953 edition notes a 1911 appointment as editor of the Woman's page, Cleveland press; fiction editor of Scripps-Howard Newspapers, 1912-1918; managing editor, Washington (D.C.) Herald, 1919; woman's editor, Newspaper Enterprise Association, 1920-1921; associate editor, McClure's magazine, 1926-1928; editor of Guide, The Woman's National Political Review, 1936-1938. She was Chairman of the National Press Committee of the Nation Council, Women of the United States, 1928-1929; member of the National Committee on Folk Arts of the United States; Co-Vice Chairman of the Steering Committee of the National Federation of Business and Professional Women's

Clubs for Celebration of 100 Years of Women's Progress in Business and the Professions, 1937; member, National Council of Women's National Republican Club, 1937; member, D.A.R. and Kappa Kappa Gamma. Episcopalian. Author, *Old Patchwork Quilts*, 1929; *The Lady of Godey's -- Sarah Josepha Hale*, 1931. Contributor to magazines. Home: 268 Palisade Avenue, Dobbs Ferry, New York. Died September 24, 1955, one day short of her 71st birthday.

The New York Times adds that in September, 1937, she began editing a new pocket-size monthly magazine called *Guide*, which was said then to be the only women's national political review. It was published by the Women's National Republican Club.

She had collected quilts for many years prior to the publication of her book describing them. She told a reporter:

"I came of an old quilting family in Ohio, where patterns were handed down from mother to daughter for generations. Here in Brooklyn and Long Island I found so much history sewed into patchwork quilts that it was well worth the trouble to study."

In *The Lady of Godey's* she told the story of how Mrs. Hale made Godey's *Lady's Book* the forerunner of the women's magazines of today and set the fashions of our grandmothers.

The Times mentions her marriage in 1910 to Emmet Finley. Brackman describes their courtship when both worked for the Cleveland Press. Ruth was working undercover as a maid to develop a story for the paper. Her employer was suspicious: why did this perfectly normal lady have no male callers? To allay these suspicions the newspaper persuaded a reluctant Emmet Finley to fill in as surrogate squire. The assignment must have suited him after all; the couple were married within months, their city editor taking credit for the match in a piece published in the *Press*.

Enter Richard Nelville Hall

Those readers who read the preface already know how Ruth Finley became a psychic medium. It happened during the Finleys' Cleveland years. Richard Hall's presence during the sessions with the Ouija board were so mind-boggling that the Finleys were a long time being convinced. Fortunately for us, they finally were. What Hall had to say was unprecedented either in or out of such a session. It had a further consequence. Quite unexpectedly, Ruth Finley became America's most important medium.

Ruth Finley describes her reaction in a letter to a correspondent who had read *Our Unseen Guest.* As in all such correspondence she carefully guards her real identity. The letter reads in part:

> After more than twenty years the thing that always amazes us is the *kind* as well as number of people who either possess psychic powers themselves or have close friends who do, and so are forced to accept the *reality* of immortality or repudiate the integrity of their own intelligence or that of trusted friends.
>
> Darby and I went all through that; some of our struggle you read in *Our Unseen Guest*, though no mere printed page could tell the story. Especially from my personal standpoint. For I am the official "receiving station" and have never been able to get over the feeling of more or less responsibility for what comes through.
>
> Like you I am of Scotch ancestry. My father, instead of my husband, was a physician and surgeon and all the men members of my immediate family were physicians or clergymen. Two of my father's sisters married Presbyterian ministers. I myself am a college woman of the Lincoln Steffans' "muck raking" era when it was "sophisticated" to view everything through a "scientifically" intellectual microscope. We

certainly were neither sophisticated nor scientific and hardly intellectual, but we enjoyed thinking we were and I suppose college students still do. Anyhow, that particular period produced a very tongue-in-cheek attitude and I developed a quite acute case of it. Darby was educated for the bar. So Stephen scarcely could have chosen two harder nuts to crack; one a legal mind trained to doubt all statements until proved -- the other, I must confess, just plain snooty! So you see the coming of Stephen was a real jolt to Darby and me, and I can easily understand and fully sympathize with your self-doubt and healthy reluctance to discuss your gift with friends. (Get *The Road I Know* by Stewart Edward White -- it's a biography of Betty, his wife who was a very great psychic -- if you want to see how very normal your feeling about the whole thing is.)

Your own experience as outlined in your letter is running so true to type -- both my own and hundreds of others reported to me just as you have done -- that I am sure it is genuine. Your power, or talent, or whatever it is that people like you and I possess -- and I'm sure I don't know what it is any more than you do -- waxes and wanes; again I don't know why. I have gone for months, indeed several years, with no "call" to attempt communication. And even in the midst of the most fluent and important dictation from the Invisibles "at times it's easy and then for days it will be very difficult", to quote your own words. A little about this sort of thing is explained in the second "divulgence" that came through me and (was) published in 1940 by Dutton's in a book titled *The Unobstructed Universe* and signed by Stewart Edward White. His wife Betty, who is one of my closest friends, died in '39 and she is to *The Unobstructed Universe* what "Stephen" was to *Our Unseen Guest.*

Named by Anne

The work the Finleys participated in transcends the importance as well as the personal ability of the Finleys themselves. It was part and parcel of a high-level orchestrated series of "divulgences" that would come to include Margaret Cameron's *The Seven*

Purposes as well as the three that came through Ruth Finley -- *Our Unseen Guest*, *The Unobstructed Universe*, and *The Content of Consciousness*.

This larger pattern was indicated by Anne in a sitting that took place in Cleveland on March 13, 1920. Present were Ruth and Emmet Finley, Margaret Cameron Lewis (Margaret Cameron's married name; in the sitting notes she is listed as M.C.L.) and a Mary E. (perhaps Mary Ebright, Ruth's sister). After some brief preliminaries, Anne said:

"Weel, I hae na sae much tae say the nicht. Ye'll be sendin' the book tae the Paw."

The "Paw" being Stewart Edward White, whose letter head from Little Hill in Burlingame, California, contained an animal's footprint done in the color blue. Anne had this in mind, but the sitters failed to make the connection. They replied in chorus:

"The what?"

"The Paw," replied Anne.

"Whose paw? What paw?" This from Margaret Cameron Lewis.

"The blue Paw," said Anne.

Still nobody made the connection. Anne grew impatient.

"The blue paw o' the white mon!"

Emmet's notes indicated that earlier in the evening Margaret Cameron Lewis had been reading extracts from some letters from Stewart Edward White and fragments of records he had sent. He notes that it was impossible that anyone present could have seen the letter-head. The sitting notes continue:

Anne: Ye'll be tellin' him frae me that I want him to be studyin' the philosophy. Ye'll be tellin' him that pluralistic monism is true, an' that I said sae, an' that i' the book he'll be a-findin' o' the message that is tae coom tae him. There is much more tae coom. We dinna repeat. When a thing's done, 'tis done. There is much more tae coom.

Ruth: Elizabeth, Bessie, Betsy and Bess, All went out to steal a bird's nest. They found the nest with noth-ing in it, . . .

Well, I never did know that one . . . Oh, I think I could say Little Tommy Tucker . . . . But what's the use of my sitting here saying trash like that? . . . Elizabeth . . . There's a woman here who says Mary should finish the rhyme. Elizabeth, Bessie, Betsy and Bess, all went out to find a bird's nest. They found a nest with three eggs in it . . . I will not sit here and try to remember a fool thing like that!

Emmet asked if anyone remembered the nursery rhyme. Margaret Cameron Lewis repeated it, noticing the persistence of "Elizabeth, Bessie," etc.

Ruth: They wish me to tell you that there is a single word in that nursery rhyme which they want you to pick out.

M.C.L.: Is the word Bess, or Bessie?

Someone unidentified now spoke. Emmet thought it was the Professor. Margaret Cameron Lewis thought it was a woman.

Voice: Yes. The reason we could not give her the name was because she hears you talking about it.

M.C.L.: Which Bess?

Voice: The Bess I have a message for.

M.C.L.: Bess of the blue paw?

Voice: I don't know anything about the blue paw. It's the Bess we are teaching. Tell her, please, to drift with the stream. A little inclined to take the importance of what has been happening to her over-seriously. Not that I mean it is other than serious, but if she tunes herself to too high a pitch, it will not be possible for her to take the messages as fast as we can . . . (Here the utterance became too rapid to follow in longhand, and Emmet lost the rest.)

During this hiatus Emmet made some facetiously scoffing remark, and the Professor remarked reprovingly that it was nothing to be flippant about, continuing:

Professor: It is quite possible that by this time you have come to a conception of the importance of the general plan of operation. I am going to tell you something more; something you would not have believed a year ago.

At this point the sitting was interrupted by a light, airy, capricious female Invisible.

Professor: The young lady has much of her old-time facetiousness. A most charming individual.

Emmet: She seems to have interrupted you at an important point.

Emmet's notes indicate he thought what follows came from the Professor. Margaret Cameron Lewis's impression was of the unidentified woman again. Not Nancy. Possibly Mary K.?

Voice: We have a very definite plan. Three persons, totally unknown to each other (Emmet: presumably at the beginning of the individual experiences.) in three different sections of the country, are being drawn rapidly, for good and cogent reasons, into this work together. To each one of you a definite phase of the message will be given. They will fit like that.

Here Ruth lifted her hands to a point about a foot in front of her bandaged eyes and clasped them, the fingers of each hand fitted closely between the fingers of the other. She held her hands thus upraised and interlocked so long that Emmet feared it would tire her and he said:

Emmet: Anne, take down her hands.

Anne: Tak 'em doon yersel', lad.

Emmet: I don't want to startle her. (Further discussion deleted here.)

Anne: *Tak 'em doon*!

Emmet accordingly tried to "tak 'em doon" and was obliged to use all his strength to force the hands back to Ruth's lap. Ruth's face was quite serene, showing no strain, and the muscles of her arms were relaxed and soft. Anne then explained that she had done this to show us that she was "material." She said her hands were beneath those of the lass, upholding them without effort on Ruth's part.

(Further experiment along this line, and some discussion of a problem of Margaret Cameron Lewis's omitted here.)

Ruth: (Apparently describing the person who had been talking to Margaret Cameron Lewis)

The woman has a very beautiful profile. An intellectual brow. The forehead is not wholly straight. The curve is very slight, but in a minute analysis there is a slight curve. The nose is not exactly prominent, but strong. A medium upper lip, with a gracious mouth. Yes, a rather large mouth.

M.C.L.: Is the nose pointed, or rounded?

Ruth: It has a little line. (Touching the point of her own nose.) The chin is decided, but not prominent. The mouth takes away the heaviness of the chin. The eyebrows are pretty. She says to tell you her complexion was a bit sallow. I can't see the hair. It's covered with something. (Margaret Cameron Lewis: See photograph of Mary K., which at that time I'm quite sure Ruth had never seen.) And now she says she has a message to give you. (Message related to some questions in Margaret Cameron Lewis's mind, omitted here.) The woman says that very soon your part of the great work, that is to be accomplished more quickly than she had planned, will begin. That you are to be the leader, to be supported by two others, one of whom you already love, the other one whom you will love. (Margaret Cameron Lewis: At that time I had not met Betty.) That the culmination of the plan is drawing rapidly to a head, and that you of yourself will recognize the two chosen to work with you.

Mary K.: Have you ever thought of the rule of three? Surely you have studied some botany?

Emmet: I have. The lily family goes by a rule of three.

Ruth: (spelling) E-T-R-U-S-K-A-N.

Emmet: (to correct the spelling) C-A-N.

Ruth: *K-A-N.* Did any of you ever study Etruskan symbols? She says they are very interesting and that the rule of three comes up in them.

Mary K. You know that in many ancient religions, even in one as modern as the Jewish faith, you find this same rule of three. It goes on into the Christian religion as Father, Son and Holy Ghost.

Emmet: But of what is this rule of three symbolical?

(Here Ruth repeatedly outlined a triangle in the air.)

Mary K.: You know that two people might be told the same thing and might lose, each of them, a piece of it. If three people were told the same thing instead . . .

Ruth: There's something about a stone that she wants me to see.

Emmet: Keystone, probably. That's sort of triangular.

Ruth: No, a jewel. Our diamonds are cut with many faces. They used, in the old days, to cut their jewels three-sided. And she wants me to tell you that the great jewel . . . .

Mary K.: I bring to you the gift of a jewel, but not with so many facets that you cannot see clearly through into its heart, but with the old cutting of three -- clear, brilliant, shining for all the world. And you have been chosen as one of those facets, and she has been chosen another, and the woman who . . . (something lost here. In effect, the woman who is coming close to each of you . . . M.C.L.) through strange and unaccountable circumstances which you scarcely understand and can not control, is the third. And the three of you are to give as your gift to humanity in the broadest sense, humanity as it represents consciousness on your plane, this jewel.

To each will be given a message that will be one of the sides -- the great triumvirate chosen. The work has only begun. The foundations have been laid by you and by her. The polishing, the varying lights, the brilliancy, the appreciation of the rarity and wonder of the jewel -- this is yet to come. But do not be mistaken. It is the fairest ever set in any diadem.

Will you give the third this message? Will you tell her that she, too, has been called? Will you ask her if she, too, will give of herself and her gift to this jewel? The great three?

Emmet, during a pause, jested about his inability to imagine himself "chosen" for any great work, and called Margaret Cameron Lewis "The Holy Daughter."

Mary K.: Do not scoff at prophecy, for I say to you that the truth shall be set high, and the light of it shall shine as from a mountain top. And those who fear shipwreck, whose sails are tattered, who look toward land and cannot see because of fog (notes incomplete) this jewel beacon will shine and lead them home. Surely you know enough now of the great plan, of the unusual and superhuman circumstances that have brought you all together in this room to know that there must be a reason. Things don't just happen.

This altogether remarkable sitting took place, as was mentioned, on March 13, 1920. Margaret Cameron's book, *The Seven Purposes*, had been published in 1918; the communications on which it was based commenced on March 3 of that year. The Finleys' book, *Our Unseen Guest*, was published in 1920, and thus was at least a completed manuscript at the time of this sitting. Its communications commenced, as was noted, on December 7, 1916. At the time of this sitting, the "education" of the third member of the triumvirate, Elizabeth Calvert Grant White, "Betty," or "Bess" as she was called above, wife of author Stewart Edward White, was scarcely begun. Her initiation has been dated by her husband as commencing on March 17, 1919.

Ruth Meets "Daisy" Cameron

Ruth Finley's own account of her acquaintance with Margaret Cameron Lewis is contained in an unpublished article entitled "Second world War Foretold Twenty-four Years Ago." The point of the article, written in mid-summer of 1942, was to bring attention to the predictions made by Mary K. while

World War I was still in progress, predictions that had been published in *The Seven Purposes.* Mary K. had said:

"The forces of disintegration are gathering for a titanic struggle, of which your Great War is only the beginning . . . ." [2]

Ruth notes: "At the moment Germany was winning; the great German offensive of 1918 had begun only five days earlier and the Allies were falling back with appalling losses."

But Mary K.'s attention is already riveted on the war to come; she considered the first already won. Otherwise: "Had Germany won, the spirits of free men would have been soiled with fear and despair, and the forces of doubt and disintegration would have held civilization captive." [3] Continuing the prophecy:

"Germany . . . chose to follow the forces of destruction, and they will surely destroy her . . . . But the forces she followed are uniting for a fiercer fight, more subtle, more deadly, more furious. Hidden beneath the garments of peace and good will they (the forces of disintegration) make ready to poison the minds of men before destroying . . . their purposes.

"This is the battle to which we call you and all who are for progress. This is the message you are to give the world, to warn of the danger at hand . . . ." [4]

---

2. *The Seven Purposes*, by Margaret Cameron. Harper & Brothers, 1918. Page 101.

3. *The Seven Purposes.* Page 101.

4. *The Seven Purposes.* Pages 101-102.

To continue the story in Ruth Finley's own words:

Today, in mid-summer 1942, I have just turned off the radio from the horror tales of the Russians' retreat in their gallant attempt to save the Caucasus. The tragedy -- and glory -- of Dunkirk are ancient history. France, Belgium, Holland, Denmark, Poland, Norway, Greece, the Philippines -- but why go on when the list is written on every heart -- all lie under the despot heel of Germany and her Axis allies. "Civilization held captive!"

Some day, perhaps soon, the United Nations of freedom-loving peoples will re-open the Western front. But at this moment of writing the only drawn battle lines are in the East.

Again read -- and note the date:

"April 1, 1918.

"A light breaks in the East -- Russia, given as a sacrifice to the brotherhood of man. A light not of star or dawn, but of sacrificial fire. Heed it, guard it . . . for by its flaming sacrifice are ye saved." [5]

A suspect statement in 1918 and for the more than two decades of "liquidation" -- a newfangled slang for group murder -- that brought the Soviet Union into being and sustained it. Portentous words -- now. Mysteriously fate has moved its pawns: at last the prophesy of April 1, 1918, seems possible of fulfillment, though we, the United Nations, still have many a mile to travel before we may count ourselves as "saved." But how illy this prognostication fitted into the picture of 1918! The Battle for the Somme was in the balance; Russia, collapsed in the throes of mass-rule bloodier than the French Revolution, had abandoned the Allies and was a cloud, rather that "a light . . . of sacrifice to the brotherhood of man."

Her account continues:

---

5. *The Seven Purposes*. Page 110.

In America a strange thing was happening, an incongruous thing. And it was occurring, of all places, in an exclusive New York drawing-room at Central Park South, many costly floors above the roar of traffic, its window overlooking the most priceless stretch of grass and trees and jewel-like bits of man-made lakes on earth.

Day after day several men gathered in this room -- and a woman. She, their hostess, would be seated at a card table across which a roll of blank wallpaper was stretched, its end unrolled end resting on the floor, its other end being gently drawn by one of the men from under the furiously moving pencil held laxly in the woman's hand. Every face in the room registered amazement, bewilderment, skepticism; the woman's most of all. General comment and conversation, in which even the woman took part, went on as her arm jerked this way and that following the galloping pencil that sometimes made letters a foot high, sometimes so small they had to be deciphered under a magnifying glass. At times the automatic writing -- for it was a case of what psychologists term automatic writing, probably the most remarkable, from a physical standpoint if no other, ever recorded -- wrote in a spiral of concentric circles that might begin in the middle like a pebble dropped in water and widen out, or might start at the edge of the wallpaper and wind itself in a web of sprawling but legible words. Often -- and this was a tantalizing stunt -- the writing was done backwards and had to be unscrambled in a looking-glass!

But this legerdemain showmanship was not what kept the woman at the card table for weary hours, hours so straining to her arm that finally a stubborn case of neuritis developed, nor did the mere act of the writing, curious and piquing though it was, particularly interest the men. Neither were they then attentive to the portions of the writing that are of paramount importance *now*. Yet all through that jittery Spring of 1918 some half dozen hard-headed, work-driven men found time to return to that drawing room again and again to hang over a card table covered with a roll of blank wallpaper which in turn would be covered with automatic writing -- purported spirit messages from an unseen world!

Why did they come?

Because the writing proved itself, almost without fail, to be three days to three months ahead of the events of the War -- let alone the published news.

Who were the men?

A couple of bankers from Wall Street; an exporter or two with international business connections; various members of Columbia University's faculty and always at least one representative from the Harper publishing company.

For the woman whose hand held the impatient pencil was Margaret Cameron, for years among Harper's successful authors. How the whole affair of automatism began need not be detailed here. It was accidentally encountered and entirely unsought. That it was startling, even dismaying, to a reputable professional writer is putting it mildly. Yet from the moment the importance of the automatic material became manifest she lent to it her days and nights, asking only, through the presence of witnesses, that her own integrity be surrounded with every safeguard possible. Within the year Harper's published Margaret Cameron's best seller of her several best sellers, *The Seven Purposes*, subtitled "An Experience in Psychic Phenomena."

It is Part II of this book that is of especial interest today. Only vaguely understandable in 1918, it comprises what the Invisible (a self-proclaimed, disincarnate intelligence) claiming to control the automatic writing called "The Lessons". There are twelve of these and they might be characterized as admonitory prophesy, particularly now when, after twenty-four years, most of the essentials of their warnings have happened or are in the act of happening. But when they were written on the wallpaper, interspersed with a mass of other materials, "The Lessons" were relegated to second place. Their beauty of language and profundity of thought were recognized, and their philosophy gave the book its very good title -- *The Seven Purposes*; but their long-range forecasts could not be understood and consequently were overshadowed by the life-after-death assurances of the rest of the "experience." Reviewers and readers alike passed their oracular import by.

There was a three-fold reason for this. First, America was mourning her First World War dead and any argument supporting the reality of immortality met emotional response; secondly, the Armistice was signed about the time the book came out -- the Allies had just saved the world for democracy -- so why worry about trials that would not repeat themselves; thirdly, Margaret Cameron was then not only a top-flight author, but her forte in both fiction and drama was farce-comedy -- about as far removed from "The Lessons" and, indeed, the whole performance, as anything could be. Her acute and not infrequently satiric sense of the ridiculous had been keeping large sections of the English reading world chuckling since before 1900. Look her up in *Who's Who* if you are too young to remember *The Cat and The Canary, The Golden Rule Dollivers, The Pretender Person* and many another lighthearted book.

A successful author to the reading public that knew her as Margaret Cameron, she was in private life the wife of Harrison Cass Lewis, who from 19-- until his death in 1926 was executive head of the largest exporting paper and type company in New York. His business necessitated wide travel and always Mrs. Lewis accompanied him. His position then, no less than his wife's, imposed many social duties, and the international contacts of the two of them made their drawing room among the most interesting in town. People from all over the globe met there. It was very cosmopolitan, very sophisticated, and very, very far from any implication of esoteric pronouncements from Beyond and just as far from prophesy whether of doom or salvation.

From 1921 on I was intimately familiar with the Lewis home. In that year my husband and I came East to stay. We were complete social strangers in New York, but Mrs. Lewis had lived all her girlhood in California where she had gone to school with cousins of mine. So I had entree. I knew from the beginning a good deal about her -- how her youthful impishness had won her the sobriquet of Mad-Cap Meg; how she had been ring-leader of the gay young society crowd of the San Francisco of her time; witty, fun-promoting, popular "Daisy" Cameron.

And though maturity had seasoned the exuberance of youth by the time I met her, her unfailing sense of humor and experienced graciousness had made her a favorite in that ever-widening social circle of New York which has learned to blend wit, talent and business achievement into a harmonious whole.

After the publication of *Our Unseen Guest* a strong bond was forged between the principal actors named by Anne during the Cleveland sitting mentioned above. A fourth couple -- Mr. and Mrs. John Gavit (Mrs. Gavit was a talented medium) -- was added, and they were a tightly knit group while any of them remained alive. One reads about this group in the appendix of *The Betty Book*. White describes a spectacular series of sittings using four mediums simultaneously. The stars of the show were Betty White and Ruth Finley. Certain of Ruth Finley's demonstrations were spectacular by any measure. She was so at home in the unobstructed universe that she was given to meandering off on her own, oblivious to what the group was trying to do. During one of such jaunts she fell into conversation with an unobstructed denizen, and reported back on what she learned.

I'm talking to someone, she said. *He has a body like anyone else. It's different, though. It seems to be lighted up from inside itself, and it's not black and white, it's colored.*

And it is somehow fluid. You couldn't pick it up. Nevertheless, it maintains its form. And it is stronger than our bodies are.

He tells me that his body is what we call the soul, and we all have one while we are still on earth. We just can't see it, that's all.

But when Emmet senses that cold feeling during these sittings, it is somebody's soul that he is feeling. [6]

This immensely talented medium did no published mediumistic work from 1922 until *The Unobstructed Universe*, which was published in 1940. She continued working as a medium, however. Richard started dictating *The Content of Consciousness*, but eventually Emmet tired of it and refused to do more.

Then Betty White died. Six months later -- it was in the autumn of 1939 -- Stewart Edward White visited the Finleys, and the Betty White-Ruth Finley block-buster, *The Unobstructed Universe*, came through.

Thereafter the Finleys remained close to Stewart Edward White. The file is full of their letters. Ruth became the editor for *The Road I Know* during the day; in the evening, Betty and her colleagues performed their own editing, sending instructions through Ruth Finley the medium on how to revise the manuscript.

White was the next to die. A few months later he also was on hand with a serious manuscript -- the languishing, long-neglected *The Content of Consciousness* -- and once again Ruth Finley it was who took the dictation.

Her Father's Daughter

No account of Ruth Finley's mediumship would be complete that did not describe her relationship with her father, Dr. Leonidas Strickland Ebright. As

---

6. *The Betty Book*, by Stewart Edward White. E.P. Dutton, New York, 1937. Pages 251-252.

noted above, when she was young she had copied out his case histories. After he died, she took his case histories by mediumistic dictation. He was such a frequent visitor to her sessions that he seems like an old acquaintance to anyone steeped in this series of books.

One of the most striking episodes in this relationship was that in which Dr. Ebright, himself long since dead, treated her for gall stones. This account is given in a letter from Ruth Finley to Margaret Cameron Lewis, dated May 9, 1939. It appears in the SFFI Journal in an article by E.W. Dykes entitled "The Fascinating Joan."

Ruth was quite sick and was being treated for pneumonia. Her temperature was 106 degrees and she had been vomiting. At that point her father interceded, saying it wasn't pneumonia she was suffering from, it was a problem with her gall bladder.

You can come with me, said Dr. Ebright. *Or I can operate.*

In the latter case, however, she had to prevent her doctors from interfering with his treatment!

She preferred to go with him, according to her letter. But he persuaded her to stay and endure the operation. He then explained the operation and the post operative treatment.

"I am telling you this now," he said, "because in your post-operative condition I may not be able to reach you so clearly. But I can make you remember it." Her father as a doctor had had wonderful hands, Ruth reported to Margaret. "I felt his hands that night as surely as I ever felt them in my life," she wrote. "They hurt me . . . then he sent me 'out.'"

But now to the text of the letter.

"That Sunday I felt desperately ill but kept on my feet. Could not get up Monday morning. Before leaving for town Emmet called the Doctor's office, learned he was away and after some discussion with me decided I had better let his associate, Dr. Held, come in to see me. Dr. Held showed up a little after lunch, immediately got both day and night nurses on the job, and began drastic pneumonia procedures at once. I was running a temperature of 106 and don't remember much about it, save the terrific pain in my head.

"The next day, Tuesday, I started vomiting, and it was Tuesday night that father put in an appearance. He had other people with him whom I seem to have known, but cannot now remember well enough to identify. It was probably his usual gang.

"Dr. Held was still diagnosing pneumonia. The nurses, of course, reported me as delirious. In this 'delirium' I carried on my side of the conversation with father, and in this way announced that 'father said the trouble was gall bladder,' and that he would have to operate -- unless I was ready to go with him. But I had to choose. Because if he operated I had to do exactly as he told me -- it would mean a great deal of pain -- a very long convalescence -- and in no case could he be perfectly sure that the docs here would not interfere with him and spoil everything. I had to understand that I -- the patient -- must be strong-willed and fearless enough to prevent that. I can see him yet, standing at the foot of my bed. He always stood at the foot of the bed when talking to a patient, so the patient could see him with the least effort, and he made every doctor who worked with or under him do the same. I had suffered so much that I was afraid of more pain and wanted to go with him. But at last he made me see that I must stay; or at least, by doing exactly as I was told, *try* to stay.

"It must have been about three o'clock Wednesday morning when I told him I would do as he wished. Because, according to the night nurse, it was at about that time that she began to 'simply freeze.' Anyway, I remember her getting her cape and insisting that the thermometer in the room 'just can't be working' because it registered 70 and '70 certainly isn't *this* cold.' she told Dr. Held the next morning that I laughed, and he told me that for me to laugh 'when you're that sick proves you are the best patient I ever had.' But that was not until Wednesday evening, when he made a final call after office hours.

"Meantime, to go back to the mysterious 'cold,' things began happening to me. The nurse wanted to call Emmet and I wouldn't let her, because father explained that, 'of course Emmet can't be with you in the operating room.' So *that* nurse sat quietly, but other nurses bent over me and I saw them -- plainly. Father explained to me what he was going to do, how he was going to do it, and what the treatment was to be when the operation was over.

"He said: 'I am telling you this now because in your post-operative condition I may not be able to reach you so clearly. But I can make you remember it. Do you understand? You are to remember it and report it to Dr. Alden, with my compliments.'

"I think I have told you of Father's noted and wonderful hands. I am not the only living person who remembers, and could not fail to recognize their marvelous touch. Only last summer, at home, a woman who used to be his patient told me how, even yet, she compared every other doctor's touch with his. I felt his hands that night as surely as I ever felt them in my life. They hurt me, but not unbearably, for he was only getting me ready, and then he sent he 'out.'

"I stayed out until the day nurse had came on next morning. Then the first thing that happened was that without retching, bile heavily deposited with black grit about the size of coffee grounds poured out of my mouth. I know all about that for I tasted some of the bile and the grit got in my teeth and had to be washed out. Somebody must have telephoned Dr. Held, because he appeared as if by magic. He pronounced it gall stones and began to talk about an 'emergency operation' right away. I said I would not be operated, but that I wanted 'a quarter grain of morphine by hypo after each expulsion, with a cleansing enema at four o'clock this afternoon.' The nurse told me afterward that I told Dr. Held 'I'd die just to spite you,' if I could not have my way -- or rather -- father's way. The next 24 hours are pretty blank because Alden kept me under morphine, but twice more I expelled the black grit by mouth, and the cleansing enema produced the jagged, three-cornered gallstone that Emmet wrote you he saw 'rattling around in a bottle.'

"Wednesday night Held ordered the dehydration treatment that nearly spoiled everything. And Thursday morning Dr. Alden, having gotten home after midnight, appeared before breakfast. He told Emmet at once that he would NOT advise operating though he was sure the gall bladder had ruptured. That day, too, is pretty blank because Alden kept me under morphine, though he and father seemed about equally there. I forgot to say that Alden halted the de-hydration pronto and began giving me citrus fruit juices immediately.

"It was next day, Friday, that I went on my famous 'morphine jag.'

"As you know, father did a great deal of consultation work. He was much over-worked and very busy, so frequently he would have mother or me telephone messages to other doctors. Depending on how well he -- and I -- knew the physician I was to telephone to, he taught me to say: 'Dr. Ebright's compliments and may I read you his report' -- whereupon in either case I would read whatever father had written for me to read, ask if a duplicate should be mailed and for any message to father. All this, of course, in less serious cases; otherwise father saw the doctor personally. Doctors didn't have full time nurses in those days. Father had a nurse in his personal employ, but kept her out doing home dressings and what not most of the time. So we at home were trained in the giving of messages.

"Well, by Friday afternoon I was enough out from under the effects of hypodermics to know perfectly what was going on, but still woozy enough not to 'edit' my conversation. So late in the afternoon when Dr. Alden appeared for the third or fourth time that day, I pipes up: 'Father's compliments, Dr. Alden, and he wishes to say he is completely satisfied with the operation. He suggests forty-five degrees elevation on two pillows -- even during sleep -- to insure drainage, with the use of small head pillows under both sides of the back to avoid strain. He says he would like the citrus fruit juices stopped and pineapple juice substituted -- two ounces every hour. No solids for another twelve hours when cottage cheese may be added. The incision -- ' and on and on, with the use of technical terms which I cannot now even remember, but I do remember Alden's accounting for all this to the nurse by saying, 'You see, she was brought up in a medical household and she's heard her father and cousins talk about such things.'

"However, he 'humored' me, asked what father thinks about this and that, all of which I answered, and to which I remember his replying more than once, 'I think you are right, sir.'

"Of course I did not know then that already he had told Emmet that he thought the gall bladder had ruptured. But I shall never forget his final question.

"'Now about this new de-hydration treatment. What did father say about that?'

"'Father said Goddam,' I replied sweetly. Whereupon the nurse gasped audibly and Alden curled over the foot of the bed and cried into my feet.

"'You've got the *loveliest* morphine jag,' he announced when he could speak. 'Hasn't she, nurse? Did you ever *see* as funny a morphine jag?'

"All of which I consider very sporting of a supposedly without-a-sense-of-humor Vermonter. Certainly it's the only time in my life that I've heard the man laugh. Last year my nurse and I used to bet with each other as to whether or not we could get him, during a visit, to crack a smile.

"The next day Alden brought the surgeon, Dr. Seamon, in consultation. I am sure Alden had been somewhat confidential, to say the least, with Seamon, because though I had never before met him, he immediately began talking to me about having been a patient of Dr. Warner's. Now, everybody who knew either one of them -- Dr. Harry Warner and Doctor Sam Seamon -- knows of their personal, as well as professional, friendship. When Dr. Warner was killed in Egypt, Dr. Seamon went to London to meet the body.

"But I wasn't having a 'morphine jag' that day, so when Dr. Seamon wondered 'what Dr. Warner would think of you now,' I agreed that 'it would be interesting to know,' and let it go at that.

"Then he examined me -- which curled me up, naturally -- and said to Alden he had no doubt that I still had gall stones and should be operated.

"'No such thing!' my voice interrupted rudely -- and loudly. 'That's post-operative swelling. Nothing but! And you know it . . .' I caught myself just in time not to add his name -- 'Sam.'

"'I'm terribly sorry, doctor," I apologized, and tried to go on stammering excuses but his hand closed down over mine.

"'Don't,' he said. 'You always were Harry's -- favorite patient. He used to tell me about you. I -- understand.'

"Then he advised Alden to have X-rays, 'just as a precautionary measure -- no hurry -- not too soon. The thing is not to tire her. And I must see them. Probably very interesting.'

"And then with a word of this and that, the two gentlemen departed. But when the nurse came back from attending them downstairs, she said: 'Well, I'll be darned! Did you see the tears in Dr. Seamon's eyes?'

"I have not seen Dr. Seamon again. But many weeks later when I was waiting in a room at the emergency hospital, on the top floor of the Professional Building, between the taking of the first and second sets of X-ray pictures, Dr. Alden came. Not a word had he said after that first day about my 'morphine jag,' though I noticed he followed father's 'suggestions' to the letter.

"'Well,' he said, grinning, 'I' 'I've just been down to the X-ray room, and I guess you had your psychic operation all right. Those plates don't show a damn thing and my guess is they're not going to. And Seamon says --'

"'Yes?' I prompted. 'Has Dr. Seamon seen them -- already?'

"'Seen them!' huffily. 'He got there before I did!'

"'Dear me,' sez I. 'How -- unethical -- of Dr. Seamon.'

"'Wait till I tell him that!' he roared. 'Is that what "father says"?'

"'You're a nice doctor!' I retorted. 'Get a patient on a morphine jag and then twit her about it.'

"'What do you want me to do? Take it seriously?' he came back.

"'Heavens, no!'

"'Exactly. So we're going to put you through every X-ray sprout we can think of.' (Which he did, even to ordering several sprouts retaken.)

"But that morning, after he had left he came back -- I was alone, of course -- and stuck his head through the door.

"'My compliments to father,' was his parting shot, 'and say to him it was some psychic operation!'

"I have seen him at least a dozen times since. To all intents and purposes he seems to have gone back to his former very serious personality. I have become just his prize patient of gall-bladder rupture. I believe that usually they don't get a cure, so he has a right to be proud of me. When he came to see me yesterday, he told me that I am at least 33-1/3 per cent better than I was at this time last year. He assured me of this with his usual gravity, but away back in his eyes was a very *un*usual twinkle.

"I have just read this over. I have been inadequate. I haven't at all gotten over the vividness of father's presence. He was here, in this room with me. I felt the strength of his hands and heard his voice. I saw him constantly. He came in and out of my room. He made me do things -- ask the nurse for things I didn't want but that he wanted me to have. And not for days after Seamon's examination did Alden touch me. He asked me how it was healing -- and I told him. Some twenty X-ray plates they took later show the gall bladder completely drained, clear and healed."

All of which adds up to an amazing incident in the annals of psychic phenomena. It is asking too much of Dr. Alden that he be required to believe the actual facts of the case. Nevertheless he demonstrated that graciousness which so often embellishes the healing art and raises it above the other professions.

At which point we can all perhaps offer our compliments to Dr. Ebright and all the others involved in this unusual case history.

Nothing So Strange

Ruth Finley buried her husband in 1950. In 1955 she followed him. In accordance with her request, her body was buried beside his in the cemetery in Salem, Ohio.

Thus ran out the life here of an astonishing medium -- a notable public woman whose special talent was entirely private -- so much so that her secret died with her, and would have remained obscure, had she not chosen finally to reveal it herself.

She picked a characteristic platform for this unveiling. Dr. Sherwood Eddy, World Secretary of the

Young Men's Christian Association, was having a sitting with the well-known public medium, Arthur Ford. Ruth Finley made an appearance at the session, giving the name "Findley," and identifying herself as the "Joan" of the Stewart Edward White books. Turning to Eddy, she told him that she had heard him speak at Oberlin college some years past. Under his influence she had been at the point of becoming a student volunteer, but chose instead to go to work for a Cleveland newspaper.

Ford reported this session in his autobiography, *Nothing So Strange*. Among its readers was Lovina May Knight, whose parents were life-long friends of Ruth Finley. The women had been girlhood friends, had in fact lived on the same street, and had gone to college together. There was an occasional visit after the Finleys moved to New York. When Miss Knight graduated from college, Ruth Finley gave her an autographed copy of *The Lady of Godey's*, her newly published book. And in all this coming and going, not once had the Finleys compromised their cover -- not once in all that time had they mentioned their interest in psychic phenomena.

So things stood when Ford published his autobiography. Miss Knight read the above "astonishing" paragraph to her mother. Did Ruth Ebright ever go to Oberlin? *Yes.* Did she ever work for the *Cleveland News* and *Plain Dealer*? *Yes.* Then she was "Joan," the famous psychic!

Even then Ruth Finley's secret was fairly safe. Miss Knight reported her discovery to the local Akron-Canton Spiritual Frontiers Fellowship group, but took no other action.

Ford's autobiography was published in 1958. In 1963 Miss Knight had an opportunity to ask Ford personally. Was Joan really Ruth Finley? *Yes,* he replied.

It was in 1988, some twenty-five years later, that Miss Knight prepared the material used above in the form of an article, "Who Was Joan," that appeared in the *Spiritual Frontiers* publication of the Spiritual Frontiers Fellowship, thus making the identification of Joan official to the world at large.

There were no more "divulgences" after Ruth Finley died. More's the pity. Anne's group prepared four; the last one is irretrievably lost.[7] We will have to discover its substance the old fashioned way.

Still, there was a tantalizing tidbit in the Ford records. He had a persistent sitter who demanded to know more than he could tell her about the nature of personal immortality. *It's like this,* the discarnate Ruth Finley told her. *There aren't really two bodies when you are on earth. It is all one thing. You are simply a mix of frequencies. Its focus is changing all the time, but it is nonetheless a single thing.*

Dying has no effect on the higher frequencies. What they do at that point is to dissociate themselves from the earth body, since they have no further use for it.

---

7. The fourth divulgence is mentioned in the chapter on The Unobstructed Universe.

Chapter 6. Emmet and Harwood

TWO other participants in these sessions bear mention. They are Robert Emmet Finley and Harwood Arend White. I give brief sketches of each below.

Emmet Finley

As husband and collaborator of Ruth Finley, Emmet had always played a key role in all of her mediumistic undertakings. He it was whose touch on her wrist signaled the start of trance which was for her deep and thorough. His also the contentious mind that chewed stubbornly on any material received until it was clear what was grain and what chaff. Not enough that the material was received; it had also to be conceived, or the job was only half done.

Finley was born May 22, 1881, in Salem, Ohio. He was admitted to the Ohio bar in 1907 and practiced law until 1908, becoming at that time a newspaper reporter, first for The Repository in Canton, Ohio, then for the Cleveland Press. From 1910 to 1912 he was secretary of the Cleveland Street Railway Commission; in the latter year he returned to the Cleveland Press as City Editor, serving in this capacity until 1916.

It was during these years that he laid the foundation of his subsequent career as a publishing executive. In 1913 he became associate editor of the Newspaper Enterprises Association, which was the Scripps-Howard feature service with main editorial offices in Cleveland. In 1920, together with three associates, he bought Publisher's Autocaster Service from Scripps-Howard and moved it from Cleveland to New York City. It was an organization that served country newspapers with editorial features. Emmet was executive vice president, treasurer and general manager until his retirement in 1945, according to the account in The National Cyclopaedia of American Biography. Curiously, The New York Times lists a cutoff date for these titles of 1939.

The Times notes that concurrently he had various other business connections. He was general manager of the American Press Association and the John H. Perry Newspapers, a small chain. From 1928 to 1933 he was general manager of the Star Adcraft Service. The list goes on and on.

In 1938 Finley and Perry purchased Western Newspaper Union. Finley became executive vice president, treasurer, and general manager of that company, as well as its subsidiary, Western Newspaper Union Sales Corporation, until 1945. Its chief activity was the placement of national advertising in small city and country newspapers. Under Finley's management it became the largest service of its kind in the world.

During the second World War that firm took care of all copy placement for the Unite States Treasury Department for the second through the sixth War Loans.

He was a member of Phi Beta Kappa honor society, a college honor offered to students with very high grades. He was also a member of the Masonic order and the BPOE. He was an Episcopalian and a Republican. His publicly admitted side interests included research in metaphysics and reading Latin and Greek. He liked to compare his own translations with standard ones. As mentioned, the Finleys were married in Akron, Ohio, on August 24, 1910. He died in Dobbs Ferry, New York, on December 13, 1950. There were no children.

E.W. Dykes reports that just before Emmet's death, with Ruth at his side, he penned this note:

So good night! my dear; we shall meet again in the morning light." . . . . Not "Good-bye," nor even "Au Revoir," but Good night."

Harwood White

Less is known about Stewart Edward White's younger brother, Harwood Arend (Beese) White. He was born in Grand Rapids, Michigan in 1895 or 1896, moving with his parents to Santa Barbara, California, at the age of seven.

He graduated from Princeton University in 1917. He then became a tennis professional; as such at the Montecito Country Club he helped coach Alice Marble, Pauline Betz, Jackie Douglas, and Keith Gledhill. He wrote tennis books. He collaborated with his more famous brother on *Daniel Boone* and co-authored with him *Across the Unknown.*

He served in the Air Force in World War I. He married the former Alexandra Tonetti (Alex) of Santa Barbara. They had five sons. All survived him except Thomas Stewart, who was killed in the crash of a light airplane he was piloting. The accident was particularly traumatic for the family, as the plane crashed on their own property.

Harwood's wife is believed to have had little interest in paranormal work until her son was killed. Thereafter she was in a sitting with Ruth in which her son explained his accident and gave other details to prove his identity. Harwood believed young Stewart was merely showing his oats -- it was his second solo flight -- and he was angry with the field personnel who let him leave the flight pattern. In a reading through Ruth shortly thereafter young Stewart appears and explains that the accident was due to a faulty part in the steering mechanism. In other appearances young Stewart said he would be a helper to Dr. E, as Ruth's father was often referred to in readings. While on earth he had indicated his desire to become a physician. In the course of his communication he identified things unknown to his parents but which were verified by his bother to be true.

Most of what else we need to know about Harwood White can be picked up from the sitting notes. He considers himself "scientific," an opinion in which Emmet concurs, and as an intellectual. Nevertheless he had an intuitive nature that was easily excited; these qualities made him an excellent foil for the rapier-like thrusts of Emmet's cold logic.

He had followed his brother's interest in psychic matters with considerable enthusiasm. He was himself psychic, and dabbled in efforts as a medium. He also was attracted by the mystic aspect of the work, having had a so-called "cosmic" experience himself of rather strong voltage, as noted in Part I.

With all of this, he was of that nature that has a compulsion to explain things in his own words, to personally re-create the world so that he could understand it. Ruth Finley's correspondence notes that Stewart Edward White had asked Harwood to scan the manuscript for *The Road I Know* and make suggestions. To the elder White's horror, Harwood instead did an entire re-rewrite of the manuscript, saying he couldn't grasp it until he had done so!

This tendency shows up in the sitting notes. Time and again he would stubbornly veto Emmet's notions, saying he wanted first to recast them according to his own lights.

On one occasion he defeated his brother's attempt to dictate important material by insisting on giving his own thoughts instead. The material not dictated is lost to us; it represented God knows how much Invisible staff work, and qualified thereby as wisdom of the ages; but Harwood would have none of it, he had to get his own two cents worth in instead.

Nevertheless, the *Content of Consciousness* would not be what it is without him. Emmet was apparently incapable of finishing it up on his own. The qualities Harwood White brought to the party provided the missing ingredient, and the sittings were consequently a rousing success.

He died January 16, 1954, at his home in Santa Barbara. He had been ill for two years.

Chapter 7. Stewart Edward and Betty White

THERE were, as mentioned, four primary actors involved in the *Content of Consciousness* sittings. They were Stewart Edward White, who dictated most of the material; Ruth Finley, who was his "receiving station," or psychic medium; Emmet Finley, her husband, acting as "conceiving station," to use White's earlier terminology -- the term implies that Emmet's job was to understand what was given in his own terms --; and Harwood White, brother of Stewart, co-conceiving station. Had we ourselves been invited to these sessions in the New York home of the Finleys, we would have seen Harwood White recording the session on his "Sound Mirror;" Emmet Finley sitting attentively by the couch, his hand on his wife's wrist; the latter in deep trance, and speaking with the unmistakable voice of Stewart Edward White, who had died the previous year yet was very much alive and eager to transmit an astounding message.

Who then were these people? All but Stewart Edward White have already been introduced to the reader. Since White relayed the message, and was himself the best known, we give him now his due, together with a brief sketch of that companion of the spirit, his wife Betty.

White was known to generations of his readers as an interpreter of the American frontier. His career commenced just as the frontier was disappearing; but its proximity permitted him to experience much of it in his own person. Thus he mined for gold in the Dakotas; punched cattle in Arizona; served as lumberjack in Michigan; ran a tramp steamer between California and Alaska; hunted big game in Africa; explored the High Sierras on horseback; and canoed with Indian guides in Canada. These activities were not those of a tenderfoot but of a seasoned professional. When he served as a lumberjack, he *was* a lumberjack; when as a cow puncher, he *was* a cow puncher. One gets a glimpse of the stern facet of White's character from his obituary in the New York Times, under the subheading "Choked Leopard to Death." "When past 50 years of age," the Times reported, "he went to the rescue of two African natives who were being mauled by a wounded leopard, and reportedly choked the beast to death with his bare hands when it turned on him."[1] The reader will get a further glimpse of this side of White's character below.

In between he wrote forty odd books based on these exploits, read by generations of readers eager to understand the era of the frontier so close to the heart of the American experience.

Readers found his accounts authentic, so much so that many a Californian claimed to be the original of wholly fictitious characters in his novels. His accounts were believable because White had himself experienced them. And they were authentic for an additional reason: that White was devoted to hard facts, and even in his novels never strayed far from them.

Since White's veracity is important to our tale, it is worth our time to explore it in some detail. One begins, then, with his early life in the Michigan woods, where as the son of a millionaire lumberman he found easy access to the life of the lumber camp.

---

1. *The New York Times*, September 19, 1946.

I say "easy access;" but rather than visit the camp as the owner's son, White signed on as any other lumberjack might; worked a lumberman's shift during the day; and wrote in the evening. I invite the reader to try this. The work is physically demanding beyond the imagination of a city dweller. The summer I myself spent in a lumber mill, I found myself confined to bed the first weekend with a high fever, the result not of infection but of the results of the unusually severe physical exertion. I was all of 19 years of age.

White on the other hand was made of sterner stuff. He spent his evenings not recuperating but writing. When a fellow lumberjack stayed up an entire night devouring one of his manuscripts, White understood that his desire to be a writer was founded on something substantial. His novel of the lumber industry - *The Blazed Trail* -- was the best seller of all his books, and still sold some 3,000 books a year 30 years after it was first published.

To return to the issue of authenticity, however. White was apparently a born naturalist. He had for example an encyclopedic knowledge of native birds and their calls. As a young man he wrote an article, "The Birds of Mackinac Island." [2] The scientific community considered the article authentic, and it gained for White membership in the American Association for the Advancement of Science.

Nor was this the only instance in which White put his many talents to ordinary affairs. His African safaris we have already noted; as a by-product of big game hunting, he mapped parts of German East Africa. The German government may have come to

2. This is an island in Lake Michigan, near White's boyhood home.

regret this; the maps were later used by the British who, in recognition of their value, conferred upon White membership in the prestigious Royal Society.

White's love affair with guns commenced with teen-age quail-hunting weekends; in his youth he found bliss in early morning tramps through cold wet brush with a shotgun over his shoulder and hand-loaded cartridges in his pocket. His prowess as a hunter was considerable; this facet of the man reflects his personal interest not just in the skill of the thing, but in authenticity, veracity, and accuracy. He was interested in the mechanics of guns. (One recalls his service in World War I as a gunnery officer.) He joined Mark Twain in debunking the stories of frontier marksmanship told by James Fenimore Cooper. ("Not only can you not *hit* a nail at the described distance, you cannot even *see* one." -- quotes supplied.)

He then proceeds to describe how rifles really work. You first bolt the rifle down to an immovable stand, then fire it several times. The bullets so fired will form a cluster in the target. No two holes will be superimposed; it is the cluster itself, called the error of dispersion, that defines the inherent accuracy of the piece.

Next, without removing the rifle, take three sightings on a target, while someone marks with a pencil the point you see. The result is called the triangle of error; it indicates how nearly you can sight at the same place every time. The results of this test, White reports, will humiliate you. It is one measure of your competence as a marksman, and you have yet to fire the piece, with all the additional errors involved in that operation.[3]

What of White's own competence as a marksman, and indeed as a rifleman? One searches his forty odd books in vain for such a report. There are references, but they are faint and oblique. In one of his African books [4] he mentions his habit of carrying his own rifle in the field; had he followed the British tradition, he would have made his bearer perform this office. White cites, in defense of his own practice, his experience in hunting on the American plains, where the time spent transferring the gun from bearer to marksman would have cost the hunter many a fleeting target.

Also in his defense he cites his first lion kill. The party saw the animal loping across their field of vision almost out of range. White flipped his rifle into position and chanced a shot. It connected. The beast fell, rolled over, regained its feet, and trotted off.

Not a good position to be in. Wounded lions kill unwary hunters. One is honor bound to follow them and finish them off.

Accordingly the party gave chase, following the wounded animal into the dense thicket into which it had crawled for cover. Into the thicket the hunters crawled also; the bush was too dense for standing. After an interminable amount of inch-by-inch progress they reached the animal, which growled

---

3. See *Daniel Boone, Wilderness Scout* by Stewart Edward White, Doubleday, Doran & Company, Garden City, New York, 1931. The reference to the nail you can't see, and the error of dispersion, are on page 24. The triangle of error is described on pages 25-26.

4. *The Land of Footprints*, Doubleday Page & Company. 1912.

menacingly perhaps 50 feet distant. A companion's shot struck a branch and went awry. The unlucky hunter dropped flat at White's urgent command; White writes that he then put a bullet where he thought it would do the most good. It seems to have been a wise choice, because the beast rolled over dead. It was, as mentioned, his first lion. [5]

What is White's personal opinion of his own marksmanship? As already mentioned, one looks in vain in the man's published works for this. The only reference I have seen him make on the subject is his report, in the same book, from the mouths of bearers. Two of them are arguing about the relative merits of the men for whom they carry guns. One says something like, "My man can shoot two shots to one for yours." The other, White's bearer, retorts: "My man only needs one."

Of this endorsement White was uncommonly proud.

So the record would rest except for evidence from an unexpected source. For this tale we go as a preliminary to Santa Barbara, California, where White as a young man is visiting relatives. A party from the East needs a guide for its excursions into the surrounding mountains. White, for reasons we can surmise, is selected to be that guide. The result is a lasting friendship between White and the head of the visiting party he led that day into the mountains. One reads about it in a tribute to White written by the son of the visitor, who reports that in later years White and his wife Betty were frequent and welcome visitors to his father's home in Washington, D.C. That home was the American White

---

5. *The Land of Footprints*, Doubleday Page & Company.

House; the father, and the Santa Barbara visitor, was President Theodore Roosevelt.

In the matter of White's shooting prowess, then, we are privileged to call to the witness stand one Theodore (Teddy) Roosevelt, twenty-sixth president of the United States and himself renowned big game hunter and African safarist.

"I never did much with the shotgun," recalls Roosevelt, "but I practiced a good deal with the rifle. I had a rifle-range at Sagamore Hill, where I often took friends to shoot. Once or twice when I was visited by parties of released Boer prisoners, after the close of the South African War, they and I held shooting-matches together. The best man with both pistol and rifle who ever shot there was Stewart Edward White." [6]

Well! It seems the man can handle a rifle after all. But there is more. Roosevelt's account explains better than White's what it means to go after a wounded lion in cover, and what it means to be a hunter of White's caliber.

Roosevelt continues:

"My own experience as regards marksmanship was much the same as my experience as regards horsemanship," he writes. "There are men whose eye and hand are so quick and so sure that they achieve a perfection of marksmanship to which no practice will enable ordinary men to attain. There are other men who cannot learn to shoot with any accuracy at all. In between come the mass of men of ordinary abilities who, if they choose resolutely to practice, can by sheer industry and judgment make themselves fair rifle-shots. The men who show this requisite industry and judgment can without special difficulty raise themselves to the second class of respectable rifle-shots; and it is to this class that I belong. But to have reached this point of marksmanship with the rifle at a target by no means implies ability to hit game in the field, especially dangerous game."

---

6. *Theodore Roosevelt, an Autobiography*, Charles Scribner's Sons, New York, 1926. Page 34.

Skipping down a bit in Roosevelt's account we find this continuation:

"What such a man needs is not courage but nerve-control, cool-headedness. This he can get only by actual practice. He must, by custom and repeated exercise of self-mastery, get his nerves thoroughly under control. This is largely a matter of habit, in the sense of repeated effort and repeated exercise of will-power. If the man has the right stuff in him, his will grows stronger and stronger with each exercise of it -- and if he has not the right stuff in him he had better keep clear of dangerous game-hunting, or indeed of any other form of sport or work in which there is bodily peril.

"After he has achieved the ability to exercise wariness and judgment and the control over his nerves *which will make him shoot as well at the game as at a target,* he can begin his essays at dangerous game-hunting, and he will find that it does not demand such abnormal prowess as the outsider is apt to imagine. A man who can hit a soda-water bottle at the distance of a few yards can brain a lion or a bear or an elephant at that distance, and if he cannot brain it when it charges he can at least bring it to a standstill. All he has to do is to shoot as accurately as he would at a soda-water bottle; and to do this requires nerve, at least as much as it does physical address. Having reached this point, the hunter must not imagine that he is warranted in taking desperate chances. There are degrees in proficiency; and what is a warrantable and legitimate risk for a man to take when he has reached a certain grade of efficiency may be a foolish risk for him to take before he has reached that grade. A man who has reached the degree of proficiency indicated above is quite warranted in walking in at a lion at bay, in an open plain, to, say, within a hundred yards. If the lion has not charged, the man ought at that distance to knock him over and prevent his charging; and if the lion is already charging, the man ought at that distance to be able to stop him. But the amount of prowess which warrants a man in relying on his ability to perform this feat does not by any means justify him in thinking that, for instance, he can crawl after a wounded lion into thick cover. I have known men of indifferent prowess to perform this latter feat successfully, but at least as often they have been unsuccessful, and in these cases the result has been unpleasant. The man who habitually follows wounded lions into thick cover must be a hunter of the highest skill, or he can count with certainty on an ultimate mauling."

A bit later:

"On the whole, I think the lion the most dangerous of all these five animals (lion, elephant, buffalo, rhinoceros, grizzly); that is, I think that, if fairly hunted, there is a larger percentage of hunters killed or mauled for a given number of lions killed than for a given number of any one of the other animals." [7]

This much I have given the reader to set the stage for what follows. We are zeroing in on Roosevelt's perception of White as a marksman and hunter. He supplies this in a review of White's book, *The Land of Footprints.*

"Mr. Sheldon and Mr. White -- whose book I shall next consider - are big-game hunters of the best type. They are not professionals, but in point of hardihood, of skill in their craft, of ability to fend for themselves, and of readiness to meet every emergency and every risk, it is not too much to say that they are fairly entitled to come in the line of descent straight down from the Boones and Crockets, the Kit Carsons and Bridgers, of the old days. Each of them by preference hunts entirely alone. Each is as competent to care for himself as any Indian. The book is admirably written by a man who loves the mountains, the great woods, and the stormy seacoasts, and who describes with power and charm what he has seen. He is the direct reverse of a game-butcher; he cares nothing for a "big bag." He kills only what must be killed. His book is of practical value to naturalists."

Continuing:

"Stewart Edward White's book deals with hunting-grounds as unlike those of northwestern America as can well be imagined. He too has written a notable book, and has given a fresh proof, if one were

---

7. *Theodore Roosevelt, An Autobiography*, Charles Scribner's Sons, New York, 1926. Pages 34 to 37.

necessary, that the fact that many first-class books about hunting in a given region already exist in no way means that there is not ample room for another first-class book. It is totally unlike Sheldon's, except in the sense that both men have a great love for wild natural scenery and good power of describing it, that each is an observer as well as a hunter, that both are thoroughly hardy men whose deeds in no way resemble those of the mere holiday hunter. I am not running down the holiday hunter at all, for he may do the best that his opportunities allow; I am only pointing out that he must not compare himself with the man who can push boldly into the unknown and do all his work for himself.

"Mr. White was for part of the time while in Africa a companion of Mr. Cuninghame, a professional elephant-hunter, who managed my safari during most of my own trip in Africa, and Cuninghame wrote me that White was the very best game-shot with a rifle he had ever seen in his life."

There you have the meat of the account. White does not merely write about the out of doors; the man is *good.*

Roosevelt does not leave it there, however. He continues with a criticism of White's optimistic advice to would-be big-game hunters.

"In the appendix Mr. White treats of rifles and equipment. In his protest against the needless luxury, in fact the cumbrous luxury, of present-day African hunting he is quite right. At the same time, in the outdoor sense of the word, Mr. White is a very "hard" man, and it would not be well for the average holiday sportsman to try to follow his example in cutting down the paraphernalia of African camping life, any more that in cutting down cartridges."

Later:

"But I emphatically dissent from Mr. White's advice to take out only three cartridges for every head of game which it is expected to shoot. His own record was extraordinary, for he got about one animal for every two cartridges fired. I believe that the great majority of animals he killed cost him but one cartridge apiece. Moreover, the antelope of the plains were killed at an average of two hundred and forty-five yards. Now I am an ordinary shot, neither better nor worse than the average big-game hunter who has had some experience. But I could not begin to approach these figures. I did not ordinarily shoot at such long ranges, and yet I averaged about three times as many cartridges to kill as did Mr. White. As a matter of fact, Mr. White at a hundred yards shoots about as well with a pistol as I do with a rifle. Unless the hunter going to Africa is a very unusually good man, I advise him to triple the number of cartridges which Mr. White thinks it necessary for him to take." [8]

Well, there it is. Big game hunting is no longer in vogue, to be sure; White himself traded rifle for camera in his later years. But in its defense one should note that hunting flourished in the shadow of the American Frontier, at a time when inability to shoot a rifle meant going hungry. I don't mean only the hunter, but also the hunter's family. Also, in those days, to be an effective woman meant among other things to be paired with a man, typically a hunter, who not only could bag game but also was willing to die for you. White was such a man. The woman he was willing to die for plays an essential role in our story.

She was born on the Isthmus of Panama of a Spanish mother and a Scotch Presbyterian father. At what point she lost them I do not know; but we do know that she was raised in the society circles of Newport, Rhode Island, by overly-protective aunts. Her entire youth she spent in the motherly care of a typical Negro nanny of the period. Her education was completed, as was the custom, at a finishing school.

---

8. *Theodore Roosevelt, Literary Essays*, Charles Scribner's Sons, New York, 1926. Pages 382 to 385.

In protecting their foundling, her aunts made one mistake, at least from their point of view; they vacationed one year in Santa Barbara, where their charge met the young writer-hunter Stewart Edward White. Vacation over, the ladies returned to Newport, but the damage was done. White had caught the scent of big game. The intrepid hunter who later would flush wounded lions from cover promptly pursued them to the East Coast.

White had apparently already wounded his lioness, and he proceeded to flush her out of the thicket of Eastern society. After a determined courtship, then, they were married, and the Whites commenced the thirty-five years of married life that was to leave its mark long after both had died.

In the main, the reader can follow this story in White's published books. For a honeymoon White naively took his Eastern bride -- Elizabeth Calvert Grant White, the "Betty" of White's Betty books, and the "Billy" of his others -- on a bridal trip taken from the pages of Owen Wister's *The Virginian* -- into the Western wilderness with pack animals, camp cooking, and outdoor sleeping -- discovering in his new wife, as he puts it, a miracle of adaptability.

They were married in 1904. Fifteen years later they embarked on what for White was his greatest adventure -- the exploration, through Betty's mediumship, of the Last Frontier, the supraconscious, that far land that informs our life here with meaning and greets us as permanent residents when we die.

Those were the days when American mediumship was producing spectacular results. The ink was scarcely dry on Margaret Cameron's *Seven Purposes*, which interpreted the century's wars in eschatological language, and while doing so re-clothed ancient religious beliefs in modern language. The sittings were already finished that would result in the book, *Our Unseen Guest*, with its philosophy of consciousness in evolution, which incidentally solves for all time the problem religion has with evolution. They were days when people's minds were reeling from the onslaught of science against religion, and from the collapse of the established order occasioned, and represented, by the first of the century's world wars.

It was during this period of international ferment that the Whites visited the Manhattan home of Margaret Cameron, socialite, prominent author, and psychic medium. There they were introduced to Margaret Cameron's friend, Ruth Finley, and her husband Emmet. It was a portentous meeting. The three mediums -- Margaret Cameron, Ruth Finley, and Betty White, together with a fourth, Mrs. Lucy Gavit, conducted the spectacular 1922 group sittings reported by White in the appendix of *The Betty Book.*

The next phase of the story concerns the spiritual development of Betty White. It was conducted for the most part in trance! Her husband, his hand on her wrist, his common sense protecting her mind and soul as his hunter's instinct protected her body -- and taking notes -- accurate, verbatim notes from the hand of the author of "The Birds of Mackinac Island." It is from the records of these sittings that we have a detailed record of one of the most remarkable examples of spiritual growth of our time.

For Betty was more than medium. She was also a highly talented student of the life of the spirit. For many, being steeped in a Higher Consciousness is the sine qua non of such development. For Betty White likewise. Her excursions into that consciousness rival those of Brother Lawrence, whose Practice of the Presence was the envy of his contemporaries. Betty's mastery of this was so thorough that at the end of her life it became her customary mode of consciousness.

Betty was a "radiator." This is the result of an incandescence of the spirit so elevated and so physical that it can be noted readily by the rest of us. This she considered her ordinary mode of expression.

Not that her associates were wanting for other evidences of her development. White details many of these in his books. She had for example St. Francis's way with animals. In Alaska she talked to ravens, or warned the party against attempts to photograph bears that had gotten up on the wrong side of the bed. In San Francisco's zoo she captivated a lion by drawing for him, she explained to her nonplused companions, pictures of the African veldt.

This Betty, then, who had become more than life to White, died in 1939. It was a fitting death for such a one, and I invite the reader to review the details from White's various works. More to the point, however, is that she was promptly chosen by Ruth Finley's Invisible colleagues to master and transmit a description of the physics of her new world. The party for this consisted of Betty White, dictating; Ruth Finley, receiving station; and Emmet Finley and White, conceiving stations. The result the world knows about; White left us a report on these sittings in his book, *The Unobstructed Universe.*

White's relationship with his Betty does not end with his published works. One needs to peruse the private papers of Ruth Finley to discover what an eminent presence she was during his remaining years. These we will in the main pass over. But his last hours bear remarking. He could sense her presence as his life drew to a close, and there were other demonstrations as well.

From the East, the Finleys watched over White's final days. In her papers, Ruth Finley left the record of a sitting on September 15, 1946, with selected portions as follows.

"This be Anne," the voice said. "Betty cannot come through direct . . ."

Nevertheless she did so.

"Oh Emmet this is Betty," she suddenly announced. "Just a minute . . . I have to go back now because the Doctor and I are keeping Stewart comfortable. He is with us psychically more than half the time now."

And a bit later:

" . . . Beesie, spend as much time with Stewart from now on as you can. And my love to Alex." [9]

We owe additional insights to a remarkable pair of letters from a W.U. Maguire, who was, I believe, White's typist in his home at Little Hill in Burlingame, California, and apparently a fixture in the household during his final days. This is presumably the Mrs. Willia Maguire of San Mateo mentioned in White's will as in his employ. He left her $2,000.

In a letter of September 16, 1946, addressed to "Dear Mrs. Finley," she wrote:

"He himself knew, from near the beginning of the year, that something was about to happen. I often noted a look of strain or worry, but he always passed off any inquiries as to how he felt. It has only been since the operation that he admitted to me

---

9. Harwood White's wife.

that he knew for six months that something was growing.

"I gathered flowers for Beese (Harwood White, White's brother) to take in yesterday, set them in a bowl on the kitchen sink until he should be ready to go. When they were put into his hands a tremendous wave of Betty's perfume arose from them -- they were roses -- as well as their own fragrance; and he said it lasted so that the nurse remarked about it when she arranged them."

A second letter from Maguire, also dated September 16, 1946, is worth quoting in its entirety. It is addressed to "Dear Friends." Harwood White is mostly called by his nickname of "Beese."

"I'm making carbons again, two days late. Harwood got here Saturday morning and has spent most of these three days with SEW. The latter is sinking steadily, but is completely conscious when he rouses from his communion with Betty, or his contemplation of what is ahead of him, as the following conversation will show. It was had yesterday afternoon, Sunday.

Stewart: Hard to figure.

Beese: What is hard to figure?

S Time.

B The time you will go?

S Yes.

B I have been trying to decide whether to go home tonight or stay over.

S Stay over. (pause)

S Too much strain.

B About going over?

S (nods) When you're ready to go -- go!

B Don't ooze out, eh?

S (Smiled, took Beese's hand)

B Are you comfortable?

S (strongly) Yes! (Looked at Beese so long and so intently he asked:)

B Can you see me Stewart?

S (raised his eyebrows and pursed his lips) Oh yes!

(Later)

S One world out of two.

B What does that mean?

S Title of book. Write it down.

"The day before Beese was sitting with Stewart, studying over a decision he had to make, when Stewart roused and said, 'Can I be of any help?'

"And the nurses tell us that sometimes SEW will lift a finger and say, 'Sh-h!'; and later explain to them that Betty was around and he wanted to hear what she had to say. They give him about another week, but Beese feels he may be able to go on before that.

Most sincerely,
W.U. Maguire

P. S. There is a feeling of complete serenity here now, and he insists he is in no more pain."

This letter is dated, as was remarked, September 16, 1946. White died two days later on September 18.

Nor does White's relationship with Betty end with his death. It persisted after the end as well. Mention has been made of the Whites' Owen Wister style honeymoon. After White's death, his Betty seems to have returned the favor. Its details are properly shrouded from view. But on their return they were invigorated and ready for work. The reader has already seen the result. Another incredible performance by Ruth Finley, the only medium besides his wife that White ever fully trusted; and a performance by White that makes his African Campfires pale by comparison.

Chapter 8. Just Betty

IT is a minor miracle that we know as much about the posthumous career of Richard Hall as we do. But what we know of Hall pales in comparison with what we know about Betty. Her husband, Stewart Edward White, documented some of it. A great deal more is contained in the papers of Ruth Finley, and it is into this treasure trove that we now propose to dig. We will find out, then, a bit more concerning her training; how she died from radium poisoning; her vigorous reaffirmation of traditional Christianity; her celebration of Easter; her war work; the spectacular circumstances surrounding *The Unobstructed Universe*; her leadership of "the gang," that small group of individuals devoted, as was she, to "the work;" and the intimate relationship with her husband until and even after his own death.

Her Training

"I've run across a treasure trove," White wrote to the Finleys in a letter dated August 17, 1940. "A filing wrapper full of Betty's own mss written 'to tidy up the subject in my own mind, to reconstruct my point of view along the way'." This material came to be the basis for *The Road I Know*, White's account of Betty's training and her recommendation for the first of the books a neophyte should tackle. It is a detailed account of the training of a modern mystic and as far as I know without parallel anywhere, anytime.

White's records show that Betty's introduction to her "Road" began in March 1919. Then, after preliminary beginnings: "I first took her wrist and she went over into superconsciousness in November, 1919," he reported to Ruth Finley. The first attempts to talk directly through her were on January 29, 1920. "As OUG (*Our Unseen Guest*, Ruth's book) was published in February, 1920, obviously my taking Betty's wrist was *not* suggested thereby," White reported -- the written record, a life-long habit of White's, having corrected a faulty memory.

The very earliest records that Betty got were from an "Uncle Calvert," White wrote to Ruth in a letter dated February 23, 1944. The uncle liked to refer to himself as "the Calvert school" in the early part of Betty's training. He was an actual uncle of Betty's, says White, and White still had a picture of him hanging upstairs at Little Hill. "Betty never lived with them but she lived very near them, and they were part of her childhood family," White wrote. Apparently Betty owes her middle name (Elizabeth Calvert Grant) to them; the neighborhood would have been in Newport, Rhode Island, where Betty grew up in "society".

"I remember Betty telling me that the old gentleman was considered 'crazy' by the rest of the family," White added. He was also something of an author, having written a book called *The Gentleman*, which was the Emily Post of its time.

White sufficiently documents Betty's Spanish connection but it bears repeating, since it will come up later. Betty's mother was Spanish, so Betty was half Spanish and might conceivably be termed Hispanic under today's definitions. How she and her sister Millicent came to be orphaned I do not know. In Newport she lived with aunts.

Other tidbits one finds on the cutting room floor: she liked clam chowder, a favorite in Alaska to which the Whites piloted a tramp steamer once a year. And she was partial to the colors yellow and gold because, she said, they had always stood even from ancient times for the highest splendor.

One would think that after such a full life Betty would have earned some rest, but that is not how it was. Her hardest work was yet to come, and additional training came along with it. After her death she quickly found a West coast medium, a Mrs. Adele Halman of San Francisco, who served as a surrogate for Ruth Finley while White was in residence at Little Hill in Burlingame, a short distance south of San Francisco. Through her Betty talked about the difficulty she experienced, immediately after her death, in understanding the talk of her new angelic neighbors.

"At first for me," she reported, "it was just like a low murmur, not a voice; just a humming sound that seemed to come from everywhere; but I couldn't distinguish one sound from another. I used to like just to go hear Stewart talk. Then I began to understand that I was not yet attuned to the higher vibrations of this new residence."

But a bit later her complaint was just the opposite. Having gotten attuned to angelic voices, she now had difficulty stepping her frequency back down to that of the "living".

"Don't you understand the wisdom of my learning how to be in touch with others than just our group?" she reported in October of 1940. "I want to give you an idea of why I feel I must study apart from you for a while. A few days ago I was taken to a hospital -- a hospital on my side, I mean. It is filled with people who have just died. An immense number of men and women. Those working there were working to put together what is missing in those people. You see, they don't come over here *complete*. It is repairing what you might call a condition of mind. Oh, I do hope that someday I can describe the picture of an advanced soul standing near one of them, and how little by little a perfect body emerges! Shattered souls -- we make them whole. But to do that you must know that person's frequency so that you can bring your own to it."

"How do you go about it?" This from White.

"I watch my chance," Betty said. "It is best when the person is calm and quiet. So I study him at night. Then I follow that person, continuously, and I can *feel* when the time comes that, when I think of a thing, he thinks of it too."

"How do you regain your own frequency afterwards?" White wanted to know.

"Anne will take me away immediately, where I can regain it," she replied."

"Where?" asked White.

"Why, home," said Betty.

"You mean our home?"

"Difficult to explain," said Betty. "I go to a place where no one can disturb me. I'm just going *home* -- with Anne. She's like a watch dog. *No one* can disturb my quietness until I am back to myself."

"One of the things that made my place here in the new mode of being so comfortable," she had reported earlier through Ruth, "is the fact that I was sponsored by the Lady Anne. I can never repay my debt of gratitude to her."

She was not always happy with her training. "I am appreciating more and more why I am being made to study with a group," she reported in San Francisco on October 7, 1940. "All my life I've been so independent, and when I started with this group, instead of being put in a front seat, I was way back! Guess I needed it."

Her death from radium burns

Betty was killed by an inappropriate use of radium in a popular treatment thought to ease the passage through menopause. We have a report by Ruth's father, Dr. Ebright, to that effect. It is dated November 21, 1937, a year and a half before she died. The text consists of a dialogue between the Doctor and Emmet Finley, so presumably Ruth is working.

"It is very difficult for me to get through what I want to say," the Doctor began, "because her mind fights it.

"The best we can do for Betty is to bring her peacefully. That we can accomplish and shall. The regrettable circumstances in the whole matter is that it is the result of stupidity. The most dangerous time in a woman's life are the years of change. Let me try to show you why. A girl child grows into puberty naturally. It is a distinct youth development. In all cases it is a delicate time but not to be compared with the cessation of growth. A woman's period of activity is long, and as a result the most habit-establishing both from a physical and nervous standpoint not to include the mental outlook. In other words a curtailment is far more of a shock to the system in every way than the initial activity of the vital organs.

"Now modern life demands an adaptation of women at this period that the human system has not yet assimilated. Over a long period of centuries man's reducing vitality became keyed to the advancing mode of living. In two at the most three generations women at this period instead of accepting inactivity have flowered to a point mentally where they force themselves to continue at a pace all out of proportion to the flagging vitality caused by physical readjustments over which they have no control. Much as modern science had advanced, many of its experimentations will be abandoned. Many of them have been abandoned. One of the worst is the use of radium for the abrupt termination of the menses instead of permitting the menopause to run its natural course. Mrs. White in the stress of meeting the demands placed upon her by a husband and friends who did not mean to be selfish underwent this operation. She did not tell Ruth she had undergone it. She told Ruth that there was such a treatment and that most women who could afford it resorted to it as a convenience. The danger lies as it always lies and always will lie in the handling of radium in burns. These need not be intense at the time, but they are peculiarly malignant. Mrs. White was burned. The result of that burn is known as cancer. I do not think this is anything you want to write to your friend. That is not my intent. If you will go back over the records or can recall them if you kept no notes, the records at the time you were visiting in Burlingame, you will find repeated suggestions to Mrs. White herself that she have attention. I did my best to get through, and to all intents and purposes failed. I can not tell you how quickly we will be able to bring her to us, but I promise you that it will be with all the dispatch possible. As for Mr. White, he shall not be left too long alone. Mrs. White knows that she is coming and her deepest concern now as always is for her husband. I shall try to communicate directly to her the fact that I have just told you."

"What fact?" interposed Emmet.

"That she need not be overconcerned about him," Dr. Ebright continued. "I have been somewhat reluctant to talk (to) you because there was nothing I could say that seemed wise for you to communicate to paper. Could it have been done by you and Mrs. White by word of mouth with softening sympathy dominating the interview, that would have been another thing. But black words on white paper are cold at best, and the situation in California is such that the truth at this time is only terrifying. I think your message to your friend is that of course I am standing by. Every possible aid is being and shall be given to one who is so dearly our own. And now unless you have questions I have said all I came to say at this time."

"How long does a case of this kind last?" asked Emmet.

"About, I should think, six months. But if we can hasten it we shall," concluded the Doctor.

There you have the death sentence. But the drama continued. In a letter dated March 4, 1939, to Margaret but intended for the entire "gang" White reports Betty's treatment with an experimental gadget related to their psychic work. Accordingly they took up residence in Upland, California, for the treatment and remained there until Betty's death in April.

"About three weeks ago," the letter reads, "disturbing symptoms sent us back to the medicos. Brunn stated the trouble had come back on Betty and that there was no more to be done. He said all we could do was to keep her as comfortable as possible. She was tapped the following day and two quarts of water drawn off. Just here we heard of a man at this place doing work with the vibrations of light and its derivatives as broken up by the spectrum. Details too complicated to go into, but the general idea is like tuning a radio. Connecting the body by electrodes with a machine that has an enormous number of tuning knows he determines, in ohms, how conductive each part of the body is, and as he knows empirically -- by fourteen years experiment -- what the resistance is in health, the difference is the disease and the amount of it. He then treats the disease with the opposite polarity. All that is not exact; just to give you an idea.

"Anything's better than nothing, so we flew to Burbank, where Beese and Alex met us and motored here. Without our telling him he spotted everything. I had him try me because I have an African bug (obscure) that manifests in an unmistakable manner in a way already medically determined. He located the bug, identified it, and told me just where and how it affected me. At least the thing indubitably worked in diagnosis. He tried Betty out; then, turning to her, said 'you have no right to be alive.' Said she, 'I have my own magic.' He looked at her sharply and said 'You have help.' Then we took our hair down and talked, and found that not only does he work with an Invisible, but that almost every phase of our own teachings -- groups and all that -- were his also. It is as if he had sat in with us for years.

"Now, that was two weeks ago. At that time Betty was dying. I thought myself lucky to get her here alive. She was in continual and rending pain; she slept only in cat naps; she could not eat. After ten treatments -- with a new 'tuning' every day-- she has only soreness, the growth has diminished over one third, the abdominal water two thirds; malignancy has dropped from 36 units to 3.3 units; she eats; she sleeps well. I think we are on our way. Pressed further, the doctor confessed that the force he uses he knows nothing about, except that it is measurable. He has learned how to use it -- quantity, location, etc. -- from observation, but more from direction from his Invisible. . . Every vital indication in Betty has steadily increased; every destructive reading has decreased. Crazy or not, there you are. And I have learned at first hand a lot of truly miraculous cures of all sorts of things given up by the medicos. Further, the day we got her death sentence from Bunn, Betty got the words 'Help will come Thursday.' She noted it on her calendar, without saying anything to me. On that Thursday we got two long letters, each written independently, telling us of this man . . .

"I have rented a house 2000 feet (up) on the slope to Mt. Baldy, in orange groves, with a most wonderful outlook. . . We are here for the duration . . . Address R.F.D. 1, Upland, California.

"We are at present a slowed motion miracle, no less; and brought about no differently, I think, than those of Christ, except for the element of time. Help us as you can."

And the Finleys do. On March 20 at Hempstead, Long Island, Ruth working, Emmet asked:

"How is Betty?"

"She has come in contact with a very wonderful doctor who will keep her comfortable," replied Dr. Ebright. "He is on his way with what he has discovered. He is beginning to harness mechanically a force that twenty centuries ago was in use emotionally and spiritually. I can't be sure yet how long or how much of a cure can be accomplished. This is the hope but in any event I promise you this -- that Betty shall tread the road she knows in peace."

But Betty was dying, this breath of hope notwithstanding. In a communication dated March 25 Dr. Ebright promised to shorten the agony, which he now believed they were prolonging unnecessarily with the new treatment.

"There is no way you can get word to Stewart Edward White that he should take his wife back to her own medical man," he said. "But you can think it hard. A bonafide physician can get Betty more comfortable and release from pain than this doctor is apt to give. We will try very hard to take her out quickly, but the present effect of the treatment is to stimulate her heart and to keep it going." And of course Betty knew what was up. These were the days she kept repeating "I've got my one bit *putsch* to make, and then -- ."

The end came on April 5, 1939. In an April 12 letter to the Finleys addressed to "My dears", he said that up to ten days before she died, the main trouble seemed to be cured. "Then, without reason," he wrote, "the liver became overactive, pouring quantities of bile into the stomach. Nothing would stop that. Had to feed by glucose vein injections. She became weaker, emaciated, and finally the physical frame was worn down to the point where only her fighting spirit held her."

The letter continues with the uplifting description since transferred to White's books, done so touchingly that nothing I can say can add or detract from it. I think he failed to mention, however, that Betty's ashes were scattered in her garden, and that he kept a light burning in the window in her memory. And in their listing in *Who's Who* he listed her, with the connivance of the editors, as still living, as indeed she most gloriously was.

There is more to this story, however, than you will find in White's books. Two days later in Hempstead Richard Hall put in an appearance. After identifying himself he said that "the Doctor will come presently. He is with Mr. and Mrs. White. Perhaps more accurately speaking he and Mrs. White are with Mr. White."

"How's Betty?" Emmet speaking.

"Very well," was the reply. "She is distressed of course over her husband but she knows it will not be long. He is having excellent care and will be able to adjust himself more rapidly than most persons who have enjoyed so close a tie, because he knows it is only his wife's body that is dead. But the Doctor will tell you more about that if you want to know."

"I was able to take Betty even sooner than I had hoped," Dr. Ebright said. "She had a minimum of suffering."

Here Ruth, although working, broke in. Notice that she considers herself at the moment of speaking to be *there*, not *here*.

"You see it's terribly hard for Stewart to be glad that Betty has come over here," Ruth said. "All the intellectual understanding can't soften the emotional break and loneliness. Of course, as soon as he can let Betty really come into his consciousness he will be more definitely aware of her as a definite intellectuality. But that, even he must grow into. I can understand that because those two or three nights when I was so very ill and father was with me he was more a fact for me -- he was even closer -- it was more vivid -- than anything I had ever experienced in life. It was almost as if his brain was operating inside my head. It was, I suppose. His *I am* came and was with my *I am.* We knew each other as we had never done before, except of course when I am over here. But I don't retain the memory of that as I do of those days when I was not over here.

"Now the thing that Stewart will come to know is just that, because on the earth plane no matter how much two people love each other, how close they are emotionally and intellectually, the barrier of the body is always there. You cannot see in my mind what I am thinking, nor I in yours. I may approximate it but the actuality of real communion never occurs. That will be Stewart's (problem) and that is the thing which you and I must explain to him and tell him. So that he can be receptive to it really -- not that he hasn't been told -- but we are to confirm it.

"That is the promise she made and that is the promise that shall be kept. The thee in me. Even old Oman K knew that."

Later Betty would say, "Never feel sorrow for one who comes here. I am *home.* My life here has been made easier by the *faithful* suffering I went through there. I left behind everything that obstructed."

Betty also talked about the possibility of alleviating pain such as hers with the use of complementary frequencies, either from a machine like Dr. Thompson's or from the ministrations of an Invisible doctor. She had both.

She was also present early in 1940 when White and the Finleys visited Dr. Thompson in Upland. There various readings were made on his machine that reflected the frequencies of the individuals involved. A reading above 50 is beyond the norm of the material universe. Ruth's normal frequency measured 39; but in trance it was 51-1/2. Betty measured 59 by herself, but 57 when talking through Ruth. In order to communicate that way, she lowered her natural frequency and raised Ruth's. Proving, according to Dr. Ebright, that the same type of frequency can be generated in the human body as is generated in the machine.

Christianity

Despite a lifetime of exotic personal development, Betty never abandoned her faith in old-fashioned Christianity. She went out of her way to make this point time and again. In this section and the next we will see that her personal demonstration of its core truths was as spectacular as anything within the religious tradition except for the earliest times.

On Long Island in May of 1940, Ruth working, Betty had this to say on the subject:

"Of all the faiths that have lived Christianity has done the most for the world -- in education, democracy, belief in self liberty, freedom. All that I have told you can be found there, but much of it overshadowed by outmoded terms and outmoded ways of life. It was expressed in the terms of the times in which it was needed, as I tell it in terms of your times when it is again needed. But without question the greatest composite accumulation of fundamental truth is in the Christian Bible. I would have you read that which we have given you with one eye, and the other eye on the Bible, so to speak. They will illumine each other."

She went on to say that the consciousness of man knows the truth but doesn't live it anymore owing to man having become too enamored of his own creations.

In November of that year she asked for Christmas cards to be sent to a few of her friends.

"I am looking forward to the festivities that are going to take place on Christmas Eve -- here where I am, I mean. Children will be gathered to hear again that the new-born babe is the same that was crucified and rose from the dead who brought the world its greatest message of all time. And among those children will be many you called men and women, who were eighty and more when they quit working in the obstructed universe!"

Was she now beginning to sermonize? She denied it resolutely. "I will never be a preacher," she said of herself in late 1940 or early 1941. "Nevertheless I do find in myself a sense of freedom when I speak, or hear others speak, on Christ. He was always the one I worshipped when on earth, and of course now we constantly come across people who live for him -- and some who died for him."

"The Bible *is* a stepladder to truth," she said on another occasion. "I don't want to knock the pins from under the religionists. Faith in God has been the greatest civilizer your world has ever known."

Her use of stepladders is not restricted to the Biblical record. The stepladders we have accumulated, she maintained, are recorded in the various bibles of the various races, as well as in poetry, in music, and in painting. "In fact," she said, "humanity has been reaching toward the unobstructed ever since humanity was."

But again and again she returns to the Biblical record. The parable of the talents, says she, illustrates the degrees of mankind. The responsibility of high degrees is very great, Christ being a vivid example. And, "'the fear of the Lord is wisdom, and to depart from evil is understanding.' Now in the days when that was written the human race was still very close to a realization of the oneness of consciousness and to the actuality of the unobstructed as well as the obstructed universe. And in the original, they tell me here, the translation of the word 'fear' is not quite correct. In your vernacular 'recognition' would be more nearly correct."

And so on and so on.

Sometimes the teaching would be old, sometimes new. On June 24, 1940, for instance, Betty had this to say concerning France and the war.

"When negative forces come to a certain point of control you have to let them work out," she said. "Like France. We hoped to stop things short of that point, but were unable. So now we have withdrawn. We do not stop endeavor, nevertheless the negative force has come to the point where it must kill itself. Further effort on our part would merely prolong and strengthen. That is the meaning of the 'resist not evil' phrase in the Bible: the resistance of evil often strengthens it . . . And it kills itself more rapidly than you would think."

Or take Anne's speech on doing one's job.

"You have been given free will, the greatest gift in the entire universe," she said. "Now you live up to it! And how can you do it by gazing off and not doing the job, like scrubbing the floor? I have no use for anybody who does not do his own job. 'He that loseth his life shall find it.' What did He mean by that? He that goes about his job every day -- no matter what it is -- and does it, thinks not on how he is developing himself -- and, lo! he is developed! . . . It is by doing things, simple things, that rubs the diamond smooth and makes it sparkle."

But sometimes the teaching emphasized the new, and when it did, it likely emphasized the view of Heaven and Hell popularized by Swedenborg, using the theme that consciousness is its own judge.

In February, 1940, Betty said:

"There is a very definite reality in 'hell' and 'purgatory', not precisely as the Roman Church has it, perhaps, but a reality . . . Free will creates its own hell." Those dying with a load of negatives such as envy must eradicate them in such a purgatory, and by their own effort, she says.

Speaking to her husband, Betty said, "I am *much* better looking than when you saw me. Well, why shouldn't I be? No cares, no taxes, no entanglements -- nothing at all like that. And such a deep surging desire to explain to those who are left without us the *utter* futility of any kind of worry. I do wish the people there could be able to understand the complete lack of such a thing as 'punishment' or 'retribution'. If I had come here knowing nothing of all this, as a raw savage, I would by now have learned this. I would know that even in the flesh there is essentially no such thing."

"Do you know," she continued, "here in this room . . . there is a peculiar atmosphere, a mixture of -- what shall I say -- well, of Oliver Lodge and Jesus Christ.

"There!" she exclaimed. "I knew that would stir you up! What I mean is, that I seem here to be on a road that somehow is divided in two. One one side I have to walk like a scientist, and on the other -- as a Sunday School teacher would say it -- 'with my hand in the hand of Jesus Christ'."

"Sorrow is the thing we do not like to come upon," she continued. "It seems to destroy the very machinery of the soul. I have yet to find out how to approach a person who has made himself blind by the blackness of sorrow."

Sometimes the theology sort of slips in during small talk. "Someone has said that he had so far advanced that he 'saw God between two walls,'" Betty said at one point. "I have not seen God. I should be terribly disappointed if I could -- it would indicate that I wasn't much. God is in everything and everybody, but one must be something to see him there and not merely 'between two walls.' I do see God in faces -- but not a face."

First things were brought to the listeners' attention time again. Giving directions concerning *The Unobstructed Universe* in mid 1940, Betty directed that they emphasize a teaching from *The Seven Purposes* that "Purpose is the Intent of Consciousness." This was no idle statement, since she considers that consciousness is controlled by a core they have termed Supremacy.

"The reason I have shied off from the emotional content of consciousness," she said one day to Emmet, "has been because I simply could not make you understand. I have just touched on your individual emotional content. I have said nothing of the emotional content of the universe. We have described the one and only reality as consciousness of which your own individual *I-Am* consciousness is the highest expression, and individually remains the highest experience. But consciousness, which is divisible individually, must have some kind of core. It must have something comparable to your atom; something sure, real, absolute."

"You could call it Purpose or Free Will," suggested Emmet.

"Yes," replied Betty. "But in any event it emotes. You can envision it as a radiation. Every being which is an individual consciousness emanates from and ties back to the core. And the core is purpose, evolution, impulse -- the best word you can find for reality."

But often the old language is best. "If we went back to the old religions," Betty explained, "we would find a simple explanation: 'God created man in his own image.' That means that man is the highest individualized expression of the consciousness that is God."

How Betty Celebrated Easter

Readers of White's books will be aware of how moments after Betty's death, on a hillside in Upland, California, he was so flooded with a sense of Betty's presence that he found it impossible to believe that she was not still alive. More than one reader must have drawn a parallel between this private experience of White's and the Pentecost of the Gospels.

But for Betty this was not enough. She believed fervently in the Easter celebration and the miracle of the Resurrection, to the point where she insisted on re-enacting the miracle in a very personal way. All of which is to enable you to appreciate the mind set of White on opening his mail shortly after Easter, 1940, a year after Betty's death. It was from Ruth and reads as follows:

Home, Easter Morning 1940

9:22 E.S.T

Dear Stewart;

A very beautiful thing has just happened, so beautiful that I am setting it down on paper before

I can forget any slightest detail. I have *seen* Betty, and *heard* her voice.

I was still in bed a few moments ago with my breakfast tray reading the current issue of Good Housekeeping magazine. Emmet had been in and gone downstairs to his breakfast. Now he has left the house -- I heard the front door slam just as I got back enough breath to jump out of bed and rush here to my typewriter -- to get the Sunday papers and post Betty's last night's air-mail letter to you. It is very cold but a brilliantly sunny morning. My room was flooded with sunshine.

Suddenly *something* attracted my attention and I looked up from my magazine. Betty was standing at the foot of the step leading to the "hole-in-the-wall" that opens into my study. She was dressed in a short white knitted sports dress -- two-piece. It was cut rather high in the neck with a sort of jabot -- soft and frilly -- at her throat. About her neck was a string of yellow beads that hung down about half way to her waist.

Beside her, so tall that the blossom made a sort of canopy over her head, was a trillium -- the wild lily that used to grow so thick in the woods when I was a little girl at the farm in Ohio. Her hat was on the stem just above the three green leaves. She said;

"Do not be afraid. This great blossom -- the blossom that Stewart will remember my telling him of so long ago, the flower of three petals that you will find in the record I had you ask Margaret copy and send for Stewart -- the record of twenty years ago -- is the symbol -- my symbol of Resurrection and of Life. *Tell Stewart I am Life*. That *my blossom* is the work he is now doing. You are helping. Keep on. Do not be afraid -- just work and leave the rest to me. I am going now to Stewart. I shall try to get him see me. But should I fail -- and I may -- because emotionally he still *wants* to see me too much -- I have to get through his emotion -- tell him that *you have seen. Don't cry (the tears were pouring over my face) laugh, laugh*! it is *the Resurrection Morning* and *you are one of the chosen to help make it so*."

Then she was gone. Not suddenly, exactly, but with a chuckley smile and a wave of her lily. She seemed to go through the door into the study. And that half spice, half flowery, perfume swept over me so strong it was almost sickening. When I got myself together I looked at my little clock and it was 9:22.

Emmet is back now and I am going to call him upstairs and give him this to read while I bathe and dress.

Dear Stewart, I have no words to make you *really* understand but Betty is shiningly, gloriously alive and wonderful."

White replied as follows:

"Dear Ruth;

I'll never catch up with you in gratitude. That experience of yours with Betty has bucked me up to a point of which you can have no conception whatever. What a job she did! That two-piece, white, knitted thing with a jabot was one she wore most about the place during the last six months she was here. The beads are of course the amber ones. Oh, it was wonderful! I don't know whether she will ever get through to me that way, I doubt it. I don't see well. And it was so well timed, your sending the letter special delivery. By the previous mail I had received a shattering letter from one who had always appeared a close friend, exhibiting him in a light completely disillusioning. I was awfully down, and yours came as a wonderful antidote sweeping away all downheartedness."

Trillium lilies became Betty's symbol of Easter. Two years later White wrote Ruth as follows:

"I've been doing some exercise by renewing the trails I made up the cañon some twenty years ago. Naturally they need a lot of hard work. Just today I arrived near the head, and there - and nowhere else in this country that I know of -- I found a whole side hill of trillium. A few of them were out, but the rest still in bud, and as next week is Easter, I expect they will be all out for that day, which incidentally is the anniversary of Betty's 'second birthday'. Fanciful probably, but remembering how she showed herself to you on Easter two years ago, with her trillium, it is rather nice."

And after Easter had come and gone he wrote Ruth as follows:

"Betty's birthday -- Easter -- was spotted. It had rained hard all the night before, but let up in the morning, though it took hold again in the afternoon. In the interim I walked up the cañon with the dogs to where I had found the trillium. The bloom on the few plants were over, but there were two or three in bud. I then went back to the forks and up the other cañon. Somewhat up the hill, off the trail, I glimpsed more trillium. Climbed up, and found a patch of them, scattered in the green undergrowth, about twenty feet or so square. From a fallen log I counted them idly; then got interested and went over the patch, foot by foot. Just to be certain, I did so four times. Each time I made the number thirty six. No sense in being fanciful, or straining coincidence, but of course Betty and I knew each other here just thirty six years. One of those take it or leave its; but there it is.

"In her letter she said, 'Easter morning look for something in or near my special tree. I'll get as close as I can.' Of course I did so, but there was nothing unusual. I did get very strongly the pervading sense of her presence, but that was all . . . "

To which he added that Rod, a close friend, sent a lily for Easter -- to Betty. And at dinner that evening Reider, the butler, made one of the tight little nosegays Betty used to do for the women at formal dinners, and laid it at Betty's place at table, saying nothing.

Nor was it only to close friends that Betty came. Betty's nurse, Johnnie, was one such. "Johnnie thought I was a nut," she had told her husband. "At first she thought I was crazy. I knew it all the time. I said to myself 'Well, I'll show Johnnie!'" So she did and this is how she did it. Johnnie had been to see White after Betty's death and, while he was working, she walked around Betty's garden. It turned out to be a tactical error on Johnnie's part. Later she told White: "You know, I'm not fanciful, but I couldn't get rid of the feeling that Mrs. White was right near me all the time. I kept looking over my shoulder. I thought it merely recollections of her. But when I came to the outdoor grill I looked at it and said to myself, 'I had an idea it was glass.' And I heard, just as distinctly as if someone were speaking in my ear, 'Look behind the bamboo, you goop'."

Now part of the screen to the grill was a clear piece of glass through which you got a view up the cañon, White explained. Betty had had a wild bird or so killed running into it, and had installed a bamboo curtain to screen it. The curtain was down, but the glass was still behind it. Johnnie was startled and impressed.

Betty could be deadly serious when the occasion demanded it, but she seasoned it with a delightful pixieishness, as the above episode illustrates. One of White's correspondents described her as "an enchanting composite of a hermit thrush and an elf." It is an apt description. There is, for example, the case of the ringing doorbell. It lacks the evidential value of Betty's other shenanigans, but otherwise is stamped with her modus operandi. White recorded the incident as follows.

At exactly six o'clock one evening the door bell rang, one long and one short. The bell system was equipped with indicators that showed which doors had had their bells rung; it showed that the reception hall and two other downstairs bells had rung. There was no one at any of the doors, and no one in the house had rung. There was nothing left to do but dismiss the evidence and go to bed. But the next night, at exactly nine o'clock, the same bells were rung again. The succeeding night there was a long ring at midnight; and the fourth night a persistent ringing, at exactly three o'clock in the morning, until the butler got up and silenced it. Not content to leave the matter there, White had an electrician examine the entire system. The electrician's report after a two-hour examination: there was nothing whatever that would permit the ringing, or account for it in any way.

And then there were Betty's dogs. In a letter to Ruth dated January 3, 1942, White wrote as follows:

"I have been having a funny time with the dogs the last two evenings," he began. "Either I have got a pair of crazy dogs, or Betty is having her kind of fun with them. They usually lie very peacefully on the sofa by my side, and still continue to do so, except that the night before last and last evening, suddenly they both leaped to their feet, rushed over to one corner of the room, stared fixedly up to the ceiling in that corner, without barking, but very earnestly. Then madly they scrambled out into the hall to the bookcase there, dug out all the books on the lower shelf, stared into the space. I was following them out of curiosity, and there were no mice or bugs or any other thing. Then suddenly they rushed back in the library, went to the opposite corner and gazed up. None of this was with any barking, or anything of that sort, but with the greatest interest and excitement.

"Well, they kept that up all of two evenings. I can't ascribe it to anything in the walls, because the places they went were too far apart, and in different compartments. Also, when there is anything tangible to be taken care of they bark considerably, so much so that I have had to discipline them for overdoing it. Of course I never do boast of my will to believe on these things, but if you and Emmet do get hold of Betty and will follow it up for me the effort will be appreciated."

Betty was so good at perfumes that one such incident bears retelling. In the fall of 1944 White detected a strong smell of violets in his downstairs bathroom. It was a persistent smell for which he could find no source. Over the following several days it would come and go. Finally he took friends down to confirm the scent. It was so faint that the test might have failed. But as they stood discussing it, suddenly it came on in the strongest sort of wave, instantaneously.

That was September 18, 1944. On the 5th of October it happened all over again. "This morning, crossing from the Ark to the house, I smelled a strong smell of rubber burning from a neighbor's bonfire," White recorded. When on entering the house the maid asked what "that smell" was, he replied that it was someone burning rubber -- sending her away with a puzzled look on her face. But she was not to be put off. "But the smell I mean is a pleasant smell," she said. "Not rubber."

"What kind of smell?" queried the unsuspecting White.

"Oh, like violets, only very strong," she replied.

"Where did you smell it?", he asked.

"The downstairs lavatory, and the blue room upstairs," she replied. (This was Betty's blue room.) "And sometimes in other places in the house."

How long had this been going on?

"Why, ever since I came."

The maid's name was Lucie, and for a report of this caliber she deserves to have her name recorded. She later said to the housekeeper, "I've always dreamed of having a place like this to work in. Somehow, in this house there seems to be such a beautiful feeling, as if someone very kind was all through it."

Which, recorded White, is a pretty good testimonial for a Swiss serving girl.

War Work

Betty died in 1939, the opening year of the second World War. She quickly made Ruth Finley her official "station", and as the war progressed she had much to say about it through Ruth. *The Unobstructed Universe* came almost at once; it is so monumental that it will get its own section. Right now I want to cover other parts of her war work.

From this point on the careers of Betty and Ruth Finley are inextricably intertwined. To begin with, then, I want to report what is known about Ruth's status as a war station. She stood alone. She was the official station for the people like Anne who were working through Betty; and she was judged the best in the world at the time, and perhaps the best of all time. I will present the evidence; you can judge for yourselves.

Discussing the material for *The Unobstructed Universe* in May, 1940, Betty said:

"We could not have done this thing with *anybody* but Ruth. When you said in the book that she is 'perhaps one of the greatest psychics' -- why, she *is* the greatest psychic, for this particular thing. Others are sometimes better about lesser things, but *nobody* for this. Even at her desk she did *exceptionally* good work for us. It was practically all automatic writing. She merely supplied a few words. We arranged for it, though ordinarily she is not nearly as good as Margaret in automatic writing."

The following month White was complaining that the dictation was coming too fast for his stenographic ability. The problem was, Ruth was faster than she had been in the past. Betty explained:

"The difficulty of slow talk -- you see, I make an impression on a magnetic field, and if it is not immediately released it crowds and runs together and the mind can't take it off. I have to make the impression on my magnetic field, and mine flows into hers and she has to take it off hers.

"What the people here can't understand . . . is that when anything of such importance as this is coming, and there are so many good stenographers in the world -- why don't you have a stenographic record?

"You see Ruth is not in the same status she was in when Richard gave his material, or even as she was when she started on this. (In late 1939.) She is considered here as *the* major station for this sort of thing, and we recognize the importance of that in a way you can't. There are a lot of us involved in this job. While these other people do not dictate through Ruth, and I am more or less like a telegrapher at this key, you must understand that a great many minds are actually operating through this station. If this is true, and if there is reality in what is happening here right now, then I say in all seriousness that right today and now the three most important people in the world are you three."

"No one would suspect it," retorted Emmet.

"Nobody would suspect that a paperhanger would play the role he is playing now," flung back Betty.

Later that month the following tidbit:

"Now we are going to shut down this station completely for a while," said Betty. "We have taken a long time to develop it for our purposes, and it is the best in the world at the present time for this particular work. We had a station in Asia that was as good, but it is oriental. That is the only other, at this time, as good. We had hopes of it, but it is too strongly colored with the oriental. It is no good to us."

Ruth and Emmet used to visit a Mrs. Carman -- the "egg woman" of White's books. Ruth left a long typed record of such a visit, which she said was at the egg woman's new home at Mellville on Route 110, over the garage just south of the Walt Whitman place. The visit was on a Saturday afternoon December 30, 1939, which places it immediately after the material for *The Unobstructed Universe* had been received. The Egg Woman breaks an egg into a glass of water, stirs it, then reads her divinations from it. She was held in considerable respect by the Finleys and White. I present here an abbreviated version of Ruth's notes.

"You are going to take a journey," said the Egg Woman. "West. . . I see . . . pages and pages of written words. Ed is there. He is depressed and his heart often aches. He can hardly wait until you come. He has had so many messages that only you can make clear for him. . .

"Who is Betty? Betty says the work is good, but that Ed has to have a living person like you to complete the contact . . .

"This work is like a key -- a key to be turned in a long locked door . . .

"Betty wants you and Ed to finish the work in May. She says you *have* to because it must be on its way to the public by the next J month. I have never seen anything as important as this work. It is amazing how important it is. Amazing."

"Don't, then, be afraid of her death," said the Egg Woman concerning one of her predictions. "She will help you *here*. She and Betty and you -- you the key. Why does the key keep coming back? Has a key anything especial to do with you? It looks like a *master key* -- a key that you are to place in other hands."[1]

"He (Ed) is devoted to you and so is Betty. There seems to be a link between him and Betty --

---

1. The draft title of *Our Unseen Guest* was *The Master Key* -- but of course Mrs. Carman had no way of knowing that.

and you come in too. You and him and Betty. . . The work you are doing with Ed is important to the whole world. This is very strange. It is a *living* work. It is not only important now but always. Don't ever dare to shirk doing it. I feel funny about it -- and you. Who *are* you, anyhow?"

"Did you know that I never have met anyone quite so spiritual as you?" she continued. "I am going to the Church in the Wildwood tomorrow. May I pray for you and myself together? Already you have brought great peace to me. You are very spiritual. I think praying for you and myself together might do me good.

"And the key is important -- very important. You won't forget the key, will you?"

So ended a memorable session. There might have been more detail but, as Ruth notes in her report, "I can't read Emmet's notes." But her own notes are more than sufficient.

There are interesting tidbits in the archives that throw some light on the process of communication through someone like Ruth. Working in Winter Park, Florida, during January of 1941, Ruth made a repeated toot-toot-toot call which identified one of the communicators. How was this done?

"Now we are going to accede to Mrs. White's request," said the communicator, "and what follows is a digging into the memory of the station to bring out of it something that has been evidenced before, but it is to show how a certain type of evidence is secured, and the technique."

At this point Ruth spoke in her own voice.

"Emmet, do you remember the morning we drove into Salt Lake valley -- the river and the mountains and the snow sheds crawling along the ledges high over the road? Do you remember how, when the train is going through the sheds, the sun caught the windows in flashes, and it went along flashing like silver in the openings of the boards? And you remember when the train finally emerged into the open its triumphant -- toot, toot."

Emmet: "You see, in all the . . . discursive fishing in the station's subconscious memories, a way is found of slipping in the toot-toot without arousing the station."

Even pets made it into these extraordinary records. Speaking on Long Island in May, 1940, Betty gave us a glimpse into what it means to be the dog of a medium of Ruth's stature. The dog in question had been Emmet's, not Ruth's, but no matter. Its name was Toby, and it had just died.

"Don't feel too badly about the little dog," Betty began. "He would have been very uncomfortable. He is a dear. He plays the toe game with me *so* nicely. He loves it because he can go so many places now that he could not before. He was in your office today. He loved it. He will be there again. He has done already what the rest of us could not do. He came back, and you *saw* him, and that was worth while. They make adjustments quickly; he understands. He told you the greatest thing there is to tell; it took him to tell you. He has a grand time with Lob. And he had to adopt Peter (a cat) too, and that made it difficult for Lob, but he made it. *He's all right, Emmet.* It wouldn't be possible for any animal living with Ruth to be confused."

"When Ruth was away on a visit," Emmet said, "Toby used to stare all about as if he saw people. I should think he would have been more likely to have seen them when Ruth was here."

"When Ruth is here she brings here a great many people," Betty replied. "She is never alone.

The dog knew that, and when she went away he was hunting for them . . . You didn't realize. Ruth took such remarkable care of him that his body was much younger than he really was. he was getting exceedingly stiff and every day she gave him currents and kept him in good condition."

"Currents" being a knack Ruth had of letting some kind of psychic energy flow from her finger tips. The group was aware of this, and considered the currents to have certain healing properties.

Next follows considerable material describing how the war was interfering with Ruth's reception and in fact threatening the very integrity of their official war station -- a matter which they took very seriously.

Betty had been giving instructions on the writing of *The Unobstructed Universe*. White made a joke to which she, uncharacteristically, did not rise. He accused her of being solemn.

"It is difficult to keep the line clear," she explained. There are thousands of newly dead trying to get through. I'd *like* to play -- I want to -- but it's only that Ruth's magnetic field is wide tonight. It's a strain when there's a battle on. (This was early in May, 1940.) We are doing work with those people coming over suddenly and they are tense and trying to get back. Those who have come today are still trying to *fight*, and when a field is open they make what is like static on a radio. This tiny little wave, that wavers and pulsates, that we must keep open, is difficult to preserve. But it's all right; I'll know when to stop."

On a later occasion she had also been giving instructions as to *The Unobstructed Universe*.

"It is not all that I wanted to say," she concluded. "But it is the best I can get through. The station is getting clogged, though it is free tonight. But the impingement on her magnetic field is becoming very strong. You have no conception of the numbers of individual entities coming here hourly out of the war. Now those who speak her language -- the English and Scotch -- are naturally impinging on the field, and we are having difficulty in keeping it clear for this work. It is a great strain, both on her and on us, to edit them out. It would do none of them any good to come through her, but you must understand that the same octave is being struck again and again and again. That is one reason why we have *shoved* you so to get this finished. We wanted the job done before there was too much impinging pressure on this side."

"At the time of *Our Unseen Guest* the station did not understand as well as now. . . There is a *temporary* clogging because the balance is off. Later on we can get better material of the same sort as was given last fall. . .

"Every line is clogged," she continued. "It isn't peculiar to Ruth and me. Why, suppose you and five or six other reporters were on a story, and there's a deadline and only one telephone --"

In June, 1940, Betty had said:

"Now as to Ruth. It took the first World War to have her listen when they knocked. It has taken this one to make *you* hear. She is emotionally involved in events now and that makes it difficult to keep the channel clear. That is why we had to hurry. It would be impossible right now to get through the material we got through last fall."

June 16, 1940, was devoted to war talk, most of which I am going to pass over. But a well-known and popular United States President made an appearance, and you will want to know about it. In the midst of the session, then, Ruth began to see pictures. She began by seeing a tin plate.

"T, as in tin plate" she said. But she also saw the thing itself, and then what the group narrowed down to shelters made of canvas -- not real tents -- with a fire between, and a man, up near the timber line, and statements that he is a nationally known figure; and in an amusingly roundabout way -- through a Major "McK," a friend of Ruth's -- it was established that the man was Theodore Roosevelt.

"This is TR," began Roosevelt. "I can see no way now, after what that damn fool cousin of mine has done, but for you to swing in with England. You must save the English navy for your Atlantic protection because you are going to need your own for the Pacific."

There followed a great deal of detail that I omit. And there were certain inaccuracies which bothered Ruth when she became aware of them. These were tidied up in a session which took place on June 24.

"For her information we wish to explain the apparent discrepancies of Saturday afternoon," began Mary K, she of *The Seven Purposes*. "We want to state that the opening of a magnetic field -- unless for something of the utmost importance -- should be guarded against until the present intense struggle is resolved. The turmoil is on both sides, which makes it the more difficult to control. The material His Excellency was pushing through became erroneous only because she could not accept the statement that the soul of France was not accepting the government's decision. . . in consequence of which she over-edited the material because she could not believe what her instinct told her to be true . . . Please explain to her, and let her know that that afternoon's work does not vitiate the accuracy and power of the station."

To which Betty added:

"We shall do no more for a year or a year and a half. This has really been a great drain on you all. You could not take anything more now. We saw what was coming, and we had to get over our stuff before emotionally you blocked it out."

"Now remember," she concluded. "THIS STATION IS CLOSED FOR REPAIRS. She must do none of this work -- on any excuse -- for anybody. Not even a line of automatic writing. Until we give her the green light."

But before the station was "closed for repairs," and again after it was reopened, there was war talk aplenty. Betty was studying; and she had become Dr. Ebright's "head nurse," not working directly with the men, but training those who did. Anne herself appeared from time to time.

"You will be remembering that I did say, 'Vengeance is mine saith the Lord'," Anne said on June 7, 1940. "Consciousness is being ploughed. It is almost the dawn of a new day. You will not be forgetting that it is only one universe, and that the day of miracles is not over. But you must recognize them. Not for the first time the waters were told to be still. (A week or ten days of calm water on the English Channel at a stretch was unprecedented but occurred during the evacuation from Dunkirk.) Not for the first time were the righteous led by pillars of fire. (Two days later newspaper reports made much of RAF navigators' statements that they navigated on bombing raids over Germany at night by burning oil tanks.) It is not written that a thousand years of fundamental decency shall be wiped out from the world. Think you not that those who have liberty fight alone. Watch for the signs and portents that you may not be caught napping.

"With you three we are well content. Do not minimize the work that has been given to you. Do not think you are a voice crying in the wilderness for that is not so. We have prepared the word and your work that it may go out at its needed time."

Betty was wont to talk in a similar vein. After discussing the welfare of Emmet's dog that died -- the tale you have just read -- she preceded to war talk.

"The only thing I am going to say about the world," she began, "is that you must not be unduly disturbed. The price being paid is high, but that for which it is paid is man's greatest fight, and so no price is too high.

"Not right away, but presently," she continued, "will strange tales be told; but the time has come for a distinct step in man's psychological and moral evolution, and sometimes it takes great sorrow and revelation to make him take that step. . . Those who oppose God -- and by God I mean the infinite of consciousness -- must again be swallowed up by their own Red Sea . . .

"Always in world crisis it has been told," she concluded. "Always it has taken a world crisis for it to be received. You have been called for this. All your lives you have been preparing and making ready. Give now all you have and leave the rest to us. And do not be afraid."

After Anne's speech given above a General "M" took the floor.

"There have been great battles before for the intent of consciousness," he began, "but this battle is the greatest of all because now consciousness is more enlightened. . . They (the Germans) were amazed at the success of the evacuation from Dunkirk; it never occurred to them that it could be done. And they, no less than you, marked the kindliness of nature. We cannot tell you how this battle will end. We cannot even tell you whether or not Paris will fall. But we can tell you this: the intent of consciousness cannot be stayed, and that democracy -- as it was practiced in our country in its inception, not as it is loosely practiced now - *will* go on, *will* spread, *will* be the form of government for you, expressing the evolutional processes of consciousness as a whole.

"But," he warned, "you men of your country must clean out your own ash pits. You must not be so limited and busied by your own affairs that you leave government to the lesser breed. You must *voice* the truth, you must *take* the responsibility."

It was a recurring theme. On June 14 Harry L. had said:

"This is Harry. I told you in Florida that the new center of civilization is to be in America, the new center of research, of endeavor of the preservation of those things for which the world has so long struggled. They are in your hands."

To which Betty added:

"Anne told you long ago -- and you took it as chit chat -- that democracy is the best parallel in exposition of the reality of consciousness reflected in government. She told you that as long as you practiced it on the degree idea, it worked very well.

"The emphasis in the chapter (she was discussing *The Unobstructed Universe*) should be that you are going to have a new pattern and for the sake of the pattern you must go back to your belief in immortality. You must follow the lines of consciousness. Each must do his job according to his capacity only, and is not expected to do anything else. As long as you have a world that does not believe in immortality, you will have emphasis on machines and not on men. . .

"Consciousness *is* being ploughed. A new pattern is going to be set. The key to the worthiness of the new pattern is restoration to the faith in immortality and its present actuality as a working principle. The American democracy was originally laid down on lines coinciding with the realities of consciousness, so on it has fallen the responsibility for the new pattern."

There is not space here for the many war details contained in these records. I present just a smattering here. For instance, on June 8, 1940, White had asked Betty what she was currently busy with.

"I'm conducting classes most of the time on the Doctor's technique," she replied. "Since the last World War much technique has been developed here. The Doctor did considerable research in hearing when he was on earth. He had even then the idea that the sense of hearing could affect the brain more than do the other senses. He followed that idea over here, and has been working on it since the last war. That led him into the development of this retroactive frequency stuff we are using.

"I want to tell you of this fact now so you will know of it when it comes out. The Germans have a siren on their dive bombers, just for hideousness. (True, writes White, but not known at that time.) Their scientists realized that of late noise has been a factor in an increase in insanity and they applied that idea to the war. The French and English have been able to discount this noise to an amazing extent. That is one of the things we here have been able to do for their morale by manipulation of frequencies discovered by the Doctor. They balance the hearing so the noise is not so frightful. Loss of equilibrium in the balance of the ear makes you sick at your stomach. You know that -- in seasickness. The Germans figured that making enough of the right kind of noise would unbalance and produce nausea, which they did in a great many cases. That broke morale because the men could not control it.

"All this will come out later," she continued. "The troops have stopped that, though the noise is still just as great. The commanders and the medical corps can't figure it out. But the fact is, we are actually able, by the use of a 'cushioning' frequency, that is used directly on the men, to re-balance the ears. But it takes one of us in specific attention to each soldier to apply this; and that means we had to train a million or so very quickly. . . So we have to have very large classes. And our people have to work in relays on the same man. We ourselves cannot keep at it too long."

Or again (May 26, 1940):

"We have all been standing around the Pope today, and just hanging onto him. You know, his poor old knees are positively blistered! Do you know, he's a *good* man. I've been in Italy all day. The thing I never understood before is the real cleavage between the royal family and Mussolini. The Pope and the king are really on one side, and Mussolini and those feeding from his trough are on the other. I do not know how it will end, but that is the present event."

And on June 15, 1940, Betty said:

"You must prepare for a shock. The news is worse than you think. (The collapse of France followed next in the news.) . . . Whom the gods would destroy they first make mad. After the last balance of sanity is gone, then Germany and Italy and Russia will destroy themselves . . .

"This is one of the moves of the center of civilization. As from the East to Egypt; from Egypt to Greece; from Greece to Rome; from Rome to Europe. Now it moves to the Western Hemisphere."

The Unobstructed Universe

Of all the war work in which Betty was engaged none had the immensity of *The Unobstructed Universe*. The subject was the physics of Betty's new world. But it was a physics no one understood then and no one understands now. Instead, its readers clasped it to their bosoms for its promise of immortality -- not for themselves so much, but for the war dead for which they were grieving, or for the servicemen who were in harm's way, or simply to give a new lease to the faith they lived by that was in jeopardy in an unbelieving, materialistic world. White and Emmet Finley considered the subject too technical for common readers and anticipated a modest sale. Instead it became a runaway best seller, its readers bombarding White with letters for years on end. We need to understand a bit about this phenomenon.

To begin with, there was massive preparation for the book on Betty's end. The physics was obviously thought out before hand and reduced to what amounted to a white paper for Betty's use during communication. But also the presentation was wrangled over by Betty and her co-workers. It was meticulously edited from beyond, and we have the documentation to prove it. In addition, there was a massive organized effort to touch the hearts of its

Have you seen this woman? *(opposite and overleaf)* She is Ruth Bissell Ebright Finley, the "Joan" of *Our Unseen Guest* and *The Unobstructed Universe.* A journalist and feminist, she was in private life an exquisitely talented medium and the official "war station" (World War II) for a group of highly placed and influential Invisibles.

In the early decades of this century, friends of Mrs. Finley saw, hanging on the wall of a Scottish castle, a portrait bearing a striking likeness to her. Mrs. Finley's Invisibles say she is a direct descendant of the individual whose portrait it was. The identity of the castle has been lost.

(top) General L.S. Ebright, Surgeon General, Ohio National Guard, shown in 1893 while serving under President-to-be William McKinley, Jr., Governor and Commander-in-Chief. Ruth Ebright was just short of her ninth birthday when this photograph of her father was published.

(bottom) Ruth's husband Emmet, her indispensable companion during a seance.

Ghostly visitors

(opposite) William James, Harvard professor and the best-known psychologist and philosopher of his day. He was the professor of *Our Unseen Guest* and a frequent visitor at Finley seances.

(right) Richard Nelville Hall, the "Stephen" of *Our Unseen Guest*. Hall drove an ambulance for French forces fighting World War I. Killed by a German shell, he showed up at the Finley's ouija board to begin a long and fruitful collaboration.

(bottom) The library at 95 Irving Street where James held seances. Ruth Finley never saw this library but described it to a "T" while in trance.

Nightly Visitations.

(opposite) Ruth Finley's father, Dr. Leonidas S. Ebright, was after his death a frequent Invisible visitor at Finley seances. The operation in which he removed his daughter's gall stones is a classic in the annals of psychic medicine.

(right) Mrs. Piper, a medium favored by the living William James. Unconvinced while alive, James became after he died an effective and frequent visitor at Finley seances.

(below) William James during a seance with a Mrs. Walden.

The Shadow of a Man. Richard Hall in France. His job: drive an ambulance to the front lines and bring back the dead and wounded. He wrote home: "It is rather nice to know I can be happy in the face of some hard and dirty work." Six weeks later he was struck by a German shell and killed.

(opposite, above) Hall with his ambulance (on the left).

(opposite, below) The remains of Hall's car.

Stewart Edward White, prolific author and male cornerstone of "the gang." His "Betty" books constitute an indispensable part of the tradition on which *Where Angels Tread* is based. Ruth Finley was the only medium he fully trusted after his wife's death.

(right) Betty White, star performer of "the gang". Betty's work was so outstanding that even Mrs. Finley was in awe of her.

(bottom) A Christmas card sent to friends after Betty's death.

(bottom left) White's scribbled message on the back of the card.

And we only wish we could deliver the message in person.

Stewart

(left and bottom) Betty and Stewart Edward White.

(opposite, top right) Emmet and Ruth Finley, Hastings-on-Hudson, 1922.

(opposite, top left) Ruth Finley as a young girl.)

(opposite, bottom) The Finleys *(center)* with Ruth's nephew, William Ebright Dague, and his wife, Margaret Beazley Dague. The photograph was taken September, 1948, at the Finley home in Hempstead, Long Island, New York, at the conclusion of the Dagues' honeymoon.

(opposite) Ruth Finley. *(above)* Julia Bissell Ebright, Ruth Finley's mother, with her grandson, the young William Ebright Dague, son of Mrs. Finley's sister Mary. William Dague eventually inherited the private papers of his aunt, Ruth Finley, and donated them to the University of Akron.

(top left) Margaret Cameron, author of *The Seven Purposes,* with her second husband, Max Kilvert. A wedding photo taken June 12, 1929. The Kilverts lived in Winter Park, Florida, and "the gang" would spend their summers there.

(top right) Emmet Finley.

(bottom right) E.W. Dykes, retired architect and formerly on the executive board of Spiritual Frontiers Fellowship. Dykes was instrumental in seeing the Finley papers donated to the University of Akron.

readers -- an angel here, an angel there -- a flurry of angels too large for our limited imaginations to encompass. You have heard Betty say that it took a million of them to counteract the Nazi noise offensive. That should give you an idea of what was done on behalf of this book.

It was 1940 and the month was June. They had been discussing a particular chapter in the book as "bait for the reader." To which Betty said:

"Now with what we have given tonight, you have a very neat, compact little angle worm. But after it is finished do not let anyone disturb you further about the book. We don't want any more done. NO! Every sentence, every paragraph, every section, every Part, has had our minutest supervision. It is beautifully done; and when it goes out it is that much better than if it was not done beautifully."

Prior to this, the close supervision Betty referred to was exercised. "Now as to the last chapter," she said at one point. "You and Emmet edit it down. It is really in three sections. The first part overbalances the middle and the last. See to that. Don't be afraid to smooth it out and to change its language if necessary to convey the meaning."

There was a great deal of this type of supervision, most of it not committed to the records and hence lost. But some remains. On June 14, 1940, Betty and a Mr. "M" requested the addition of material that became chapters IV and XXXIII. The introductory chapter was also Betty's idea. Why not? It is the delightful tale of the Chinese box. There was a shipment of them in New York, and Betty wanted a particular one for her sister Millicent, because there were swallows on it, like the ones the two of them had watched from the eaves as children. So Betty maneuvered the unwitting Ruth into buying it, much to the latter's exasperation -- until she found out that she had been manipulated and "had" by a dear friend. Of course neither White nor the Finleys understood the significance of the birds until later, when the box was delivered to Millicent and Betty's brilliant piece of evidential was unveiled.

Summing up Betty said to White:

"All that you have done in your work has been in order that your name might stand as a guarantee of this thing that I have been permitted to do. Do not think for one moment that you are not, even yet, serving and taking care of and standing back of me. No single job we ever did together was as perfectly synchronized as this one. None so important, and none that will bear richer harvest. I think you and I are unique in our marriage, don't you? Do you know of any man and woman -- any man whose wife is where I am who works as closely with her as you and I?"

Always they were urged to hurry. A message that arrived on the East Coast talked about giving White, then on the West Coast, a kick in the pants. "Huh!" he replied indignantly. "I've just finished Part II. . . Seventeen days. Thirty thousand words . . . What do these people want, anyway?"

There were detailed instructions on how to promote the book. "Start with $3000 and feed it in," Betty said. "You put a pot on to boil, and as it gets low you put in more water. If they think they've got a lot of money, they'll have big ideas."

The Unobstructed Universe went on sale the 18th of October, 1940. It sold 5,000 copies during the first two weeks and proceeded to become and remain a best seller. It became an inspirational text for many, especially in the armed forces. A letter from Ruth addressed to "Dear Gang" points this up. It was dated January 18, 1942.

"I am duplicating this letter to Margaret and Jack because I have neither the time nor energy to write to everybody individually," she began. "And anyway this is the only interesting thing I know."

She proceeded to relay a glowing report from her housekeeper bearing on *The Unobstructed Universe*. The housekeeper's name was Mary, and Ruth shared her with a family, the Davidsons, that lived in Garden City. One of the Davidson's sons, Randy, was in the service and stationed nearby at Mitchell Field.

"Everybody at the Davidsons are all excited about a book of Mr. White's that Randy brought home from the Field," Mary Began. "His mother bought him a copy for himself and one for each of the other boys and two for the house. Mr. Davidson (a World War I veteran) keeps one on his bedside table all the time and has it all marked up and won't let anybody touch it. Mrs. Davidson has loaned Sarah her copy (Sarah being the Scotch-Canadian nursery-governess who had been with the Davidson's over twenty years) but Sarah can't loan it to me. I wondered if you -- Mr. White visiting here and being such a friend of ours you must know about it and have it?" she ended plaintively.

Recall that this is the Ruth Finley whose secret identity is so closely guarded that hardly anyone in the world knows that she is White's collaborator.

"Probably I have it if it is one of his late ones," Ruth replied. She was feigning an innocence she did not feel. Did it show? "But Mr. White has written over forty books, Mary, and I have only a few -- not more than eight or ten. Which one is it?"

"I can't remember the title," replied Mary. "It has a purple cover. Sarah showed it to me in Mr. Davidson's room and told me not to move it and at lunch she said she was reading it. She thinks she's going to buy herself a copy and if she does she'll loan me that. But from what she told me -- somehow -- I'd like to read it right away."

I forgot to say, Ruth added, that Mary's son has been in the Marines three years, is a noncom, and that his Christmas leave consisted of a long distance call from Newport News to say that he was leaving on two hours notice for San Francisco.

"I expect it's *The Unobstructed Universe*," Ruth replied to Mary. She had covered her tracks and could now mention *the* title with blowing her cover. "What did Sarah say about it?"

"She says it just makes you *know* that you go on after you die," Mary replied. "That you can *understand* it for *yourself* -- not quite all of what it says -- but enough, like reading a newspaper, to *know* that what the priest keeps saying -- it's kind of hard sometimes --" She broke off.

"Exactly," Ruth said briskly. "I'll loan you a copy if you really want to read it. But won't you have to 'confess' to having read such a book?" Mary was born in Dublin and both she and Sarah were *very* staunch Catholics.

"Oh Sarah told *her* priest," said Mary, "and he knew all about it and said it probably was the greatest book written in modern times. He talked to her a long time about it the other evening when she was at his house having tea with his housekeeper. You have read it of course?" she asked Ruth.

"Yes, I've read it," Ruth deadpanned. "Several times."

"What do you think of it?"

"Just what you say Sarah's priest does -- the greatest book of modern times."

"Do you believe the dead can communicate with us?" asked Mary, who knew when to get down to brass tacks.

"With some of us," confessed the greatest medium of modern times. "And at certain times. Not with everybody nor at all times."

"That's what Father (name forgotten) told Sarah," rejoined Mary. "He said there was nothing really new in the book. All the writings of the Saints and the Church were full of the same thing. The difference in Mr. White's book, Sarah said he said, is that it takes into account new scientific discoveries and makes old truths reasonable according to the way people think today."

"Yes," agreed Ruth. "Though I think it goes a little beyond that. However what Father --- says is just as true. And you say Randy Davidson brought it home from the Field?"

"Oh yes," replied Mary. "That's where he first got hold of it. He says everybody is just crazy about it at the Field. He says they all discuss it and argue and fight over it -- fight over who's going to have the book to read next, I mean. And Randy says visiting officers steal them. They had a lot in their mess -- ten or something like that -- and now he says there's only two. Randy doesn't know it, but his father has ordered some for him to give his mess."

Ruth ends with a fervent plea to "the gang" to preserve her secret identity as Joan, the outstanding medium who had taken both *The Unobstructed Universe* and *Our Unseen Guest*. "*Please* everybody, be careful!" she pleads -- having been warned by her Invisibles that if ever her identity was discovered, she would be of no further use to them. And they were indeed careful; Ruth carried her precious secret all the way to her grave.

Betty and The Gang

"The Gang" that carried on this work consisted of Margaret Cameron, the original star; Ruth and Emmet Finley, whose prominence was originally owing to the publication in 1920 of *Our Unseen Guest*; the John Palmer Gavits (Jack and Lucy -- you can seem them working in the appendix of *The Betty Book*); and the Whites. After her death Betty became the acknowledged star of the group and in a very real sense its leader. This evidence not having been presented by an overly modest White in his books, I will sample a bit of it here.

Since you have already been apprised of the spectacular events surrounding *The Unobstructed Universe*, the basic text of which was received in the latter part of 1939, I will commence a bit later, with an October, 1940 letter from White to Ruth. In it he attests his confidence in Mrs. Adele Halman of San Francisco as Betty's chosen West Coast station and Ruth Finley surrogate.

"Mrs. Halman knows of us and our activities only what she might glean from the books," White wrote. "I have not seen her since Betty died, and never really talked to her before that. Of course to me, her picking up Betty's instructions just where Betty left them off is the remarkably convincing part. Mrs. H had no inkling of all that. And there was a lot of internal evidence that I could not get down. I think I would be harder to convince than most, but I have no doubt that Betty had (taken) charge. By the way,

Mrs. H had not before had anyone take over that way."

White sent to the Finleys his record of an October, 1940, sitting. It is so interesting that I include it here verbatim.

At Home, Oct 2 1940.

(Sitting with Mrs. Adele Halman. She is a woman of education and refinement, an acquaintance of Betty's. We knew her mainly as a psychometrist . . . and had seen her at the houses of various friends. Lives in San Francisco. Has in her home a small room with chairs and a sort of slightly raised platform at one end with a table behind which she sits, resting her forearms on a large opened Bible. Here she meets a small group of people in what I should describe as semi-religious meetings; that is, they are not formalized with dogma, and seem to be mostly for the purpose of help in a very wide field. No fee charged, but contributions accepted which, I understand, are devoted to "the cause" of help. No emphasis on usual spiritualism. Very pleasing and straightforward personality. Plenty of humor; no portentousness.

Led to visit her through a friend of us both; by the fact that this friend wrote me that through her Betty "wanted to see me" there. Thought I might as well go see.

Externals of her communications interestingly characteristic of Betty -- her sidewise bird-like poses of the head, etc. Content of communication still more characteristic. Not all taken down.

"I am so tempted to go near Ruth," Betty began. "I have not done so, for you see I am under orders, and I obey orders -- doesn't that surprise you, Stewt? You'd like that! In about three weeks from now I shall approach her, on tiptoe, very quietly, like a little angel, and just *touch* her so gently! It would be so easy for me to take her with me, but I am not to do that again just yet.

"You see, I have so much of my own work to do here in preparation for out next work together. I have been made to join a group, which is not entirely to my liking, for I much prefer to work by myself. The lessons are rather hard. But I'm competent! I have progressed lately, and I have gained an assurance of strength in combination. At the moment we gain more by listening than by talking, and just now I am listening. But the day is coming when I shall express myself again, and I'm telling you that our work of today will look like child's play.

"I don't know whether you will understand this. My job is to lay solid stepping stones. So many people come over here half prepared. They seem to think that at once when they die, they are going to be able to fly! They need under their feet -- I am talking literally -- a solid foundation of cobble stones to *walk* on, and they have to be laid one by one. The ideas -- spiritual ideas -- they can really possess there, which have no what you call solidity there, have real solidity here, cobble stone solidity. They make the road for them to walk on. I am helping lay those cobble stones. That is my job, just laying cobble stones; and of course there are architects and engineers who plan the road, and who are over me, the road, the bridge, from one world to the other. The people who read and who understand our books that we are doing will use the ideas they get from them, when they pass over. That is what I mean when I say I am laying the stones between us. Do you understand? Now don't say you do if you don't. It is to tell you these things that I got you here."

"I think I understand," replied White.

"All right," said Betty. "Now I want to add this. Ruth is the very best instrument possible for me to use in doing this. I cannot even imagine doing it without Ruth. I cannot imagine anyone taking her place. For one thing, If I did not *love* Ruth I could not do it. If she did not love me and if you did not -- and Emmet -- it could (not) be done. Love is the thing best fitted to manipulate a station.

"So you see the importance of obeying orders. That is why Ruth has a rest period. But here is something important too. We cannot make the mistake of letting too long a period intervene between Ruth and me. We have to come together and practice. I must keep my footing through her. She requires rest; she must go ahead and do everything that pleases her. When the time comes to start again I will tell you. But once a month -- exactly that -- I want her to let me talk through her, with Emmet. Not long. And not just yet. . . I will let you know when to begin."

"Me?" asked White. And Betty assenting he added, "How? I wouldn't trust a hunch."

"I'll fix it," replied Betty. Perhaps through this woman."

Then Betty repeated her orders for Ruth, adding:

"I obey orders here; will you obey orders there?" It should be kept regularly *once a month.* I must keep my way back to her.

"As long as you are there on earth, I am to work with you. There are books yet to write. It seems probable that the next book will go more into detail of my life here -- make it clearer and simpler. The reason is that my life here is no different from anybody's, and it might very well serve in essentials as a *pattern* for better living there. I do not know; that is how it seems. When you come, then I am to go on, have a sort of cleavage from the earth in my work. But while you are there, I am with you on the earth job.

"Don't you think I'm a *wonder*, chattering away like this? I did not think it possible, for when Ruth is able she is the best *possible* instrument for me. When I came into this room I was amazed at the difference in method. You see, Ruth's job demanded her training to be able to hold steadily on definite frequencies so she could communicate at her best through a few. But Adele's job -- it's silly to call her Mrs. Halman -- demands that she be able to shift frequencies easily, from high ones to low ones, because she has so many different kinds of people to work for. It is amazing."

And indeed White followed "orders." His problem was, he got too few. He would constantly badger the Finleys for them, wondering what he should do next, complaining that "I don't like to break orders." Still, orders there were in abundance. You have already seen the detailed instructions given as to the writing of *The Unobstructed Universe*.

Betty had been an avid gardener and it seems appropriate at this point to say a few things about it. She used to collect exotic African plants while accompanying her husband on safari, and under her care they would flourish in her garden at Little Hill. She had one gardener, but other women in her social set had three. And she used to beat them in the annual competitions of the local garden club.

Still, isn't it surprising that after she died the garden club established an annual medal to be called "The Betty White Award" to be given each year at their show for something different?

The medal was established in 1939. As late as the Spring of 1941 White wrote to Ruth:

"Such a nice thing has happened. Members of the Garden Club, friends of Betty, have been up here working like nailers 'putting Betty's garden in shape for her.' They did not let me know; I just happened to see them. They were weeding, tying up, trimming -- doing dirty hard work; and the time they selected for it was when they knew I am always busy in the Ark. They weren't doing it for me, but for Betty."

And in April of that year Betty won a prize for her flowers! White's report was:

"At the annual rose show here, two of Betty's Garden Club friends put it up to the board of governors whether they would accept an entry from Betty (I am not a member and hence not eligible); and after some deliberation they made an exception and permitted it! Allee samee Who's Who. Out of four entries in roses Betty got two blue ribbons and one red."

Now as to Betty and Ruth: it is difficult to talk about one without the other. You have seen above how Betty regarded their relationship. Of the mountains of evidence of this I will present a smattering.

"The Gang" by now had an elevated notion of Betty's place in the order of things. So it is not surprising that Ruth consulted an astrologer in an attempt to determine Betty's "degree."

"Your astrological findings as to Betty's 'degree' is interesting," replied White to Ruth's report. "It is what I should expect." But no details are available.

Early in 1941 Ruth had an impacted tooth. Betty intervened with suggestions. How she did it is instructive. She chose Mrs. Halman and her chapel for the demonstration. White's report to the Finleys is as follows:

"Began with a hymn and the organ; Lord's Prayer; then a brief and simple dedication of the room to construction -- evidentially a ritual," White's letter reads.

"Then Mrs. H said in effect that the usual procedure was off for the day; that the meeting would be conducted by 'a very lovely lady, who came this morning to tell me so'; that this was unexpected, but she could not refuse -- did not want to refuse. She ended by saying that she pledged herself to do her best to be a good reporter for this lovely lady. Then followed a short talk. Mrs. H did not mention Betty by name until after it was finished. The talk did not mention healing, which was supposed to be the subject of the meeting. . . It was a darn good talk, and very Bettyish, and made them sit up. At once it struck me that possibly here was Betty's promised attempt on a 'gathering.'"

"But here is really what this letter is for: After the meeting I stopped to talk with Mrs. Halman. Suddenly she stopped short.

"Have you heard whether Emmet is in good health?" she asked me. I said I hadn't heard lately. She looked puzzled. "I get a feeling that something is a little wrong, something that delays your work together" -- *then she placed her hand against her jaw*: "there is pain -- no, more ache or discomfort -- here," said she.

"I too was puzzled for a few seconds; and then I remembered your letter, in which you wondered why you had written so much about yourself, and a great light broke through my stupidity; and *Betty* herself took charge of Mrs. H and cried out triumphantly: 'There! I knew you'd get it!'"

"Now I submit that is something. I knew nothing of your impacted tooth until I got your letter day before yesterday. You yourself did not quite know why you told me about it. And unless you assume a highly complicated brand of involved and selected telepathy on the part of Mrs. H, she was blankly ignorant of everything. In fact she ascribed her own impression-- before Betty took over -- to Emmet. It was good evidential, and also it gave weight to what Betty had now to say, I think. And perhaps that is what it was intended for."

"She really must get that fixed as it interferes with the kind of rest I want for her," Betty had gone on to say. "It does not seem that it should be necessary to have a general anesthetic; they ought to be able to do it with a local.

"It will not be necessary for her to work once a month with Emmet, as I thought. I could not work well with her and Emmet without your being there too. I need the three. I find that I can keep my own way (through or back) by coming here occasionally to practice. (i.e. through Mrs. H) Now listen: you will begin again in March -- just begin. I will start the new book the first of April. I would like it published about the following Easter."

With Ruth's astounding talent it should surprise no one that she was capable of seeing visions. She was, and of course Betty was involved. Betty wanted to send a squirrel of some sort to White as a present -- squirrels being a Bettyish sort of animal, it seems.

"The squirrel got here all right," White wrote Ruth early in 1944. "I wrote you quite a long letter apprising you of that fact and that he sat on my desk below the two terra-cotta squirrels holding the pencils very neatly just as Betty showed you in the vision." The letter referred to apparently having gone astray in the mails.

"I think the squirrel came out remarkably brilliantly," he continued. "From what our letter said I thought he would be rather dull in appearance but he fairly shines. Anyway, he is so exactly and typically the Betty type of squirrel, as evidenced in the other species, that it is most astonishing and amusing."

But again and again she would return to Ruth.

"Now as to Ruth," she said in late 1940 through Mrs. Halman. "She is not resting quite as she could. It's sort of half resting. It's a sort of house-cleaning I want. I want her to take out of her mind everything that we said that is in the book. You see I don't want the next book to have in it from her any trace of what is in this one." And so on.

And again:

"This is a message for Ruth and Emmet. The first thing I want to tell is that I spent a few hours with Ruth last Tuesday and helped her to rest and to sleep because, in our next divulgence, we shall deal at length with the activity of the beta body during the resting hours of the alpha." (A reference apparently to the Content of Consciousness divulgence that forms the first part of the present book.)

"Until the month of February," she continued, "no work will be possible except only the night work. As to that, do you know I have had the unmitigated joy of having you there with me, for discussion in our beta bodies; and it was most interesting to see how much of our conversations and discussions remained in the alpha minds all through the following days."

And early in 1941 came this with respect to Ruth:

"I have refrained from going too much near her," said Betty. "She feels me so quickly, and I perceive a peculiar tremor passing through her -- a sort of little shiver -- when I am near her. Emmet has felt that also."

"Now I want to say to Ruth that when she does begin work Anne says she is to be taken care of, and that some very advanced people are going to take charge of that with her. Emmet is just a little worried about her undertaking it, but you tell him she is to be watched even more carefully from this side than ever before. We have doctors here, remember. When Ruth is in trance it is not her physical body but her beta body that requires attention. And when one is not well in the beta body he cannot be cured with pills."

You all know by now who the core members of "the gang" were. What I despair of describing is the sense of camaraderie that glued them together, the sense of elan that permeated their work and welded them into a single working team. A lot of this is evidenced by letters emanating from Winter Park, Florida, where Margaret, by now a semi-invalid, lived with her second husband, Maxwell A Kilvert, and where the Finleys, the Gavits, and White would gather during the Winter whenever possible. Margaret was a good letter writer. Why not? In her heyday she was accustomed to penning best sellers. In the piece below you can see the writer's insight into White's character. They had Ruth in residence but not Emmet; Margaret's letter is to the latter.

"We were awfully disappointed that you couldn't come back," she wrote Emmet, who apparently was tending to business in New York. "And hope you will a little later.

"Stewart also was disappointed, and yet -- as I told Ruth the other day, he had a sort of cat-that-ate-the-canary look, probably attributable to the fact that when you are not around, Ruth certainly won't psych and therefore it was no longer incumbent upon him to stay here sitting on the lid. His hell-bent determination that no one but Betty shall ever use that station again is funny.

"However, he has discovered that sitting on the lid wasn't really the whole purpose of his being here. Just now he is doing errands for Ruth, among other things, and being very useful."

In contrast to White, Margaret is relaxed and ever so informative. Without her letters we would have no inkling what a gathering place Winter Park had become. The next letter -- this one to Ruth -- goes all the way back to the early years.

"I know I need a new typewriter ribbon," she began. "But I keep thinking I'll get over to the marts of trade in a day or two and select it myself. I've been thinking that for months and still can't get there, but . . .

"Yours of day before yesterday -- black magic! -- just here. Your serene -- and not unnatural -- assumption that Stewart will write me this and that gives me to grin. He might mention that you'd been getting wonderful stuff from Betty, but his letters -- welcome though they always are -- couldn't by any stretch of the imagination be called chatty.

"I went upstairs and looked at a long row of record books, wondering how under the sun I could find that Cleveland stuff, which I remembered but couldn't date, and then my eye fell on that blessed card index -- and in five minutes I had the stuff. I haven't looked into those books for years and had forgotten they were indexed. I wish to Pete I'd had sense enough to index Betty's records from the start, too. . ."

"That egg woman is a wonder!. . . I chuckled over her not liking Florida for me after June, however. June and July are all right, it's August and September that get a bit thick. But as between staying here and traveling, packing and unpacking, living in hotels and suitcases, in my present state of decrepitude give me the home fires. Besides which, going away from here for the summer means fussing over rugs and woolens to keep them from moths, silks and books to keep them from mildew. Every book has to be wrapped in paper and put in as dry a place as possible - and with our library that's some chore. And when you get back you wear yourself out getting things back in place . . ."

"Yesterday, having felt pretty well for several days, I got gay and went to a luncheon given by Mrs. Sanford Bissell -- the lady who asked Josephine whether I was all right mentally -- and thought last night I'd got away with it all right. This morning was another story and I've been a wreck all day.

"It's Max's birthday, but we are not celebrating, as he is dead tired and has been out night after night with a heavy week coming. We decided to lie low tonight and go to bed, but there are some pests over in Orlando who are more than likely to come in for a chatty evening!

"He says that hereafter he's going to leave town at the end of January and stay away until early March. February here is a riot. Things doing day and night and this year he got into them and can't get out. Being an invalid has its compensations. Ten minutes ago a woman asked me if I'd go to her for cocktails before a big Institute dinner on the 21st and was obviously shocked when I said I doubted that I should go to the dinner. They just run around like squirrels in a wheel fagged to death, tongues hanging out, but miss anything? Not they!"

"We look naked and bare now. The lovely hibiscus outside my window died of frost and has been cut away, hedges at the back are gone and I feel sort o' indecent. Everything open to the world."

Having promised Ruth to copy the Cleveland record and send it Santa Barbara -- the Finleys were visiting White in California -- she stopped to read it. The following postscript records her reaction:

"My land! I hadn't read that stuff over when I wrote the letter -- but twenty years after, it's more interesting than it was when it came. Some of it astonished me. Of course I was the leader only because I published the first book -- and so became a sort of focal center for the group -- because at the moment I was in the spotlight. And I wondered a good many times since why I insisted upon signing that book in spite of Harry's qualms . . . Maybe this is the reason.

"Certainly the 'more to come' came all right -- and with it 'the polishing the varying lights, the appreciation of the rarity and the wonder of the jewel.' And between us all a good many shipwrecked or fog bound mariners have found the way home.

"Golly, why aren't we out there with you!"

The reader was introduced to the Cleveland records in the chapter devoted to Ruth Finley. The "jewel" was described as having three facets, each an outstanding medium from "the gang." The date: March 13 1920.

So how can the invalided former leader assist the rest of "the gang?" More than one would think. The next is from Betty via Mrs. Halman.

"Now tell Margaret our abounding thanks for all her splendid work she is doing over here. She is working with people here who would perhaps never come to knowledge there in her everyday life."

This looked like bad "coloring" to White , who protested that Margaret is here, not there.

"Of course," replied Betty. "But darling don't you know yet that work can be done here while you are still in the body? Even when the body is tired out and sick and stretched on the bed? But only, of course, if you have earned the right, by your earth doings, to work that way. Why, you do it yourself. It is so discouraging, when I try so hard to make you remember, to have you wake, and it is all gone. Except perhaps a little impression, more vivid than usual, of companionship.

"Ask Margaret if one morning, on awakening, she heard a chorus. If she heard it, it was from a lot of us seeing her off from her work here. I wonder if she heard it.

"What you do there has its effect here," she continued. "The book that you wrote is very well known here."

And they worked while in Winter Park. The sessions were frequently devoted to small talk, but they were never dull. The following session took place early in 1940. World affairs were on everyone's mind. Ruth was working. Prominent among the guests was Harrison Cass Lewis, Margaret's first husband, now dead. In life he had been a successful businessman with international connections.

"The preservation of the integrity of the South American nations is dependent on the solidarity of the Americas," Lewis said. "The center of civilization has moved. The U.S.A. has not realized yet that it is the axis. It must realize it and it must take the lead. It must be above war. The ideological fight of Europe must not be allowed to affect this country sociologically nor -- to put it baldly-- commercially. The best position for the South American countries is to stand strong with, for and back of the United States. They are not so dumb that they do not realize the superiority of the North American civilization and methods. . ."

"One of the things that can be best done is the introduction into the public schools of Spanish. Once they taught French and German. Now the Americas need Spanish and English. One of the worst dangers to the South American countries is the introduction of North European professors into their schools."

"How?" Max wanted to know -- he being Margaret's current husband.

"The danger, for instance," Lewis replied, "of German chemists in their Universities. They are there for only one purpose..

"The balance of the world has moved," he continued. "I said that before, but I want to emphasize it. The production balance has moved. The cultural balance has moved. The ethical balance has moved. The social balance has moved. The educational, the mercantile, the research balance, likewise have moved. We do not look to Germany now for scientific advance: it is centered in the United States. Once you looked to Russia for wheat; now you look to South America. Europe is done -- for several generations. And people like you who understand this must voice to the two Americas the importance of their own stability. . ."

"You see this is a kind of gathering spot. I have been much impressed by the type of mind that comes here for rest. They take away from here, back to busier and more influential places, the ideas that seep in during a period of suspension from work-a-day things. Their minds are very fertile and lax -- easy to penetrate while they are here. You get their attention here when you couldn't possibly get it in New York or Chicago."

Betty and her "Stew't"

"Stew't" for Stewart -- it was her pet name for her husband. Ruth hadn't known it while Betty was alive -- they had had few social contacts, living a continent apart as they did. But after Betty died her nickname for him became known, and Betty used it time and again to reaffirm the intimacy between husband and wife.

In one of her more spectacular stunts, Betty managed to write White a private letter that everyone at the seance was dying to see but which no one did, not even Ruth. It was signed and sealed, posted and delivered, sight unseen -- and even then White revealed only part of its contents. Ruth describes the circumstances surrounding its production as follows:

"I'm glad the birthday letter clicked," she wrote White. "According to reports it was a most unusual performance. I never did automatic writing in trance before, and as I never have been too good at it under any circumstances, I was pretty nervous when told of that two-ring-circus attempt. Foolish, of course. I suppose sometime I'll learn to *completely* trust them! And this will interest you as it does me.

They told me that the writing of the letter itself was fairly rapid and completely unhesitating; that I only fumbled a little in changing the sheets of paper which Betty sharply insisted on doing herself. Somebody -- Emmet probably -- evidently wanted to supply a fresh sheet when one was covered with writing. How many pages long was the letter, by the way? But when she had finished, put the sheets together, folded them, put them in the envelope and sealed it, they said she was inordinately slow in writing the address -- now that you say that here she actually forced through her own hand writing, this deliberateness is explained. As I understand it Emmet's copying of the record and Margaret's writing of her letter were accomplished while Betty wrote HER letter; that the outer envelope was addressed and Emmet's and Margaret's contributions folded in it by the time Betty's envelope was sealed and addressed, and that she insisted on putting her note into the outer envelope herself. I believe she permitted Emmet to lick the flap of the outside envelope, but I do know that it was sealed, stamped and ready to mail when I was taken out of trance. I never saw *any* of the contents -- and I don't think the others saw even the address Betty wrote on the envelope in which she herself sealed her note. I doubt if I would know Betty's handwriting. If I had three letters from her in my life that's two more than I can remember. Once or twice on a Christmas card she scribbled a message. But these were never saved after the immediate season was over. I have a dim recollection of getting one letter from her asking me for the pattern of a wood-carrier she had seen us using at the Hill -- she wanted it for some work-group she was interested in to make for sale. I sent it and *you* replied saying she had found it practical and was grateful for it but was too busy to write at the moment but would later. She never did -- that I remember -- and there was no reason for her to do so. I remember the somewhat caustic remarks you made concerning my ability as an artist, for I had attempted to sketch the darn thing with logs in it to show just how it was used, in addition to the ruled pattern with the measurements. I remember howling over your letter with Emmet -- and that was that. So even if I wanted to I couldn't imitate her hand writing to save my soul, for I simply don't know it. When I stop to think it seems funny, doesn't it, that she can be so much a part of me now, so familiar, so intimately real, when all the years she and I knew of each other here our meetings were so few and our in-between contacts practically nil. I wonder if you really realize how little I knew her -- none of her friends, none of her tastes, none of her habits.

"Do you know, I think she spoke to me just now! As she did to Johnnie. And what she said was this -- 'But it was planned that way. THEY didn't want you to know me *then* because you were to know me so well *now*. Don't you see? Just this one fact makes or work together so much more authentic and valuable.'

"I get the idea -- only I would so have enjoyed her 'then'; and remembering her."

The above was in response to White's acknowledgment that he had received Betty's letter. In it he wrote, "I don't know whether you noticed, but the address on the envelope -- "Stew't" -- was exactly in Betty's hand writing. . . It was a fine letter for a birthday; and it contained her code words, and much that she said she would give me when the time came. Also she pointed out -- which I had not noticed -- that in the telegram not only had she got over two items of her code; but that she had repeated them in a sort of anagram, which she explained!

"By the way, in the said letter Betty stated categorically: 'This will reach you the morning of the twelfth'; and it did. So your-all speculation as to whether it would or not is out."

Well, as Margaret pointed out, he was anything but "chatty". Still, he opened up a bit in a subsequent letter. "As to Betty's letter: I repeat that the handwriting on the envelope was hers. Your letter enlightens me as to one thing she said. You write, 'As I understand it, Emmet's copying of the record and Margaret's writing of her letter were accomplished while Betty wrote *her* letter.' In the first part of the letter she said: 'It's just killing Margaret that she can't see what I am writing, and I must think of a job she can do.' And toward the end, 'I must stop because Margaret has finished, and Emmet has finished, and they are all yelling and so darn curious that it is no good trying any more.' The letter is three full pages of rather small writing."

So much for another spectacular performance by their star performer. But then she was good at letters. Consider what White wrote next in the letter just quoted:

"You remember she dictated a long letter to Millicent (her sister), which I did not include in the record. In it she said: 'If you have decided to upholster that chair, why don't you let Stew't send you a piece from several brocades and homespuns I have folded away. They are of no use in the box, and might be much better enjoyed by someone. There is one particular piece with a brownish goldish sort of tone that I think would be very adequate for you.' While waiting to hear I asked Reider (the butler) whether he knew of any such. He did not. So having confidence in the woman by now, I set him to searching. He found it, finally, as described, laid away. Mill wrote: 'Now *how* did she know I was just sending a chair to be recovered!' Ho hum! What price mere evidential!"

And through all this Betty kept up her work, with White's help, with troubled people. Although she declared that she had no time to go to strangers -- there were hundreds who thought they had heard from her -- still she seemed available to help when help was truly needed. White wrote the Finleys in 1942 that he had been forced to ration visitors -- there were simply too many -- and from then on he would see only those that really required help. At such times he would summon Betty and say, "Now you rally 'round. This is your job." And amazingly, he reported, he would find the proper thing to tell them.

"In the past week," he wrote, "I have had three wonderfully intelligent women here to whom I gave about two hours apiece, all of them in the depths of something or other that really was on the edge of suicide, but who now have written me telling me that they have gone forth bubbling with joy, rapture, energy and so forth on the road of life and all the rest of it." All of which he ascribed to Betty's intervention.

And always they took care of their own. One such was Lucy Gavit, a charter member of "the gang", who died in late 1940 or early 1941. Betty had instructions to give regarding Lucy, and she summoned White to Mrs. Halman's to receive them.

"First I want to say something of importance as to Lucy," Betty said. "She wants very much to help, but she is not yet able. Tell her to go and rest and get ready; that later she is going to help a great deal, but not yet. It would only muddle things, if she tries to do so now."

"You mean for us to tell her?" This from an incredulous White.

"Yes," replied Betty. "She needs that assurance from you too.

"Lucy left this with me for Jack, "Betty continued. Jack being her husband. "When she passed over she felt first of all the touch of a hand and she did not travel alone to here. Someone held her hand and made it easy, very easy for her. She was then placed in charge of a group that had been awaiting her. I tell this last so that no one will feel he must think *too* much of helping Lucy from there. All such thought of detail for Lucy is useless, and must be eliminated. I say this so we can have a clear sight of the coast. You remember on the yacht, when vision was confused by mists?" she concluded.

White survived Betty by seven years, dying on September 18, 1946. The reader has already been apprised of what he and Betty did subsequently. From our limited point of view they created another masterpiece for us, *The Content of Consciousness*, which forms Part II of this book.

Betty's other principal collaborator, Ruth Finley, alias "Joan", was still very much alive. A year after White's death she responded, as Joan, to a White fan letter that had been forwarded to her by Harwood, White's brother.

"I cannot tell you anything of Stewart's passing for I do not know," she wrote. "My feeling is that he just went to sleep. When I learned how ill he was

I asked my father "the doctor" of whom Betty speaks to take him out as quickly and easily as possible and Darby told me that father came and promised to do so. I know that he (SEW) went quickly; I think father would be able to take him easily. I also know that Betty was with him constantly throughout his (SEW's) last weeks here if his nurses are to be believed. They reported to his brother that he frequently would say -- "Just a minute -- just till I finish talking with Betty" -- or something to that effect.

"Yes, he has 'come back' most gloriously. He finished dictating through me the concepts for at least one book -- all entirely new ideas though naturally based on the Stephen and Betty philosophy -- by the middle of June of this year. Darby is at work on it this minute. I can hear the click of his typewriter over in the ell that makes an upstairs sunroom just across from my windows. I do not know how soon it will be published -- but it is amazingly good stuff and quite as revolutionary as the new concepts in *The Unobstructed Universe.* Being a librarian you, better than most people, will realize that the editing and structural presentation of such notes no matter how copious they are -- and these are very copious -- is quite a job.

"Yes, I think SEW found things quite as he expected in the Unobstructed. He and Betty went off on some sort of jaunt from the time of his passing until just after Christmas. We were never told much about that -- save that we could get no work out of him or her either. Then he suddenly came back with a bang and through the late spring kept us so busy that I was a rag when he finished. The general presentation I mean. I know from working for Betty and Stephen that there are spots to be further elucidated and that SEW will be along with bells on to clear them up to his own satisfaction."

But that was never to happen. We have "Joan's" notes but not "Darby's" manuscript. The present book is an attempt to make amends for this, so that such material will not be lost to future generations -- the ever believing, ever hopeful, ever aspiring young that make it all worthwhile.

Chapter 9. Of Angels and Archangels

THERE were so many lively angels involved in the work described in these pages that it is difficult to single out a particular one for special mention -- especially since so many worked anonymously just for the sake of the service they could render. And yet among the many honorable foot soldiers of the spirit were a sprinkling of archangels -- those individuals whose development had proceeded so high that they stood at the pinnacle among human beings not yet incorporated in Supremacy.

The "Twelve Lessons," that jewel of *The Seven Purposes*, was said to arise from individuals of such eminence. And in the work of these pages there was a great stir among those who were intimates of archangels. Richard said so early on; told the Finleys about the lively interest in his revelation being shown among angels of higher degree, describing it as a happening of the greatest moment among his contemporaries and associates.

Yet with all that it is still possible to single out an individual who more than anyone else was the instigator of those things chronicled herein. Of all the individual contributors to the work of *The Content of Consciousness*, then, none rises to that lofty eminence occupied by Anne o' Perth. This assessment of the situation was not immediately apparent to the Finleys. It took Betty White to point it out; that it was a rare privilege indeed for all concerned to be associated with so grand a spirit, one already poised for that final flight into Supremacy, but who had paused instead, during a crisis of the human race, to direct a work both practical and sublime.

All three divulgences are a tribute to her industry; any attempt to add luster to such a body of work can only fall short of the mark. Nevertheless it is necessary to point out that she was and is the chief instigator of these things. And, after the introductions, we will let her speak in her own voice: to begin with, as she first appeared long ago to the Finleys; and finally, as she said her good byes to us while *The Content of Consciousness* sittings were drawing to a close.

Anne was for the most part content to let the youngsters do the talking. But on occasion she would interject a bit of her own philosophy, and when she did, it tended to go to the heart of the matter. Her statement that we conceive our world, she hers, is treated elsewhere in these pages. It is the finest epistemology I have ever seen, and no doubt also the shortest. I'm not sure it was possible for the modern mind to grasp its meaning prior to the trail-blazing work of Thomas Kuhn. Certain it is that I could not have done so.

It was I believe Anne who said that what she and her colleagues strove for in the world of people was not great books, but harmonious lives. Perhaps also hers that to settle into a true evolutionary pattern, it is necessary for each of us to accept help with our individual problems -- again capturing a cosmic concept in a handful of common words.

In *A River Runs Through It*, [1] the author's father, a Presbyterian minister and a Scot, mixes fly fishing with the Westminster Shorter Catechism.

---

1. Norman Maclean, Simon & Schuster, 1976

"What is the chief end of man?" he would demand of his sons. "Man's chief end is to glorify God, and to enjoy Him forever," they would reply, which is easy to do, I suppose, if you are a preacher's son and eager to get on with trout fishing.

The question, however, is a perennial one, and always worth asking. Scottish Presbyterians answer it one way. But Anne was herself a Scotswoman, and she had a different answer. Stewart Edward White, in the sittings from which this book is drawn, answered it a third way. The folk who prepared *The Twelve Lessons* from *The Seven Purposes*, which is also an integral part of this general philosophy, answered it a fourth way. Each answer is individually valid as far as I can judge.

The folk who gave us *The Seven Purposes* were doing large-scale civilization-building things. "Choose ye!" That was their Old Testament challenge. Their notion was that we have reached a point in our development where it is to our advantage to separate the sheep from the goats in the here and now, rather than wait for the traditional Biblical end of time. Doing so will make it clear to all what each individual stands for, and on that basis we will be able to sort things out and get a better world going.

The answer of the model in this book is as microscopic as the *Purposes* is cosmic. Achieving the good life and the furtherance of human evolution are, in the sense of this book, synonymous; and evolution as so conceived proceeds by the accumulation of quantity; thus our individual job is to accumulate it. How? By storing, quantum by quantum, bits of experience in our subconscious minds. To make these bits count, each one must be accompanied by a decision on our part. We have to take a point of view with each drib and drab before it slips into the subconscious and out of our conscious purview. As with the *The Seven Purposes*, the answer is, *decide*. But there is a difference in scale there.

Anne's hot button was *control* -- individual control of one's self, societal control of civilizations. Here we see perhaps the long view of individual development as it proceeds into the stratosphere and becomes a candidate for Supremacy, where individuality is untrammeled and personal control complete. I don't think any of us achieves a very high degree of control in this sense while living here. It is by all accounts a tough nut to crack. But Anne puts it on the front burner.

Now for the voice of Anne. This initial passage is from the manuscript of *The Master Key*. It was omitted from *Our Unseen Guest*.

I, Anne o' Perth, wha mair than twa centuries as earth counts time ha' lived beyant th' sting o' death, say untae thee wha readet i' th' book: --

This be th' master key.

Place it i' th' han's o' philosopher or priest, scientist or man o' letters, artist or artisan, an' it shall unlock frae them th' door at which they ha' knocked. An' wi' th' op'nin' o' that door a new licht shall be thrown intae th' foursome corners o' th' room -- that room where ha' been imprisoned their lang sought knowledge.

Many things which ha' lain under th' shadows o' mysticism, o' dogma, o' hypothetical reasonin' an' o' mon's own emotions shall be revealed. An' frae out th' dust that litters th' floor th' pearls o' truth shall gleam an' mon shall separate them at last frae th' untruths an' shall string them on th' golden chain o' his daily livin'. [2]

---

2. *The Master Key*, page 2

The next passage is also from *The Master Key*. Most of it was also omitted from the published work. It is Anne's first appearance.

And then there came to the Ouija board's tripod a moment of strange technique, such a moment as Joan and I have learned to recognize for the herald of some new friend.

"There is one here," announced Stephen, "who calls herself Anne o' Perth."

"Guid e'en tae ye, sweet gentles. Th' hearth be wide enou tae rest ane mair."

Thus spelled Anne o' Perth, making her initial bow upon Joan's and my Ouija board.

"The Lady Anne," Stephen broke in, "lived many years ago in Scotland. She is Joan's grandmother, distantly great."

In truth, Joan had told me of an ancient ancestress of hers, one whose portrait hangs in an old Scotch castle. To us the grandam had been noteworthy because friends who have seen this portrait aver the features pictured might well be Joan's own. Also we had been mildly curious because of a family legend which reports the original of the portrait to have been possessed of second sight, whatever that is.

Stephen continued: "You will find the Lady Anne a whimsical soul, but be not deceived; very close is she to the supreme degree."

"Anne o' Perth," said I, "be welcome. We'll give you free rein to race across our Ouija board."

"A' dames' tongues hae sic 'tis taled," the tripod spelled.

"And doubtless," I suggested, "you are like all other women, Anne -- doubtless you like to talk."

"I be dame," she answered. "Th' guidmon says, "Tongues o' a' dames do clack.' 'But,' I answer, 'where's th' difference 'twixt cup o' tea an' pot o' ale?"

"Anne," I laughed, "they tell me that in this life you had second sight."

"Witch!" confessed Anne.

"Indeed?", Joan exclaimed. "You were, then, a witch?"

"Sae, th' clatterin' tongues i' th' market place whisperet. But hush, laddie! hush, lassie! I'll spin ye a tale."

Then did Anne o' Perth set down upon our Ouija board this fable:

"Noo th' guidwife plantet her gayrden, an' i' ane pairt o' her gayrden she plantet th' maize for th' makin' o' th' paraitch, an' i' anaither pairt o' th' gayrden she plantet th' thyme for th' season o' th' roast, an' i' anaither pairt o' th' gayrden she plantet th' flowers for th' decoratin' o' her hoose. An' a' were green an' were fair an' fruitfu'.

"By th' door, then, o' th' cot she plantet a guidly number o' honeysuckle seeds an' she wateret them; an' th' sun shone upon them an' the' vines coomet up frae th' mold an' climbet o'er th' door o' th' cot. An' th' young tendrels fastenet their fingers i' th' thatch and runnet o'er th' eaves and on tae th' roof; an' some o' th' vines grew na sae high, but wound across th' casement an' peeket i' th' pane an' tappet o' th' glass.

Noo then, when th' sun haen shone fu' mony a day on these honeysuckle vines, th' buddies burst i' tae bloom. An' th' vine that haen grown th' highest were closest tae th' sun, an' there th' flowers bloomet th' mickle maist. They were gorgeous whatever.

"Weel, noo then, under th' eaves betimes aither buddies burst an' they, too, were fair, but lacket o' color, for they ha'na seen th' fu' glory o' th' sun, an' o'er th' casement they, too, bloomet an' peeket i' th' window at th' guidwife an' th' laddies a-playin' on th' floor. But th' vine that grew na tae th' sill, that falteret an' turnet back and laid itsel' o'er th' groun' bloomet na.

"An' when th' hummin' birds coomet i' th' marnin' dew after th' sweetness that was th' vines' gift tae th' world they sucket first th' flowers that haen grown highest, that haen th' greatest depth o' warmth i' th' hearts o' them, for they haen gien much o' their strength tae reach th' thatch, an' i' th' climbin' theretae haen they gatheret untae themsel' a gran' appreciation o' th' winds that fannet them an' o' th' rain that kisset them an' th' sun that warmet their hearts.

"An' sae th' birdies that were a-seekin' after sweetness sucket where th' greatest sweetness were. An' there coomet some that drank o' th' blooms under th' eaves an' aithers that lovet them which tappet o' th' pane; but no mon nor bird gave aught for th' vine that crawlet o'er th' sward, for it ha'na fu'fillet its blossomin's.

"An' th' guidwife coomet tae th' door o' th' cot wi' her bairns a-clingin' tae her skirties. An' ane laddie said: 'Maither, for why do th' honeysuckle be a-bloomin' more beautifu' at th' roof than on th' groun' where I could a-reachie o' th' blooms?'

An' th' maither said tae her laddie: 'My ain bairn, the honeysuckle climbet high an' bloomet i' th' fu'ness o' its sweetness beyant yir reach noo, but i' th' days when ye fu'fill th' growth o' yir ainsel' ye will be a-pickin' o' th' blooms that be above ye noo. Ye, too, maun grow, laddie. Noo a' ye can do wi' yir wee han'ies be tae water th' vines for maither, but next year methinks ye'll be a-gatherin' a bunch frae them that tappet o' th' pane. An' when ye come, laddie, tae yir monhud ye'll ha' grown i' stature e'en as th' vine ye can then pluck o' its flowers 'neath th' eaves.

"It be ane step after anaither, laddie, an' 'tis a wrung each day, sae that when ye coom tae th' realization o' yir desires they be as beautiffu' i' their attainment as they were i' yir dreams."

The tripod halted and in a moment Stephen was back.

"The Lady Anne's little tales will bear study," he said. "Look upon the maize and the thyme and the flowers that the goodwife planted as symbolical of various degrees of consciousness. In the honeysuckle Anne has shown you a degree of consciousness striving upward toward a higher and higher development and promised success as it puts forth the effort that ever is ready within it to be put forth. In the little boy you are shown the human vine; it, too, must strive. And accept the assurance of the goodwife, in whom for the moment behold the whole of consciousness, that individual consciousnesses have but to seek development and lo! it is theirs. Much more of knowledge there is in the Lady Anne's allegory."

It is no easy task to take down the spellings of a rapid-fire Ouija board. Anne o' Perth dictates even more rapidly that Stephen; and her many Scotch forms render more difficult a difficulty great enough when least. At first Joan and I tried the plan of interrupting "The Lady Anne," whenever we were doubtful of her exact orthography. These interruptions were soon discontinued because they resulted in broken sentences and confused context. At first Anne told us to verify and correct her spelling "frae th' bookies"; later she said that this would involve much labor as the Scotch dialect has been one thing in one age and another in another, one thing in one district and a different thing in every other district. She advised us to do the best we could at taking her dialect and then to stand on that best. And that is what we have done. -- Darby. [3]

Finally, there was the following long conversation with Anne at the end of sittings for The Content of Consciousness. It is reproduced here as it appears in the sitting notes. In this transcript H.A.W. is Harwood White; Darby is Emmet Finley; and Joan is Ruth Finley.

---

3. *The Master Key,* Pages 88-92

ANNE ON CONTROLS

ANNE: What is it you want to know about controls.

H.A.W.: What you want to tell us.

ANNE: Well, I suppose in one sense you would call me the Lass' control. Just as we have told you that for every one that comes here, there is a person sent to meet them and tell them what has happened, so for all, particularly those who do this type of work, some individual here is delegated to look after them and protect them and guide them. There must be, for this to happen, a common bond. It is true that I have gone beyond the degree to which the lass will graduate when she comes here and that I have developed quality since I came here. But both her quality and mine are alike in kind though mine is amplified. And when I was on earth we would have been what you might call twins as to degree and quality. It is true that a direct physical line is traceable from me down to the lass.

This does not mean that all sorts of suitable persons may not talk through the lass, and they have.

With Stewart, he had a group, though there was one of that group that had the particular task of protecting the station. With Betty it was a fairly close relative -- an uncle. With Margaret it was a close woman friend. And by close I mean as you call time. With Stewart the individual termed "Gaelic" was not related to him by blood, and he was on earth long since as a teacher of philosophy.

Now the type of controls or imagined controls of professional receiving stations are usually -- not always -- an impersonation by the station itself. All the Little Bright Eyes and the Indian braves, etc. are the acme of emotional hypotheses instigated by a frustration on the part of the receiving station. For instance, all these people are taken care of by some one here. And that some one is given a personality by the receiving station as a direct result of an emotional frustration. The woman who has a child as her seeming control has been frustrated either in wanting children or if she has had them, they have not measured up to what they should be, and she translates that into this outside entity that serves her so well and so satisfactorily but whom she does not really know.

Or it may be that the receiving station has a great longing or wish for strength, for fearlessness, the result of a sort of inferiority complex, as you call it. And so to the one here who serves them, protects them, give them a little more important contact with their fellow men than they would have in any other way, they give that big, bluff Indian personality.

I have only given you two types. It is enough, because you are quick of understanding and you can readily see how it comes about.

Take the more honest mind such as Mrs. Piper, for instance, even she, who acknowledged that she had the communication of a group, even she named that group Imperater -- the imperial, the imperious.

But it is true that each of you has a sort of guardian angel. That is the easiest way to express it. There is a direct affinity between you as an individual of the Obstructed Universe and this individual of the Unobstructed Universe. And it is also true that in many cases, though not all, the mediumistic receiving station, and of course you understand that all people get some reception, translates the personality of the unobstructed entity to fulfill either a lack which they recognize in their own obstructed personality or a frustrated emotion.

H.A.W.: Who is my control?

ANNE: Your control is one of the Gaelic group -- no one, I think, that you would recognize. But do not get the misconception that this guardian friend is the only one who works through you.

H.A.W.: Will Stewart, Jr. be able to work with me?

ANNE: Yes, when he is through school. You can get a great deal of help in the way of stark workmanship from your brother. He was quite a good craftsman.

Darby: Anne, you once said you lived some 200 years ago.

ANNE: I said two, three centuries ago.

Darby: We have rather gathered that only those close to earth do much communicating.

ANNE: Depending entirely on the capacity, qualitative and intellectual, of the station.

Darby: Why doesn't Richard come back and communicate?

ANNE: He could if you asked him to. But he is doing other work.

Darby: Have you stayed in touch with the obstructed universe in order to serve Ruth? Has that been a motivation with you?

ANNE: It is part of my job.

Darby: If you had taken some other course, could you have got beyond either the possibility or desire to communicate?

ANNE: No. We never get beyond the understanding of service. We grow in service.

Darby: If some one came and said he was Julius Caesar, I would not believe him. But why don't the ancients bob up in communication?

ANNE: Because they have evoluted to much higher frequency and because their earth contact was in a different tongue. The impression of an idea in the same language is easier.

Darby: What did you do with yourself before Joan was?

ANNE: I was developing and evoluting in quality. I still am. But there are many kinds of service and there are many more of us than of you and you earn the privilege of caring for one like the lass.

Darby: I believe you once told us that you had tarried, chose to, for the purpose of caring for the lass. What did you mean by tarrying?

ANNE: Just what I said, that I might have gone on with the ancients. Consciousness is in degrees and there are those here now who would fain take over my job.

Darby: I am trying to find out what it is that you have done but did not do because you elected to look after this station.

ANNE: We have free will. We grow in evolution. So we develop in understanding and consequent desire for service. I have been privileged three times now to make it possible to bring to man an evoluting and developing truth than which there is no greater thing to do.

Darby: I suppose that in your concept of time you could foresee that opportunity maybe 200 years ago, so that you considered the opportunity worth waiting for.

ANNE: When I was on earth, they called me fay. They who are fay can see the pattern. And you will not forget what you have been told many a time that you are a part and a furtherance of the pattern.

Darby: How can we be sure that even Gaelic was not a translation made by Stewart either out of frustration or lack?

ANNE: Because Gaelic was a group and was so recognized. The real leader of the group was never isolated.

H.A.W.: Gaelic was in the background when I received communication.

ANNE: Very simple. You just got the impression of what was happening.

Darby: Granted that each station has a guardian, is that guardian necessary to communication? Is control an essential element of communication?

ANNE: Aye.

Darby: Why?

ANNE: To keep the line clear as possible, to edit out as nearly as possible clamoring entities. The station's mind would not be able to focus clearly without direct assistance of Orthos.

Darby: But could not that assistance be given by the communicator?

ANNE: That involves a technicality about which I have not words to tell you. There is chela.

Joan: I am Anne's chela.

Darby: What does the word mean? It is entirely new to me.

H.A.W.: Chela is a Hindu word for pupil.

And so we say farewell to a grand lady, and wish her all the best in her further career.

Book II. The Content of Consciousness

Chapter 1. An Overview of The Model

session 1

THE best thing is to start some dictation, said the Invisible.[1]

"Yes, let's get on with the job. Hello, this is Stewart . . . We have a tremendous job . . . Let's take it easy and begin to work. The title is *Content of Consciousness*. In order to make this book go over, the dictation is going to come from me . . . Dutton's will take it -- I can see to that -- but you can't let it go too long."

This is how it started. The date was December 14, 1946. Only the Finleys, Ruth and Emmet, were present at the session. White had died three months earlier, on September 18, and previous attempts to reach him had failed. Now he is announcing that at long last the book Stephen[2] had started dictating more than twenty years earlier was finally to be finished.

Harwood White, younger brother of Stewart Edward White and a principal collaborator with the Finleys in these sittings, had not yet come East from his home in Santa Barbara, California; he would

---

1. See biographical sketch in the chapter, Of Angels and Archangels.

2. Communicator of *Our Unseen Guest*.

not do so until March of 1947. But prior to his coming we get an overview of the project from Stewart Edward White. The basic notions of the model of human consciousness are here, though certain of its details will be changed as the sittings progress. Apparently the Invisibles themselves were not of one mind on how to flesh out the underlying ideas.

"There are three divisions of consciousness from your mundane standpoint," White continued his dictation. (They are) Consciousness, Super-consciousness, and Sub-consciousness.[3]

"And there are three aspects of man: the soul or spirit, which is the real ego, the physical man and the mind man. One thing must be remembered: it is, that trilogy and trilogia[4] run through all consciousness.

"At this point I suppose that the easiest . . . approach is to give definition of the various divisions. Consciousness is the instant of awareness of the physical world. Super-consciousness is that consciousness with which a man is born -- instinct, race heritage and that *ding-an-sich*[5] knowledge that every ego possesses and which is above and beyond the ordinary operation of his physical awareness mechanism."

---

3. Later the team will standardize this nomenclature as consciousness, the subconscious, and the supraconscious.

4. This word is part of the special nomenclature from White's book, *The Unobstructed Universe.*

5. Immanuel Kant, German philosopher, used this phrase to mean the underlying essence of a thing.

Here the dictation faltered on the attempt to define the subconscious, White saying that Ruth knew too little about it to permit the dictation.

"Might I suggest," put in Emmet, "that the subconscious is the various involuntary physical activities, such as circulation, digestion, etc., and also personal memories."

"That's right," said White.

But it wasn't right. They would change it later. Nevertheless White's response kept the conversation going, which seems to be an important consideration in this business.

"Another thing that we must get clear," said White, "is that the borderline, the cut-off, is movable."

"As between conscious and subconscious?" asked Emmet. "And also as between conscious and superconscious?"

"Correct," said White. "Another point: the normal . . . band of awareness consciousness varies in width in different individuals. It varies also with the same individual under different circumstances."

To which Emmet noted that an artist sees details of a landscape of which the ordinary man is unaware.

"Yes, but that's another subject," said White. "It has to do with talent, and it will be discussed later.

"Now there's a peculiar thing. I don't want to mislead you, but think of consciousness as a three-color rainbow. You know how in a rainbow the colors shade in. Well, in the case of our three-color rainbow, the middle color we'll call Consciousness-awareness. Now as the intellect of the individual is educated and developed, this middle band contracts, becomes sharp. That is, the edges are sharpened, so that a man has to voluntarily step over the border to get instinctive elements that have been educated out of him."

Emmet didn't like the way this was put, and said so. Contract? No way! To which White agreed, saying he simply meant that the edges of the band of awareness ceased to blend into the subconscious and superconscious.

"Take a concrete example," White continued. "With advanced education and civilization, the question of hunger . . is sublimated. You don't think of it much; you expect to be fed and you like good things to eat, but the actual taste sense is dropped deeper and deeper into the subconscious.

"For instance, a wild animal will satiate itself and that will last over a period of time; then the sustenance desire (Emmet has made White substitute this phrase for 'taste') becomes again a main awareness. In fact, in animals it is always to the fore . . .

"You see, all the five senses, even in the case of man, are a defense mechanism. As civilization advances, acuteness of these senses is not so necessary. They can of course be trained back to acuteness. Hearing can, and touch, and sight and the others. But ordinarily they are sublimated. They drop below the instant of consciousness much of the time.

"But if you were a cave man dependent for safety on hearing the slightest approach of an enemy, your hearing would be different from what it is. A horse gets through its feet the vibration of an action occurring quite distant from it. This is true of other animals. Man too once had that gift. Hunters and trappers still have it to a degree."

Emmet noted that irrespective of such blunting, experience does seem to have a tendency to drop into the subconscious.

"It is the reservoir of individual memory," replied White.

"Could one say that the subconscious is memory?" asked Emmet.

"It's more than memory," replied White.

"In what respect?" asked Emmet.

"You must think of awareness-consciousness, subconsciousness and superconsciousness as trilological aspects of the individual ego. If you could think of the three-color rainbow I postulated as a triangle, the superconscious and the subconscious feed each other at the apex."

This conversation completes page three of the twenty-two or so pages of records taken by the Finleys prior to Harwood White's visit. Already significant portions of the model -- to be described in detail later -- are evident. The triangle presentation will persist throughout. And the notion of the subconscious and the superconscious feeding each other, quite beneath the notice of individual consciousness, is a main contribution to the structure of the psyche, as will be seen as the discussion develops.

"You have a problem," White continued. "You call on past experience and memory and what you know of other people's like experience to solve it. And you think about it a lot and you don't solve it. And you possibly decide that there is nothing you can do about it. And then quite suddenly comes to you precisely what you are going to do about it, and the solution is a thought -- or two or three -- beyond what you had formerly thought about it. Now all your original thought on this problem had been based on empirical knowledge. The two or three thoughts beyond this empirical knowledge came out of your subconscious, all right, but they had been enriched and fed by that degree consciousness of yours with which you were born and which is the silver cord that is never broken and which really is the superconscious.

"At the time of individualized consciousness birth, the superconscious is supreme. In order for individualized consciousness to assimilate earth experience and operate free will, education away from superconscious is immediately begun. If this were not true, man's consciousness would operate with choice but not any very high degree of free will."

This marks the end, more or less, of the evening's work. I have not presented it all. It is an enormous amount of material for a single session. Introduced immediately above is the model's notion of child development. To my knowledge, this is a unique contribution to the field.

Also presented was White's notion that once born, the individual may subsequently become temporarily "unaware," but he or she never ever again loses consciousness.

And you will also find in these records the beginning of his technical definition of immortality, as well as other gems to be developed at the appropriate place in the model.

"A man is born with his superconscious, which is his quality," White explained. "He operates in his awareness mechanism, and he stores his quantity in his subconscious."

Again he said, "When a man does what you call die, he is still consciousness individualized. He is given a new awareness mechanism. But, by golly, his subconscious and superconscious go along with him."

Session 2

The date is December 15, 1946, and the time is right after breakfast. Ruth had dreamed during the night that White had something he wanted to get over quickly. So the Finleys started to work at once.

Anne: "I like this house. I feel at home in it. And it's part of the plan. Accept it as such. There is work to be done here. Work of great service. Do not think you are not to take this work seriously."

SEW: "Good morning. You said last night that each of the other two books with which you had to do had a definite aim. *Our Unseen Guest* -- immortality. *The Unobstructed Universe* -- true universality. The aim of *The Content of Consciousness* is to prove the one and only reality. That is its aim.

"Until we can find a better terminology we will call the individualization of consciousness which is man's, simply ego. Ego is an attribute of consciousness, of course. Nonetheless it is consciousness and is of consciousness. It dwells in consciousness and consciousness dwells in ego. Now just as consciousness has the three great co-existents of time, space and motion, or receptivity, conductivity and frequency,[6] so ego has three great co-existents. I am not entirely sure that the terminology I am about to give you can obtain. Certainly we must put new content into the words if it does. But for superconsciousness substitute instinct, for consciousness substitute self-awareness, for subconsciousness sub-

---

6. These are notions taken from White's book, *The Unobstructed Universe.*

stitute memory. This makes a triangle of the ego. The triangle is formulated by memory and instinct coming together at one apex. At the other two apexes, or the base of this isosceles triangle, memory and instinct touch the side that could be named self-awareness. Now the thought I want to leave with you for you to consider is that memory is analogous to time or receptivity; instinct is analogous to space or conductivity, and self-awareness is analogous to motion, or frequency. This is very far in advance of where you were last night with me. So you can use you mind to jump the step."

There followed a squabble with Emmet over terms, which I omit. And the reader should be cautioned that terms and concepts introduced above are subject to revision as this divulgence progresses.

Note, however, that at this session we have introduced the key notion that emotions are a border activity of the superconscious.

"Emotion is a race heritage," White explained. "It depends upon the qualitative degree with which you are born."

Well, then, take grief, suggested Emmet.

"Grief has to do with the race heritage of fear," White elaborated. "If you could only understand that your emotions are in the superconscious; that they are a part of the quality inheritance with which you came into the world.

"You know that some people experience deeper grief than others -- more lasting, more shattering. Other people have a violent grief, but it's shallow. You know that that runs through all types of individuals, as to grief, love, happiness, humor. These are what you call God-given. You are born with the capacity for them.

"Now your self-awareness handles them, conditioned by your quality. The same emotion will disturb one person more than it disturbs another.

"Let's get another thing straight," said White, apparently aware that he was on a roll. "In the *Our Unseen Guest* days you thought that the Invisibles communicated through Ruth's subconscious. The fact is, we come through the superconscious. The flow of conductivity has been opened up.

"Though you realize it," he continued, "still I want to point out to you that any person, any ego, with a high talent, music, painting, psychic communication, has the potentiality of most acute emotion. It is only when people of that type, or egos of that type, are highly self-disciplined in the realm of self-awareness that you do not have an erratic personality."

So how does the concept of quality fit into this scheme, Emmet asked.

"I want to give you an illustration," White said. "Something happens -- say an auto accident. Four or five people are in the vicinity. One of them immediately gets out of the way as fast as he can. Another starts to scream. Another beats it to the nearest telephone for help. Another plunges into the mess and tries to get out whoever was back of the wheel. All of these actions are automatic and instantaneous. They are not emotional reactions. They are reactions of the quality of consciousness. They are instinctive, you say. They are very closely tied up with the emotions, yes. The quality of consciousness is the endowment of instinct with which the ego is born. The man who recognizes that can quantitatively correct, enhance or subdue any of these things which his intellect judges."

Session 3

There are five more sessions prior to the first participation of White's brother Harwood on May the eighth. When he arrives, the hard work starts. The results of that hard work are captured in the formal description of the model, which is presented in subsequent chapters. Not every one will want to struggle through that detailed description. But you can get an adequate overview in the material developed before Harwood's arrival and presented here. So relax and have a bit of fun.

All of which is by way of introduction to the session of December 20, 1946. Emmet's editorial persona, a stabilizing element in these sessions, is particularly helpful here.

"At this meeting, while there was a sense of SEW's[7] presence and guidance," he reported, "the speaker seemed to be largely Joan herself." He then proceeded to label what came through simply as "dictation."

In order to enhance the reader's sense of participating in this session, I will withdraw my own editorial presence and present the session as Emmet recorded it.

Dictation: There is no such thing as a fourth dimension. Consciousness is the reality. Always it obtains with a trilogy of co-existents. These may be time, space and motion; solids, liquids, gases; instinct, awareness, memory. ----- There's a white house on a hill. You go up a winding drive. The house has a porch across the front with square pil-

---

7. Stewart Edward White.

lars, not too heavy. The architecture of the house places it just before 1870. I don't know what it has to do with anything.

Darby: (who thought that SEW might be trying to impress evidential material as to his identity): Please give me more detail.

Dictation: Alongside of the house pretty much up the hill, that is, between where the drive leaves the road and the side of the house, there are a lot of raggedy bushes. It seems that the house has quite a lot of ground attached to the back. And there's a great big barn, painted red and trimmed in white. It has a funny door, with a gable over the door. Somebody is talking about a well. The place is pretty much run down. It's like the bushes -- all raggedy. -- You are to send the description of this house to Beese.[8]

Dictation continues: Now the reason scientists have been enamored of the fourth dimension is because they tried to add reality to all of its phases of trilological co-existents. ---- Somebody upset a bottle of liquid shoe polish on the rug.

Darby: What rug?

Dictation: I don't know, just a rug. -- Here's another house. I look down on it from up on a hill. It's made of stucco -- a foxy affair with a heavy front porch, arched. And it has sharp maroon red shutters. As I look down on it, the house faces my left, and off in the distance, in a wide valley, is an industrial village of some kind. I see no sense in this. Now here's a church, and it's low-roofed for its size. It's built of yellow brick, and entrance is at the extreme left-hand corner -- a square tower

---

8. This is the family nickname for Harwood White.

topped with a very high sharp spire. In the middle of the church, facing the same way the tower entrance faces, is a jutting-out gable. And up under the eaves is a round window. Craziest looking thing you ever saw. It has colored glass in it.

Dictation continues: You weren't satisfied with the analogy of time, space and motion with memory, awareness and instinct.

Darby: Is there an analogy other than the fact that both groups are co-existent with consciousness?

Dictation: We might discuss the extent of instinct -- what its nature is. Instinct is your degree label, sort of. You are born with it, and it contains what it says it does -- the instinctive knowledge of the human ego. Now it is in evolution, and according to the use put to it by the awareness mechanism it is broadened. (Here the dictation became confused as the result of Darby's inability to write fast enough.) Let's go back. There are two kinds of education. There is the education that develops instinct. It's through this portion of the trilogy that you tap the Source, that the ego recognizes his dependence on the whole and the possibility of using the whole for one's own benefit. Any act or thought by the ego reacts in two ways -- it goes to the Source and draws from the Source. The other type of education turns entirely away from this portion of the trilogy, teaching the ego to operate its awareness consciousness.

Darby: I suppose that the latter is the education of perception and reason -- mental education.

Dictation: Correct. People so educated are cold and unfeeling.

Darby: Not necessarily so.

Dictation: Well, they don't have the feeling of understanding responsibility.

Darby: Then we are certainly miseducating a lot of people.

Dictation: Yes.

Darby: Just what is covered by the word, "instinct"?

Dictation: Race knowledge, degree knowledge, the emotions.

Darby: Anything else?

Dictation: The ego's knowledge of its individuality.

Darby: Meaning by that what?

Dictation: While everybody knows he is an individual, some people have an acuter realization that the mechanism through which they operate, that is, the body and the senses, is merely an attribute of the real self.

Darby: Do the body and senses come under the heading, "instinct"?

Dictation: No, they operate in the subconscious. You remember I told you the whole trilogy through which the ego operates was like an eye. Awareness is like the range of vision at any one instant.

Darby (still fussing over terminology): I don't like instinct, memory and awareness. Why not confine ourselves to the words Sub-conscious, Superconscious, and perhaps awareness?

Dictation: Better yet, subliminal, superliminal and liminal.

Darby: What does liminal mean literally?

Dictation: It means focused.

Darby: Yes, but literally? Someone there ought to know. It means pertaining to the threshold.

Dictation: This whole thing must be thought of as a circle. This circle is divided into three parts. We'll call it a wheel. The hub is the ego, and it has three pie-shaped pieces running out to the rim and then three spokes or dividing lines. The way the wheel is set up is that on either side of the liminal is the subliminal and the superliminal, which means that the subliminal and the superliminal come together. They touch each other, just as each in turn touches the liminal. (Here Darby volunteered an explanatory diagram, but the record does not record it.)

Dictation: This is important. Everybody knows that the subliminal and the superliminal touch the liminal. But what has not been discovered is that the subliminal and superliminal touch each other, and that the spoke or dividing line is just as shifting and malleable as the two dividing lines between the liminal and the subliminal and between the liminal and superliminal. The thing we have to discuss is the shifting line. Sometimes the liminal is very broad or wide, and then again it will contract.

Darby: Do you mean in the same person at different times?

Dictation: Yes.

Darby: And what is the significance of the shift?

Dictation: One thing I want you to think about. I want you to think about the shifting line between the subliminal and the superliminal. They react on each other. So your experience is valuable to you according to the degree of inheritance you have in the superliminal. That inheritance is fixed. It is qualitative and more than qualitative.

Other Sessions

The next session was on January 11, 1947. At the suggestion of Professor William James[9] the Finleys formulated questions to be posed to the Invisibles. Ruth wanted to try for answers through automatic writing. I present below a selection of the results. The terminology here is as follows: *Liminal*: the conscious mind. *Subliminal*: the subconscious mind. *Superliminal*: the superconscious mind. *Q* = question. *A* = answer.

Q: Is the superliminal of the individual qualitative or quantitative?

A: Qualitative.

Q: Do the liminal and the subliminal have equal power to contact the superliminal?

A: The subliminal of modern man operates more in accordance with tradition than does the liminal, which has been educated out of the traditional contact with superliminal, vouchsafed to all animal life.

Q: Does the subliminal or the superliminal oversee and regulate involuntary physical activities such as digestion and circulation?

A: It is the subliminal guided by the superliminal. The superliminal is the seat of creative life, the ego or the individual entity which lives in the body during earth experience. It is the boss, so to speak. The subliminal is the director, the liaison officer, the link between life force and the operation of the various organs of the body. The subliminal makes the direct contact.

---

9. See the Chapter on Two Professors.

Q: Since it is easy to comprehend dropping a liminal experience into the subliminal, the fact of the subliminal seems apparent to us. How can we get an equally clear vision of the superliminal?

A: In modern times men have done so, for the most part, by prayer, meditation, and ultimately, faith. Upon occasions of great emotions or need they frequently have flashes of a power greater than that which they habitually operate. This greater power they themselves can call upon or tap. To you, the most illuminating answer probably would be to point out that awareness of self is awareness of the superliminal.

Q (No. 6): Why isn't the old classification of conscious and subconscious sufficient?

A: Because there is an active third division not taken into account in the old classification.

Q: Is the superliminal as individual as you have seemed to picture it? Or is it rather a cosmic or at least a degree type of consciousness?

A: The superliminal *is* the individual ego. Earth, we have told you, is the "borning place" or the evolutional phase of individualization -- the manifestation of pluralistic monism for the development of quantity.

Q: When I say, "I am," I speak out of my liminal but from a deeper well of selfhood. How is the deeper well related to the subliminal, and how is it related to superliminal?

A: That deeper well is the superliminal. From the superliminal you control both the liminal and the subliminal. *You* are always in control.

The January 11 session was a very productive one. After the prepared questions were disposed of by automatic writing, the Finleys continued the session in the customary way, Ruth in trance, Emmet taking notes. In the records, Emmet, not knowing who was speaking, indicates the replies as coming from "J", for "Joan." Later in the session we have an indication as to the actual speaker.

Emmet commenced, saying it was a simple question, why the old classification of conscious and subconscious wasn't sufficient.

"Very simple," was the reply. "If we went back to the old classification, we might say that the superconscious (using that word only for this moment) was the authoritative portion of the mind that is not in acute operation at any given waking period. The superliminal is the repository of the I AM. It is the highest control. It is the qualitative inheritance. It is the degree link. It is through the superliminal that man, operating his earth awareness, can contact his degree power, his degree strength.

"In the old phraseology of the Bible there is a phrase 'I am that I am.' Now the 'that' is the superliminal

"I want to take a concrete illustration for you. Take a musician who is a genius. He has an idea for a symphony. That idea is impinged upon his liminal by his superliminal. He has developed his liminal for the composition of music, but he has done something more than that. Through his superliminal a man of that type, that degree, deliberately seeks contact with sound and then his liminal translates what he hears into the composition.

"It is the color of the superliminal that makes an individual what he is.

"Now the individual superliminal is in a high degree of evolution. The quality of the degree of an individual is not changed, but a man's superliminal can be developed.

"In the air corps of the various countries certain individuals developed superliminally to a very high degree, when it couldn't have been the subliminal that acted because the occurrence was above and beyond the individual experience and yet required instantaneous judgment.

"This is, by the way, one of the things that has attracted modern Christian civilization to certain phases of the old Eastern philosophies -- those philosophies' recognition of the superliminal and their attempts to teach their followers how to contact, use and profit by this degree power. Everybody has it. Everybody can develop the use of it, and it's quite an asset. There's nothing new about it; it has been recognized always. Men have given it such names as the over-soul, the overself, etc. But that is too detached from the concrete individual operation.

"Modern psychology has divided the mental operation into two divisions -- conscious and subconscious. Now there is in reality a third division, which the modern psychologist has lumped with the subconscious."

At this point Emmet stuck his oar in.

"It seems to me," he said, "that the difference between your idea and that of the Eastern philosophies is that with you the third division is just a part of the individual consciousness while with the Eastern philosopher it is something seemingly outside himself -- the Cosmic Source, God, etc."

"It is not outside," Joan replied.

"Is there anything outside?" This from Emmet.

"There is the whole consciousness," Joan replied, "and it is through the superliminal that the whole can be contacted. But in the meantime, whether or not you deliberately seek to operate your superliminal as you do your subliminal, it is always working, always active, always a part of you. It is the stronger part of the not-impinged-upon awareness of you.

"You remember that last night we had the picture of the triangle and the little pink bead that went to the apex and got redder. That additional redness is symbolical of the constant operation of the superliminal upon the subliminal. The superliminal is always judging, watching for the valuable beads that are dropped into the subliminal. Some of the beads become pretty much submerged. Some are enhanced for future use, because the superliminal knows their value and that they will be needed.

"In other words, the individual consciousness is three-dimensional, and it never operates in a single dimension. It operates in all three. The subliminal, the liminal and the superliminal are co-existents of the I am."

"I claim that's a bad term in this connection," claimed Emmet, who had to take this all down in longhand. "And who is it who has been talking tonight?" -- Emmet having inserted into the record that there was little of Ruth's own personality in the above remarks attributed to Joan.

Anne showed up to reply.

"Perfectly competent individuals who would not awaken her recognition or emotion," she said. "The subject is quite abstract, and should be, for her."

Then Emmet asked, "Will this divulgence be confined to exposition of the liminal, subliminal and superliminal?"

The voice that replied was the one who had been speaking before Anne.

"Not unless you wish it to be."

"That's hardly a good answer," said Emmet dryly.

"The answer is no," the voice replied.

Then Emmet said, "How soon can we leave this phase, to be returned to later, for other phases?"

And then the voice: "If consciousness is the one and only reality and the individualized consciousness known as man is also reality, then relation, coordination with, use and operation of the accepted coexistents of consciousness per se naturally must be discussed. His relation to the attributes of consciousness must also be discussed. Many of these attributes that man uses he is perfectly cognizant of, and of his use of them. Of others he is not cognizant."

A heavy session, and a most productive one.

The above material provides an adequate overview of the model of the human psyche detailed in part II of this book. There is a natural break in continuity at this point, and it gives one pause. Was Emmet affected by a writer's cramp of fatal intensity? You may reach that conclusion on your own when reading the minutes of the March 6 final session, which I present below. The records end abruptly at this point, on sheet twenty-two. They resume on sheet sixty-four. We have no explanation for the hiatus. Sheet twenty-two covers the March the sixth session. Sheet sixty-four records a March the tenth session. That session, and a subsequent one held on April twenty-four, are an interlude. Of the Invisibles present, the Doctor and Margaret Cameron of *The Seven Purposes* are old favorites. The discussion of the model, however, was taken over by a new personality, Knisely, who was apparently someone the Finleys had known. Stewart Edward White is missing from these interim sessions.

Then there is nothing until May eighth, which marks the entrance of Harwood White, and the start of the intense activity which resulted in the technical description of the model.

Based on the mass of material thus developed, Emmet the author worked diligently for a period. Did he complete a manuscript? We will never know. None survives, and nothing was published.

It is in the light of these facts that you should read the minutes of this final initial session. Anne is there urging Emmet on, as is Betty. Whether or not they succeeded, the reader must judge on the basis of the book they hold in their hands.

It is March 6, 1947, then. Anne is speaking.

"You have heard of the seven deadly sins," she began. "The three that are most important to avoid and overcome are remorse, which is nothing but a type of self-indulgence; next, lack of respect for the endowments and growth of same that is the individual's present evolutionary inheritance. The tools each has been given are those with which he must work. You may sharpen those tools and you may learn to use them with more dexterity, but you cannot change them. It is ungrateful not to appreciate and care for your tools. Another great sin against yourself (and these are sins against yourself) is intellectual and spiritual pride. He who is not willing to learn, who is bumptious, will stultify his own evolutional growth. I do not mean that he can stop it. I do mean that he can create for himself much unhappiness.

"Another sin against man's self is discontent and lack of appreciation of material possessions. No matter what be preached, the fact remains that on the earth plane, material possessions are up to a certain degree a criterion. They are comfortable. If they are beautiful, they feed man's sense of beauty. It is true that man cannot live by bread alone, but it is certainly true that he cannot live without bread.

"Now bread means to one man one thing and to another, another thing. I find in the lass's mind as I speak a story of the French seamstress who went without bread to buy a hyacinth. You and the lass have created here for your dwelling place, with a good deal of assistance from us, a hyacinth. You cannot do without bread and wheat. You need both. You have both, and in those two you must work; for work is the salvation of consciousness.

"All consciousness has to work," she continued. "It is the process of evolution. Consciousness, of which you are an individual manifestation, operates in rhythmic cycles; that is evolution. The cycles may change; the rhythm, never.

"Now your rhythm, as all rhythm, was created or is created by mundane habits. At a certain hour of the day, five or six days a week, you sat down at a desk, and not always could you immediately get to work, but you did ultimately every day."

Ah, yes. Emmet is newly retired and having trouble working at home, eh?

"Go back," continued Anne. "Go back to that habit for the re-establishment of the Rhythm. It could be that for quite a few days you may not get to work; that is, you might destroy whatever you did. But if you had a broken wrist, after it was taken out of the cast and you wished to make the muscles of the fingers and the palm of the hand, the wrist itself, and even the arm, strong again and usable, you would gradually and persistently try to force those muscles back into their habitual rhythm, and you would succeed.

"You are not so stupid that you do not ken what I am saying to you and why, and ye will not read this part of the record to the lass; that is an order.

"But we created for you an office. It is unfamiliar as yet, but it is not the first office you have made your own. And this I promise you that the very second you start to try to obey these rules you will have from me and from all of us here every aid that you permit yourself to encompass. That is all."

So much for Anne. But she is not the only superstar present at this remarkable session. Betty is also there.

"Things are all right here," she commenced. "Only we would like to get on with the work."

"We do seem to be held back," said Emmet.

"You see," said Betty, "I know how difficult it is. It is only when you can get a real conviction that the job is important that you make it important. It was awfully hard for me to make my job important for myself because, you see, Stewart so overshadowed me."

"How did you do it?" asked Emmet.

"By just doing it," replied Betty. "I just said to myself: 'Well, after all I'm an individual too. I have a human soul, which is of paramount importance to me; I don't mean to take anything away from Stewart's ego, but why should I sit and rot?'

"It's right," she continued, "for people to help create a background. Doormats are exceedingly useful for cleaning the feet; they are not intellectually inspiring. I'm not suggesting you were ever a doormat. I'm only telling you I just forced myself to make what I ultimately came to call the first dead lift. You do have to do that, and you have to do it for yourself.

"But let's get on with the job. The time is so ripe."

At which point she plunged into a discussion of the model.

"You were discussing with Stewart the superliminal, its content and its method of use." said Betty. "One of the things to always remember is that always back of focused attention, back of the subliminal and the superliminal, is the I. It is *your* focused attention, your subliminal, your superliminal, above and below.

"One of the interesting things of the focused attention in modern education, true education, is its elasticity. Modern man has learned through necessity to widen or contract his focused attention. Primordial man did not have this facility or faculty. He depended upon a fairly limited range of focused attention, but (and this is a big but) he was also able to employ his superliminal faculty. Man has been enticed away from that employment.

"The focused attention of a dog or cat is narrow," she continued. "It's contracted. All you have to do is watch them when they are interested in something. But how do they know when danger approaches and do they ever fail to know? Domesticated, they too lose a bit of the superliminal faculty. But if you lived in the woods as much as --"

Here this wonderful voice failed abruptly. The technical material -- in particular, the subject of focused attention -- is not fully understandable in this introductory setting. Readers who want to follow the argument will see it discussed in greater detail later in Part I.

Ruth's father, the Doctor, finished off the session.

"We were glad to have Ruth for this hour of treatment," he said. "She does pretty well consciously giving herself into our hands, but it is not nearly so effective as when we can work on her in this type of anesthesia.[10] If for no other reason, and this is important, than that I can have her in trance condition for an hour a day to give her physical treatment, see that that condition obtains.

"There is no need to read her this record," he continued, "but, if you possibly can, pump up a little enthusiasm over what you have received.

"What Betty gave you about the elasticity of modern man's focused attention is worth thinking about."

Thus ends the record of this, the last of the preliminary sessions. The reader is invited to ponder what the Doctor said about focused attention, and the so-called "anesthesia" of the entranced Ruth. Both subjects are discussed in detail below.

---

10. See the discussion of anesthesia in the chapter on tipping the triangle.

Chapter 2. The Model's Diagrams

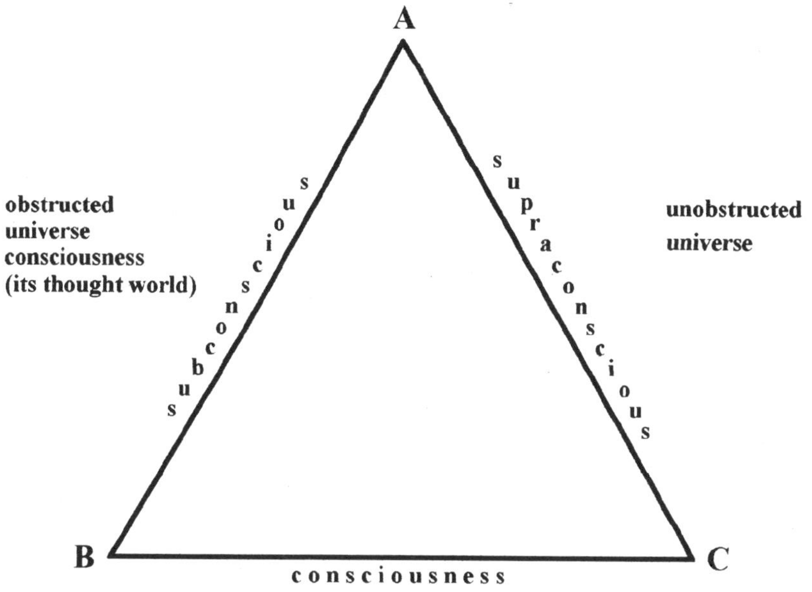

Figure 1. The ABC triangle

THE equilateral triangle shown in this diagram represents the basic structure of the human psyche. Its three sides correspond to the trilogy described in *The Unobstructed Universe*, where the human subconscious represents time, the human supraconscious represents motion, and human consciousness represents space. The sides of the triangle represent the limits of the psyche's mechanisms for dealing with its environment. Outside is the world of impingement from which, computer-like, the psyche draws its inputs. Beyond consciousness lies the perceived world. Beyond the subconscious lies the obstructed universe consciousness -- its thought world. Beyond the supraconscious lies the unobstructed universe.

How the psyche processes the inputs from each of these three facets of its environment is the point of the model. For example, inputs on the BC line (labeled "consciousness") travel along the line toward the left and right to its hinges, where possibly an information exchange takes place with one or the other of the other two basic parts of the human psyche.

The label "consciousness" is a studied choice. The BC line represents the physical senses and is the psyche's connection to the physical world. The study team decided to call it "cognizance"; "perception" was their second choice. The Invisibles stated for the record that they thought "consciousness" was the correct term, but agreed to be overruled by the study team. Since the study team is now among the original Invisibles, I have let the original Invisible choice stand. The reader should keep in mind that the term "consciousness" thus has two separate meanings in the context of this divulgence. The other meaning is its use as the name of the "one and only reality" in the earlier work of the Invisibles, of which the present divulgence is an integral part.

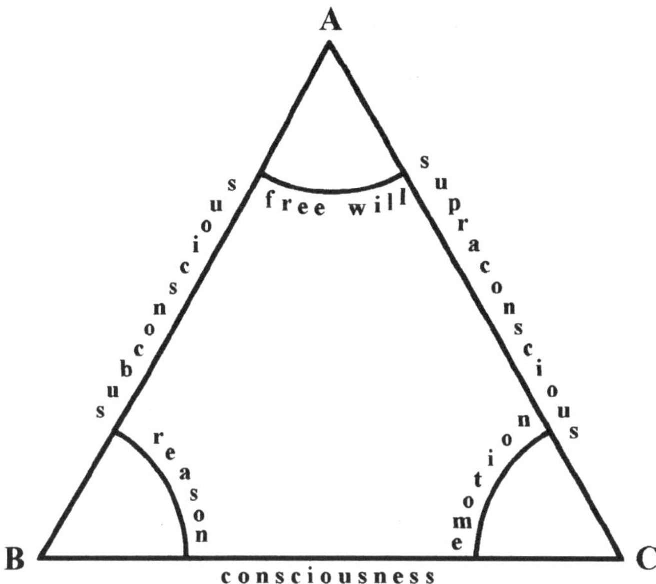

Figure 2. The ABC triangle enhanced with arcs

Three functions are added to the model with this drawing. The functions are represented as arcs that connect adjacent sides of the triangle. Each function also provides a two-way path over which data can flow between adjoining sides. Thus the arc of reason connects consciousness with the subconscious, for "reasons" which will be explained below. The arc of emotion connects consciousness and the supraconscious. The arc of free will connects the subconscious with the supraconscious.

Each of these arcs will receive a fuller exposition below. Emotion plays a particularly full role in the day-to-day working of the psyche. But free will also gets a detailed exposition, and cannot be left out of the model, since the underlying philosophy of the model is based on a notion of evolution in which Homo sapiens is the free-will degree of consciousness.

Incidentally, the use of the word "function" to describe these arcs is deliberate. A function is a black box that processes an input and outputs it in modified form. Many parts of the model represent functions, which first of all describe real goings on in the psyche, and secondly, are representable in the software of a computer model. You can run the model to see what the psyche will do on particular occasions. Where parts are not functions they are usually either data paths or storage units, unless they connect directly to the environment, in which case they may be two-way impingement antennae.

The psychological side of Homo sapiens is depicted in the fully enhanced ABC triangle drawing of Figure 3. The mind is here divided into three parts: The *awareness* mind, equivalent to the *awareness mechanism* of White's Betty books, whose inputs are from the physical world and arrive via the senses; the *recall* mind, whose job is to retrieve memory and knowledge; and the *aspiration* mind, which deals with the supraconscious and represents the higher self.

A new term, *Monas*, is introduced to denote the central observer and executive whose mind this is, and who controls its operations. The term comes from the Greek, and points up the atomic

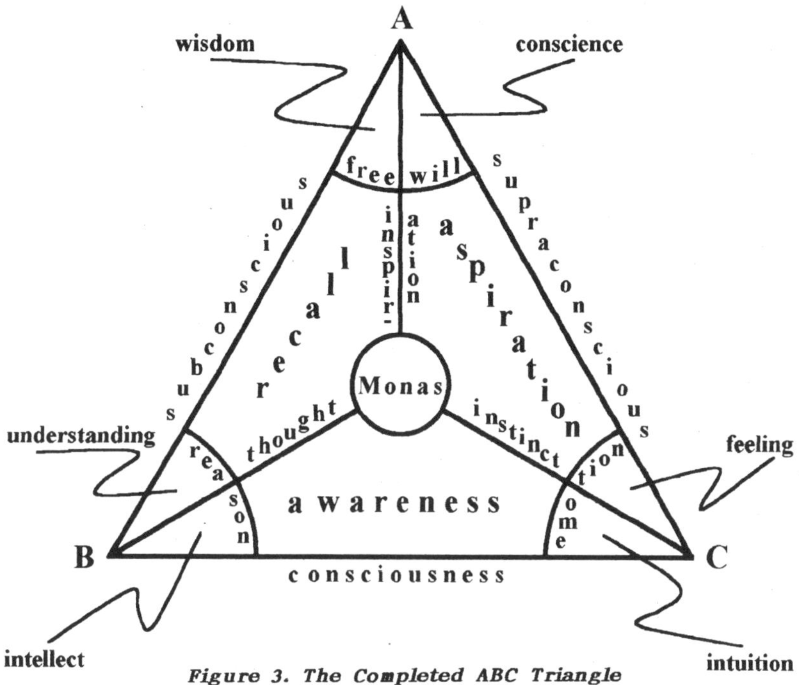

Figure 3. The Completed ABC Triangle

nature of Monas, as contrasted to its physical body which is an aggregate of billions of living cells, each possessed of its own species of consciousness.

Three new data paths are introduced: *thought*, *instinct*, and *inspiration*. These data paths serve also as the sides of secondary triangles used to divide the mind into its three component minds. (In notation form these secondary, or sub, triangles are AOB, BOC, and AOC, where "O" stands for the central circle occupied by Monas.)

With these structures in place, we can commence to exercise the model. For example, an apple falls. The sight and sound are registered on the BC line. The impingement travels to the "C" hinge and evokes an emotion, which travels up the instinct line to Monas. Monas evaluates this event by passing it in the form of a thought down the thought line to the reason function. Reason reports perfunctorily that, okay, an apple has fallen, but no big deal. With this reassuring report, Monas puts the emotion on ice, but waits for a more complete report from its reason processor. The latter has in the meantime dumped a preliminary report into the subconscious for an evaluation -- are there similar reports, for instance, with which the current event can be compared?

What comes back depends on the content of the subconscious, which depends on the age and experience of the individual, the previous evaluations which are stored, and on the characteristics and quality of the individual. One such report might indicate that we have here a potential snack, a windfall as it were, that must be acted on quickly lest the tree's owner arrive and claim it. Another mind will report that the apple's fall is remarkably like the orbit of one of Kepler's planets, and should be looked into in further detail. Monas accepts these reports, and after consultations with its supraconscious dumps them, emotion and all, and together with its own evaluation of the event, down the thought line to the AB line, which is the subconscious, and thus into permanent storage. The fact that Monas has rendered a *decision* is a significant factor and a key to the individual's mental health, as will be seen below.

Also introduced in this diagram are six arc subprocessors. These are defined by the lines that border them. Thus *intellect* at the "B" hinge takes its character from the fact that it is bounded by reason, by the thought line, and by consciousness, representing impingement from the physical world. Its sister processor, *understanding*, is also bounded by reason and thought; but its third side is not the world (the BC line) but the subconscious.

Similarly, *intuition* at the "C" hinge is bounded by emotion, instinct, and consciousness; its sister processor, *feeling*, which is defined here as excluding anything related to the sense of touch, is bounded by emotion, instinct, and the supraconscious.

There will be much to say about the "A" hinge in the detailed discussions. Here it is only necessary to note that *wisdom*, a word much favored by White's invisible correspondents, is bounded by free will, inspiration, and the individual's store of memory and empirical knowledge in the subconscious. Its sister processor, *conscience*, is bounded by free will, inspiration, and the supraconscious.

To complete this part of the model it is necessary to note that the sides of the basic triangle are actually bands, and as such serve as storage units. The band contents are as follow:

The AB band is the subconscious. It contains:
memory
empirical knowledge

The BC band is consciousness (synonyms: cognizance and perception). It contains:
the "five" senses
a sixth sense described below

The AC band is the supraconscious. It contains:
race experience
degree experience

The records left by the study committee include the following description of the triangle by SEW (Sheet 176):

"The lines of the triangle are the boundaries of the possessed mechanism of Monas," White began, "just as the lines of a State become its boundaries. The BC line faces the perceived world. The AB line faces the obstructed universe consciousness. In other words, the AB line is the boundary dividing the individual from all the thought world or consciousness of the obstructed universe, just as the BC line divides him from the physical world.

"The AC line is the boundary of the individual between himself and the unobstructed universe. The subconscious and the supraconscious of Monas combine at the apex A, with which he finally pierces orthos. [Ed.: This term is defined below.] It is his pointing toward the stars.

"The base of his triangle BC is his reaching into the world of matter for his quantitative evolution," he added. "The term awareness-mechanism that was coined by Betty can be expressed in this new divulgence by the sub-triangle BOC. It is there that the day by day cognition operates.

"But it must never be forgotten, he continued, "that the longest line of the BOC sub-triangle faces the material world, it is bounded on one side by the sub-triangle whose longest line is the subconscious, and on the other by the sub-triangle whose longest line is the supraconscious. The lines are really bands, not lines. Even the arcs at the angles must have space. For instance, the arcs of emotion and reason have degrees in them, for there are different types of emotion and different kinds of reason."

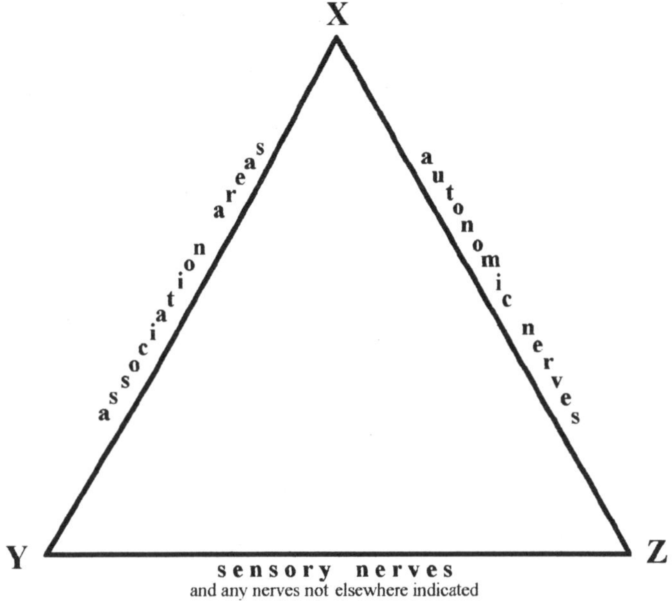

Figure 4. The XYZ triangle representing the physical body.

The model is mainly concerned with the psychological side of people; but since there exists a close coupling between it and the physical body, a triangular representation of the body as a system is here presented.

In this triangle, the XY line represents the association areas of the brain regardless of actual location in the brain. This line's ABC correspondent is the AB line, or subconscious. The XZ line represents the autonomic nervous system; its ABC correspondent is the supraconscious. The YZ line represents the sensory nerves; its ABC correspondent is the BC line, which is Monas' window on the perceptual world.

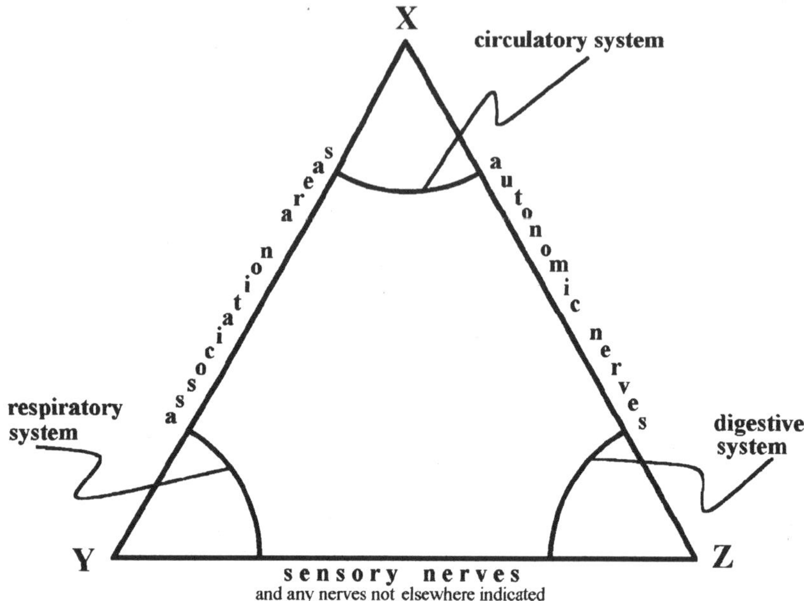

Figure 5. The XYZ Triangle Enhanced With Arcs

The arcs in the XYZ triangle are assigned functions with natural relations to the triangle sides. Thus the arc at hinge "Y", the respiratory system, being partly under conscious control, connects the brain's association areas with the sensory nerves. The digestive system is assigned to the arc at the "Z" hinge because of the close association of the "Z" hinge with the "C" hinge of the ABC triangle, which draws constantly on the racial heritage that largely drives unconscious functions such as digestion; the "Z" arc connects the sensory nerves with the autonomic nervous system. The circulatory system is assigned to the "X" arc partly because of the correspondence between the circulation of the blood and a comparable circulation in the psyche; the arc connects the autonomic nerves on one side with the association areas on the other.

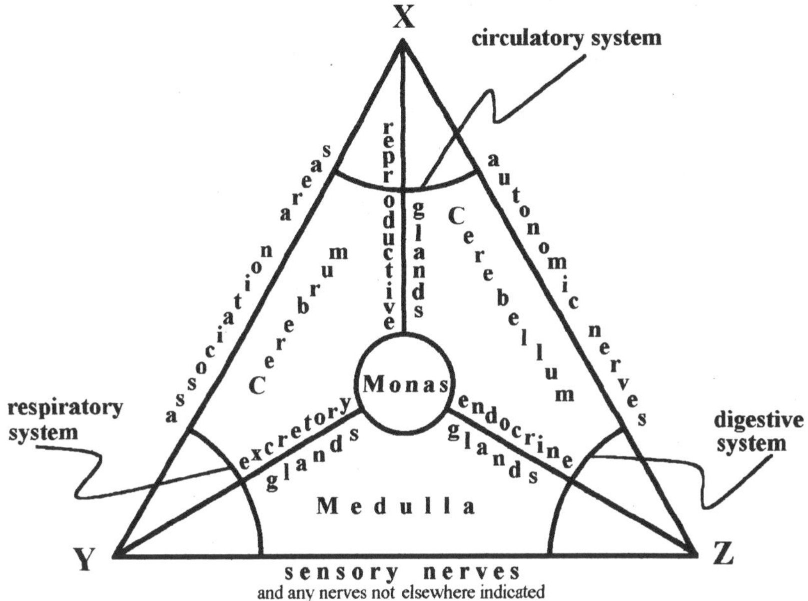

Figure 6. The fully enhanced XYZ Triangle

The completed XYZ triangle adds Monas in the center as the directing agent, a role it plays in any and all triangles in the model. The cerebrum has been assigned to the XOY secondary triangle; it corresponds to the recall mind. The medulla is assigned to the YOZ secondary triangle, corresponding to the awareness mind. The cerebellum has been assigned to the XOZ secondary triangle, corresponding to the aspiration mind.

The data paths connecting Monas with the triangle's hinges have been assigned to the glands.

The endocrine (ductless) glands include the thyroid, parathyroid, adrenals and thymus. The study group (including the Invisibles!) was unable to assign a function to the thymus; its role in the immune system was not yet known. The excretory glands were assigned to the OY line.

A surprising assignment is that of the reproductive glands to the OX line, corresponding to inspiration. These glands include the pituitary, and also the pineal; the latter is indicated as the switch between brain and mind.

As an algorithm for classifying the glands, the Invisibles indicated generic functions as follows:

ZO - stabilizing glands
XO - creative glands
YO - winnowing, editing, sorting out and discarding glands

Also important to note is that the close connection between the XYZ and ABC triangles is at the "Z" and "C" hinges; and that the XYZ triangle is a drag on ABC.

This concludes the discussion of the XYZ triangle. We next introduce the triangle that represents the spiritual life of the individual and is a unique contribution of this model.

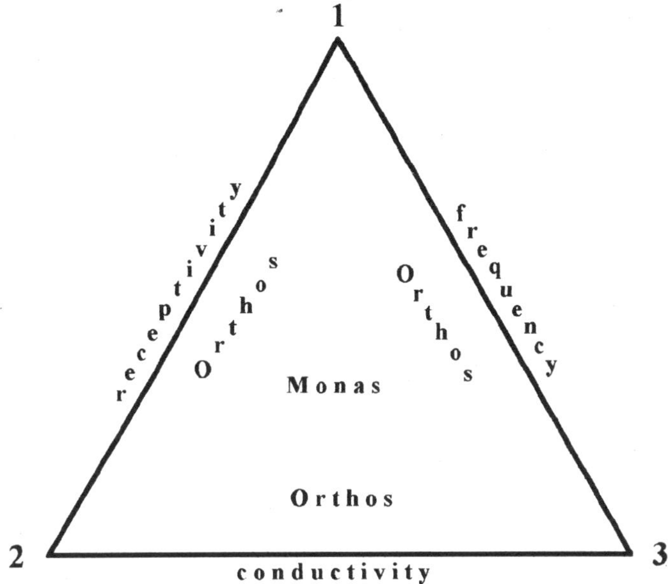

Figure 7. The Orthic (or 1–2–3) Triangle.

As the XYZ triangle represents a step below the psychological (or ABC) triangle, so the Orthic (or 1-2-3) triangle represents a step above. SEW said of this triangle: "This visualizes the individual's capability for penetration into the fringe of the Unobstructed while still in the physical body."

Orthic is a term introduced in *The Unobstructed Universe*, *Orthos* being the environment in which White's Invisibles live. The 1-2-3 triangle's sides bear the names of the three co-existent essences of consciousness in Orthos: receptivity, conductivity, and frequency. These translate in the obstructed universe to time, space, and motion. We thus have a correspondence between receptivity, time, and the subconscious; between conductivity, space, and consciousness (defined here as "perception"); and between frequency, motion, and the supraconscious.

The ABC or psychological triangle deals with the other two triangles as representations of physical worlds. The XYZ triangle is its window on the every day perceptual world. The 1-2-3 triangle is its window on the Orthic world, which in its sphere is every bit as "physical" as the XYZ world. In the full model, the XYZ triangle stands between the other two. Thus positioned it represents the drag it imposes on the ABC triangle.

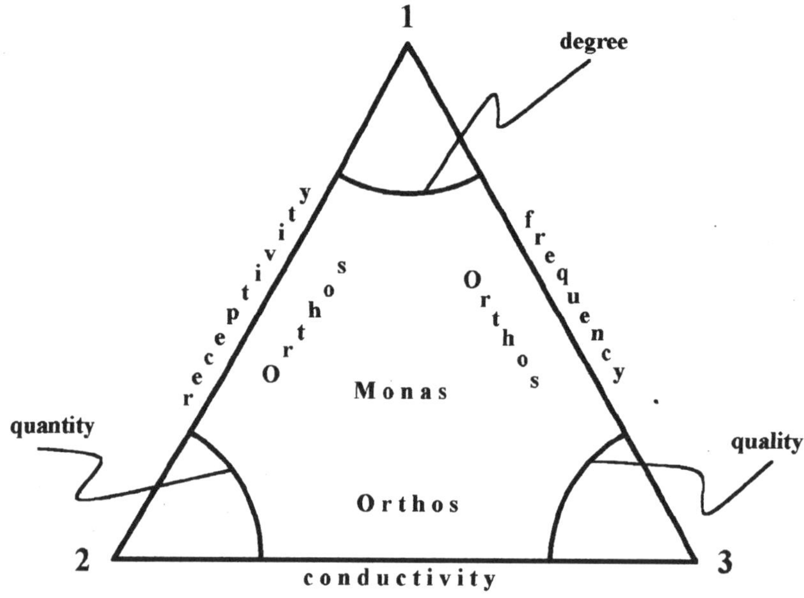

Figure 8. The Arc-Enhanced 1-2-3 Triangle

The arcs added here were first named by "Stephen," the communicator in *Our Unseen Guest*, the first of the divulgences of which this is number three. The arc at hinge "2", quantity, is largely self-explanatory. "Quantity" represents the accumulated experience of the individual, and is roughly equivalent to the individuation of Jung. In the model quantity is "quantized" thusly: an impingement arrives via the YZ line of the XYZ triangle, represented in the above diagram as conductivity; Monas makes a judgment, a decision, concerning it; then Monas drops it into its permanent storage of memory and empirical knowledge, represented in the above diagram by receptivity. The three steps: impingement, decision, storage -- represent the accumulation of a quantum of quantity, and satisfy the primary purpose of each individual's presence on earth.

Quality, also introduced by "Stephen", is properly placed at hinge "3", in association with such things as intuition, feeling, and the supraconscious; quality being the innate qualitative endowment you bring with you when you are born.

Degree is also properly placed at the apex, or "1" hinge, where it is most closely associated with the highest spiritual aspects of the individual. Degree is a fundamental notion of "Stephen's" evolutionary scheme. Just as consciousness is the one and only reality, so also consciousness exists in degrees; and each of us is born out of a particular degree.

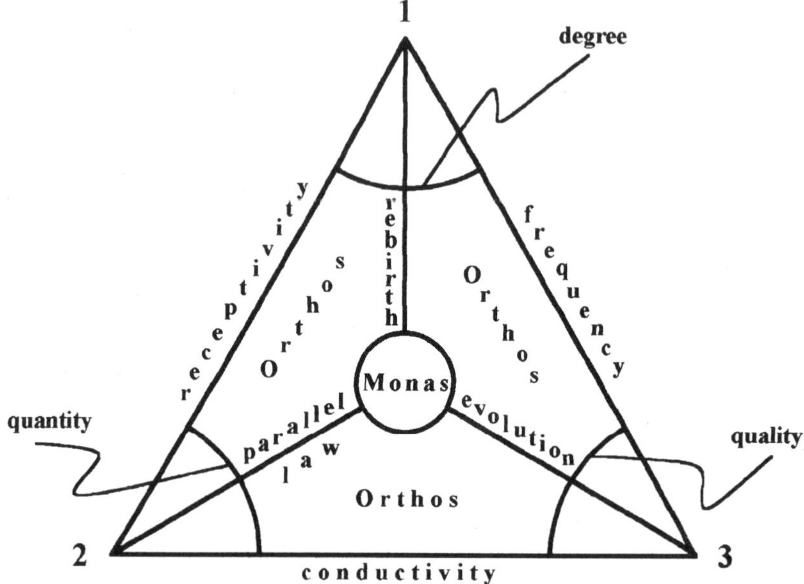

Figure 9. The Fully-Enhanced 1-2-3- Triangle

In the completed 1-2-3 triangle, Monas is indicated as always in the center as the triangle's directing force, surrounded not by mind as in the ABC triangle, but by Orthos.

The sides of the secondary triangles are also indicated. "Thought" is replaced by "parallel law". This notion encapsulates the dictum that all laws are universal; that any law we discover here also operates in Orthos; and vice versa. Parallel law is the theme of the missing Fourth Divulgence.

Evolution takes its natural place on the O-3 line, whose correspondent is instinct. Rebirth was placed on the 1-O line by Anne herself; it corresponds to inspiration in ABC and reproduction in XYZ.

There is not much detail available for the 1-2-3 triangle. It was given as context only, with detail assumed but not provided, so that the group could devote their time and energy to the ABC or psychological triangle, which was the topic of the divulgence.

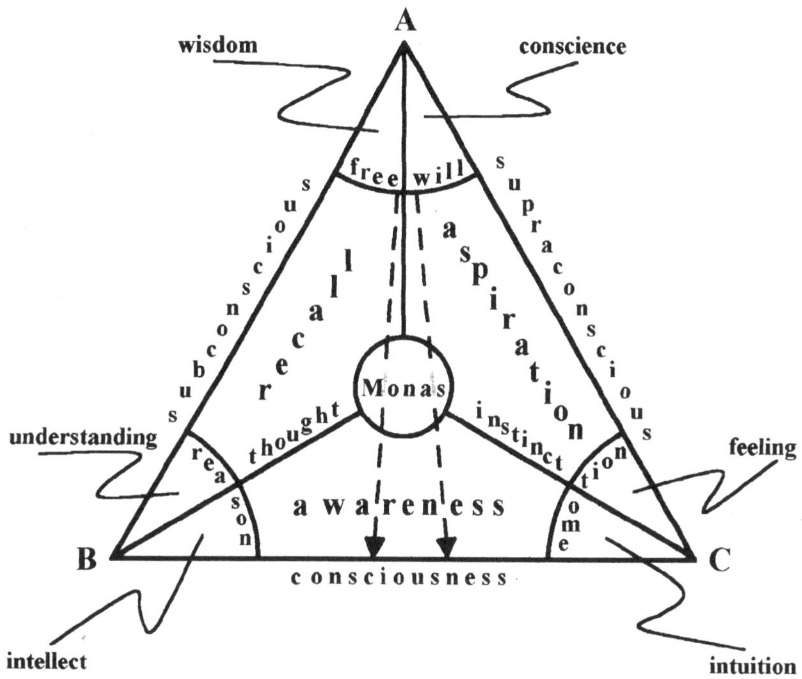

Figure 10. How Monas manages its attention

During ordinary waking activities Monas directs its attention by means of an attention line originating at the arc of free will and pointing -- directing Monas's attention -- at the BC line, where the outer world impinges. The arrow head, which is where attention is active, searches along the BC line looking for anything of interest. Inputs from BC are reflected in the awareness mind.

There is one such arrow for each of the three divisions of the mind. When the recall mind is active, as during sleep, the attention line originates at the arc of emotion, passes through Monas and the recall mind, and impinges on AB, the subconscious. When the aspiration mind is active, as during meditation, the attention line originates at the arc of reason, passes through Monas and the aspiration mind, and impinges on AC, the supraconscious.

Only one arrow can be active at any given time.

Chapter 3. Exercising the Model

ALTHOUGH the presentation of the model is far from complete, it can still be exercised to some extent. This is illustrated in the following conversation from the record commencing at Sheet 171. Harwood White kicked off the discussion. When he woke up that day he had been seized with a flash of intuition -- a rather clever one, as it turns out.

"This morning I woke up with an idea that seemed new to me," he said. "Namely, that impingements on the BC line not only travel along the line down to "B" and also down to "C" but also travel straight across the triangle BOC to Monas. In other words, the triangle BOC could be taken to represent a part of the cognitive mechanism."

This prompted a speech by his brother.

"You have in your entire triangle," said White, "three pie shaped pieces, if you draw your lines from 'O' to the three apexes. This whole area, bounded by the BC line at the bottom, which is your impingement line, immediately gives an upsurge to Monas.

"But it also travels in two ways along the line and, depending on what Monas does about this immediate upsurge that comes to him, he will get or not get an emotion out of the arc. This is the present over-developed portion of the triangle. It is the most sensitive part -- the BOC portion. Again the BOC portion of the triangle is what you shut off when you sleep."

This speech sparked one of the numerous clashes between Harwood and Emmet which characterized these sittings. The record calls it alternately "an acrimonious discussion" and "a large discussion." The area of disagreement seemed to concern a distinction between Monas and its faculties. It was thus a technical discussion on the further definition of the model. They seem to have resolved the argument by agreeing that the model was a valid if simplistic way of representing the real-world relations between Monas and its parts. The thread of the presentation was presently picked up by White.

"All with reservations," he said, by way of agreeing with the truce between Harwood and Emmet. "We have Monas possessing his triangle. He sits in the middle of it like a spider in a web, and down here on what we have been pleased to designate as the BC line we get, say, an impingement of fear."

"You cannot get an impingement of fear on the BC line," interrupted Harwood. "You get a sensory impingement on it which arouses fear."

"Wholly aside from the emotion, the thing that happens outside immediately awakens fear," said White. "For instance, you are in a motor accident or, let us say, you see the motor accident coming. Monas is on the job through his mind. He immediately gets a reaction. But maybe the fear does not happen until after the thing is all over. Now what are you going to about that?"

"I would say the sensory impingement at the BC line had stimulated the AC and the AB lines," said his brother, forgetting his bright idea of the morning.

"No, sir," said White, remembering. "You have got an upsurge. What I told you about the pie shaped pieces appears to have gone all over your head."

"I am trying to get around to that," Harwood hedged.

"Well, you get an immediate mind reaction, in the case of the motor accident," said White. "You get more than that because you get a subconscious reflex."

"That is what I was trying to say," said Harwood.

"Suppose," said White, "we don't talk about the triangle at all for a moment. Let's just talk about an impingement of fear. You drive down the street and you see you are going to get into a motor accident. Something happens in your consciousness and it is instantaneous."

"Well," said Harwood, "you are simply scared."

"Yes, you are scared," said White. "But you have to avoid the accident and you are not scared really until after the thing is over. Because all the time the likelihood of an accident is going on Monas is operating to save you from having a real accident.

"The upsurge of the pie shaped piece, the glow of a mind as it were, the illumination of the mind, concerning the occurrence about to happen, is contributed to Monas instantly across the pie shaped piece. The pie shaped piece is, as it were, a flash of light. Then Monas begins to operate the other two lines, and the BC line of impingement begins to operate and you get something that is going this way (to "C") and up this way (along "OC") and down this way (along "OB") at the same time. In other words, your little triangle inside the big triangle is operating."

"Take it easy," said Harwood, as the dictation was much too fast. "God help the poor stenographers on a night like this."

"Yes, but now supposing there is a weak woman at the wheel instead of a strong man," he continued.[1] "When the impingement on the BC line floods across the BOC triangle, the major portion of the flood, instead of going into the intelligence at the "B" hinge or up to the will at the top, will all go roaring over to the "C" corner and there is a large yell. And that is the totality of the situation."

"Yes," said White. "You have that happen sometimes, or if you are in a skid for instance, the first time you skid you don't know what to do and you may have a pretty bad accident as the result of it. But you learn, and in your subconscious finally is placed the method by which you avert a skid or with which you handle a skid, and the next time or the third time you have a skid you automatically, as they say, turn the wheel in the opposite direction to the skid."

"That is the AB line functioning," said Harwood.

"Yes," agreed his brother. "But during the skid that occurs after you have learned how to handle skids, you don't have much fear, if any. You master the fear immediately. I can find an incident illustrating this fact in Ruth's conscious experience."

White then related the facts concerning a fall by Ruth from a horse, occurring years ago. At the time of the fall, she had no fear whatever. She went home, took care of the horse, went into the house and then proceeded to faint.

"She fainted from emotional reaction," said White. "Now what would be the operation of the ABC triangle in that instance? That is a problem for you to

---

1. This is a direct transcription.

think about and give me the answer at the next session."

The next session was three days later, on May 29, 1947. (Sheet 174) There was trouble with the Sound Mirror; it seems that Harwood didn't set it properly, and no one noticed. The upshot was a full-length session with no record. Instead, the sitting notes provide us with a summary.

The session began with White asking for the group's solution to the horse question. Getting no response, White gave his own solution.

"At the time of the crisis," he said, "the entire ABC triangle was instantly activated from the BC line. But Monas, being thoroughly aroused, took immediate charge, suppressed the fear reactions from the "C" hinge of the triangle, and operated through its other elements.

"As long as these were kept under tension they dominated the situation. But once the horse -- a great favorite with Joan -- was adequately cared for, the tension relaxed.

"Now here is where the interrelation of the ABC and XYZ triangles comes in. The various organs, the very cells of the body, have a semi-independent life of their own. During the crisis, their fear reaction to the situation is suppressed by the domination of Monas. But once the crisis is passed, the way is cleared for the dynamics set up in the XYZ triangle by that first instantaneous fear reaction. This now surges backward over the ABC triangle, causing collapse."

This completes the illustration on exercising the model. The notes on the remainder of the session are of interest mainly because of the light they shed on the personality conflict between Harwood and Emmet.

White had changed the subject for the usual reason, which was to prevent Ruth from becoming too interested in the subject matter being dictated. He then took up the subject of the withdrawal from the world of monks and adepts. The purpose of this, he said, was to reduce the impingements on the XYZ triangle and so facilitate concentration on the ABC triangle.

"The same holds true of the artist's desire for seclusion," he said. "It clears the way for operation on the OA line."

At this point, Emmet brought up his perennial question as to just how one goes about operating on the OA line. This was too much for Harwood.

"I have been studying this guy for some time," he said. "And I think I am now qualified to give some pertinent conclusions.

"Whenever he meets a new idea, his reaction is invariably the same, and consists of two phases. First he sits down hard in the BOC pie and assumes a truly remarkable condition of violent immobility. This is fundamentally a highly emotional state originating at "C" but is immediately overlaid with a rapidly proliferating rational structure emanating from "B". To get him off this spot requires the combined efforts of all the king's horses and all the king's men, armed with sharp sticks.

"Thereupon Phase Two sets in. At this point, Emmet executes a lightning withdrawal into his OA line whence he hurls torrents of coruscating inspiration. Only then, of course, he is on fire and doesn't realize where he is at".

In reply to this, White remarked that Emmet's was a complex case and would be better considered later.

Chapter 4. The Subconscious

THE nature of the subconscious is receptivity, one of the trilogia of consciousness as described in *The Unobstructed Universe.* It should come as no surprise, then, that it functions as the storehouse for thought. It receives individual thoughts by a route shortly to be described. A thought newly-arrived in the subconscious finds itself at the model's "B" hinge. From this hinge it may travel along the line AB to the apex at "A" and elicit a response from the supraconscious.

The thought thus modified or "edited" is now ready for permanent storage. In uncomplicated cases it is deposited next to the "B" hinge, from which location it is readily accessible to the recall mind. Over time you expect it to work its way along line AB toward the "A" hinge, where it is less readily accessible. Or it may go there at once if Monas desires to suppress it.

The content of the subconscious is available on demand to the recall mind. These thoughts also impinge on line AB, the latter serving as a two-way antenna, radiating the individual's thoughts into the thought world of the obstructed universe, and in turn accepting impressions from that thought world.

The subconscious is not entirely static. It has its own algorithms, which it pursues out of sight of the awareness mind. Its spontaneous activities include, as mentioned, querying the supraconscious so that a new thought may get one more editing pass prior to storage; the comparison and coalescence of thoughts, partly in response to the reason processor but also partly spontaneously; the solving of problems, perhaps from a conscious request, perhaps not; and the spontaneous regurgitation of thought flagged on arrival for suppression. The latter -- thoughts flagged for suppression -- will have a strong emotional content, and may be stuffed by Monas so deeply into the subconscious that they are retrievable only with the greatest of difficulty.

A surprising function of the subconscious is its relation to free will. It is the free will processor's primary input. Thus the exercise of free will is a subconscious activity, not a conscious one as we would have supposed.

These aspects of the model will be discussed below under the following headings:

1. The Path of a Thought
2. The Everyday Use of the Subconscious
3. Reason in Perspective
4. Problem Solving
5. A Flood of Memories
6. The Subconscious in Sickness and Health

Other topics of interest will be discussed in separate chapters. Thus dreams and their interpretation will get its own chapter. The topic of sleep will be expanded in the chapter on tipping the triangles. The recall mind will be discussed under the topic, The Types of Attention.

The Path of a Thought

The subconscious plays a key role in White's model, as it did in the earlier work of Sigmund

Freud. The two systems are similar, but diverge in significant ways.

If you revisit Freud's own description of his work, you will see his emphasis on the reality of thought.[1] White's work reiterates this emphasis and raises it to a level comparable to the reality which a modern physicist accords to matter. *Thought is a thing*: this is an earlier statement of the principle in his work. In the model the ante is raised again: *Thought is the primary volitional act of man.* [Sheet 163]

In the model, every thought is eventually deposited in the subconscious. It is instructive to retrace its path en route. Disregarding for the moment its origin, the thought proceeds out of Monas down the thought line to the subconscious. This is not an absolute statement. It takes this route because it is conditioned to do so.

Why? On Sheet 89 of the sitting records an Invisible gives this suggestive explanation.

"If you can imagine this as a flow," he began, "the conscious mind flows down into the subconscious mind, that is your present training. That is what education has done. It has taught you to drop all of your stuff into the subconscious mind and it is there for consideration. That is where memory is and that is where your education is. You have overdeveloped your subconscious mind because you want memory. You want accurate memory. There are certain things that you have to use an accurate memory in a mechanistic world for. Now the supracon-

1. He writes, "Worte sind auch das wesentlich Handwerkszeug der Seelenbehandlung," translatable as "Words are also the essential tool in the treatment of the psyche," in *Darstellung der Psychoanalyse*, Fischer Taschenbuch Verlag, 1969, page 14.

scious, if you could directly contact it, could tell you all those things without that. Thus for those who think -- our present ideal -- we have thought proceeding from Monas down the thought line to the subconscious."

The individual thought is headed for storage, but it is not there yet. The mind gets an additional shot at it, a chance to exercise its spin control on it, before it becomes a permanent memory. This is introduced on Sheets 115 and 116 in a speech by Stewart Edward White which will be quoted at length later. The gist of it is that thoughts flow along the AB line to the apex at "A", where they are edited by the supraconscious before final storage.

There are thus two chances the individual has to influence the input to his permanent subconscious store: first as the thought passes from Monas down the thought line to the reason subprocessor; and subsequently as the thought propagates along the AB line of the subconscious to the free will arc, and the "A" apex, encountering the supraconscious and the judgment processor behind free will. Thus modified, the thought is ready for permanent storage. White covers these points in an extended speed on Sheet 170.

"Now Monas comes into the world with his gift that is contained in the AC line," he said. "He has two points in the triangle which he can himself operate to increase, decrease, or stabilize any impingement that comes in over his BC line or any impingement that, via his BC line, stimulates a portion of the AC line, such as an emotion. He can let that emotion do with him what it will, or he can let it run down the thought line to reason, consider it there, and drop it into the subconscious after it has been reasoned out and he has made a decision concerning it. That of course brings into play his will power immediately, but there is another function of the will. The will, too, is at the top of the triangle. It is as much attached to the subconscious as to the supraconscious. If this particular man, or Monas, develops his supraconscious with the intent for the use of free will, even after the thought has been dropped into the subconscious it can stimulate the will. So that it will come to Monas in such a way that he will realize something must be done about it. So he has two chances with every thought, every emotion, every impingement. He can do something about it before it goes into the subconscious and he can do something about it after it has been received by the subconscious."

The discussion thus far has aimed at following the history of an individual thought prior to its deposition in the subconscious as a permanent memory. Its subsequent history is also of interest. The subconscious is the store of the individual's memory and practical knowledge. It is the substrate on which the recall mind operates, whether in recalling what we think of as memories or in habitual activities such as driving an automobile. It is also the substrate for the recall mind during dreams. And it has a dynamics of its own, both in health and pathology. It transmits thought to the "A" apex where free will is brought to bear -- an operation in which reason and awareness are excluded! And it is where repression and obsession occur, which impact the individual through the recall mind as the subconscious goes through its basic dynamism or algorithm, which is to surface all thoughts buried within it.

It also operates as a two-way antenna, in which the individual's thoughts are radiated into the thought world of the race; and in which the mass thought of the race may impinge so strongly that the recall mind may present it to Monas.

The Everyday Use of the Subconscious

We use the subconscious constantly in everyday life. It contains all our empirical knowledge; and it is rife with stored subroutines for everything from brushing our teeth to how to pronounce "stored subroutines." These subroutines are constantly presenting themselves to the awareness mind "hoping" to get used. You can demonstrate this quite satisfactorily to yourself. Sit in a comfortable chair with a cup of tea or coffee, but engage your mind in another activity, say, reading a book. Whenever something in your mind suggests taking a sip from the cup, disregard it, but casually. Sooner or later you will discover that you have taken a sip. Look into your mind: *you have not given explicit permission for that sip!* Instead, it happened automatically. Your recall mind, having presented the subroutine a couple of times, found a softened response and went ahead and called the subroutine on its own.

And what a subroutine it is! If you don't believe this, try programming a robot to do it. A small child cannot master it. Given the typical handle of a fine china cup, the wonder is that anyone can do it. Finely tuned nerves and the musculature of a prehensile hand are involved. Not just any hand, mind you: your favorite one. The same hand that in another might wield a violin bow. And an excellent feed-back system from the proprioceptors of the muscles is involved (they sense weight), so that the cup engages the lips at the same place whether the cup be full or empty. Don't think too hard about it, though. Your subconscious has the know-how to do it, not the awareness mind. (The latter can program it, but can't do it!) The subconscious: constant companion of everyday living.

The recall of learned patterns demonstrates their presence in subconscious memory. Stored patterns that are readily available are said to be stored, as stated, near hinge "B"; those less readily available have migrated nearer to hinge "A". On sheet 92 an Invisible put it this way:

"It is perfectly true," he said -- he was speaking to Emmet Finley -- "that you use your subconscious mind constantly, that you drop into it for, how to work your fingers, how to use a pen, how to use a typewriter, all how to do this, how to do that. All of those things are in your subconscious. You call on them a thousand times a day with every move you make, with every thought you think. Now if you can keep those up close to the B and they do not get clear down to the A, you have a more active awareness mechanism than if they were away off where you have to dig for them."

Emmet Finley resurfaced this train of thought at a later session. "There is an every day normal use of the subconscious," he said, "that is distinct from dreams, reveries and etc. We have had only limited discussion of this ordinary use of the subconscious."

White took the cue to expand on the subject.

"Every thought has a response from the subconscious," he began. "All your comparisons and all your reasoning are done with the aid of the subconscious. No judgment is reached without a comparison, without the present problem of Monas being brought to the subconscious for that purpose."

Thus begins a train of thought that will give reason an operational definition in terms of the model. No antipathy between reason and feeling, no dark hints as to whether the path to Truth follows Plato or the Aramaic-speaking Israelites of antiquity, no chest beating, no histrionics -- just a simple algorithm you can write a computer program for, plus a few hints as to how the individual and the civilization can strike a useful balance at a particular point in the evolution of the race.

"Now the ordinary process is this," White continued. "You have here the long leg of the subconscious, memories and etc., then you have here your magnetic field, namely, the AOB field. Now if you have a problem or have anything coming to your attention, Monas immediately sets in operation the thought line.

"Monas can only reason in one way. The arc of reason goes from the BC line over to the AB line. It is in touch with the presently existing situation, plus the situation that Monas finds similar or opposite or apposite in the AB line. After he has operated both these lines, he goes on down and drops the matter into the hinge, into the actual AB line. He has put his judgment and cogitation to work and then has dropped the result into his subconscious, after his attention has dealt with the new impingement. The attention of Monas can be again attracted, not by the same thought by way of reason but by an occurrence out of the AB line. When that happens, the upsurge across the AOB triangle is where it will hit Monas. In other words, the AB line will send a message over the AOB field. Memory will occur to Monas in that fashion.

"You were speaking of various depths of subconsciousness," he continued. "I think one of the first things you were told was that the subconscious kept pushing memory back or up toward the "A" hinge, that there is where it gets less acutely useful to Monas in his everyday operations. It is there that your triangle is smaller and your field is smaller. Also you are closer to the supraconscious and also that is where the supraconscious can inflow and have something to do with the thought-become-memory that Monas has dropped into the AB line over the OB line."

This completes the discussion of the ordinary, "trivial" uses to which, following the model, we put our subconscious, and without which we would not get very far into our day. Other uses, those made popular by Freud's work, will be described below in separate chapters.

Reason in Perspective

As mentioned, reason acquires an operational definition in the model. This is the subject of a lucid discussion direct from the record. The date is June 13, 1947. The speaker is White.

"We are going to give you within the next few recordings the uses of the three apexes of the ABC triangle," he began.

"Since the record was lost" (this refers to an occasion when Harwood failed to press the right button of the Sound Mirror) "and the dissertation on wisdom the other day was sort of a side issue to the main point, I think we would better start with the angle "B" because it is there that man best understands his processes of the use of the triangle. The "B" arc is reason and to the left of the arc bounded by reason, sensory perception and thought, is intellect. And on the right, bounded by reason and the subconscious (or Monas's own empirical knowledge) is understanding. I don't know how vivid a picture this makes to your mind but to me it is tremendously vivid."

I want to pause briefly at this point to let the previous remark soak in. To anyone wanting to model the mind of White as it existed during this discussion, it is a wonderful cue. The vividness of pictorial information is a recurring theme. Nor is it necessary to join White and his colleagues to experience this. One has only to recall Jung's experience in the Baptistery of the Orthodox in Ravenna. He saw the walls of the Baptistery decorated with mosaics of breathtaking beauty, and they left in his memory an indelible impression. On his return home he determined to obtain a picture post card of the treasure, and commissioned a friend to do so. Impossible, his friend reported back. Such mosaics don't exist and never did. But for Jung, they did. Till the end of his life he remembered them in undiminished detail.[2]

But to return to White's extended speech.

"I used thought, not only as a daily living apparatus, but as a tool. And I used my intellect as a tool. Now the thing that I have come to realize since I came here is that man can use both thought and intellect and use them exceedingly efficiently and yet not have too much understanding. If you will examine the pairs at the arc, each bounded on its base by a piece of the arc, you will note that one of the two in each corner most people use and understand and talk about and consider familiar. And they

---

2. *Memories, Dreams, Reflections*, Vintage Books, 1965, page 284-285.

develop it to a degree. And the other one is more subtle. You develop it and you know it is there, and you think you have it fully within your grasp. And yet it is that one that has something very specially to do with what Beese calls Emmet's $64 question.

"Now in this "B" arc, with which you are most familiar, which you use most every day -- the thought line, reason, sense perception at the base, and even your subconscious -- is that little chap, understanding, stuck in there, that requires a great deal of nursing -- a great deal of care and building and attention and prodding by yourself to get him into the same shade of development as intellect is. Because, believe me, understanding is the important side of this arc."

The foregoing presentation prompted a discussion between Harwood and Emmet on the fact that White had turned left into right and right into left. A glance at the diagram of the ABC triangle seems to confirm their suspicion. But White stood his ground.

"Looking down the thought line from Monas," he retorted, "your objection that I had the positions of intellect and understanding incorrectly placed, left and right, is invalidated because I am looking down the thought line. If you sit in the place of Monas, you do look down the thought line, you look down the inspiration line and down the instinct line. But to go back. Let's discuss this apex."

"I have a question," said Harwood. "How do you distinguish between intellect and thought?"

"All men think more or less straight," White replied. "Likewise men vary as to their capacity of intellect."

"But," said his brother, "what does intellect do that thought doesn't do?"

"The intellect intensifies thought for one thing," White replied. "It builds the thought. It retains thought. It acts directly on reason and reason acts directly on it. It is bounded on one side by reason. It has perception, and all of these have to do with the color of a man's intellect, with the kind of intellect he has. Now some men do not have a mathematical intellect at all. Some do not have a musical intellect. Perhaps there is a lack or overbalance, because it is in here that you for your daily operation get the cast that is the color of what you are going to do with your mind."

"Well, why not say that intellect is the capacity for coordinated thought?" This from Emmet.

"Excellent," replied White.

"Now what is understanding?" continued Emmet. It must be the appreciation of the significance of the conclusions reached by coordinated thought."

"Yes, plus," replied White. "You must remember that understanding is bounded by the subconscious. And it is not only the conclusions reached by any one coordinated thought or any series of coordinated thoughts. It is taking the significance of a particular conception and adding to it something of the content of the subconscious."

"A good idea," said Emmet. "That certainly does add to my definition."

Here the tape ran out and the group paused while a fresh one was installed. When the session resumed, White took up the discussion.

"Now we were discussing understanding. We got to the point where to have understanding we added something of the subconscious, to which Emmet seemed to agree. Now let's go on from there. What is your next question? There is another one, you know."

"Well, you read my mind," replied Harwood. "I was about to pop it. It seems to me that understanding would contain not only subconscious content but also something from the "A" hinge. True complete understanding."

"Yes, it would," replied White. "You have a direct line there and you have the pulsation of your whole AOB secondary triangle, which directly touches understanding. So you would have some of it, of the "A" hinge, but the amount you would have of it would depend on what you had done in the "A" hinge. You see the whole thing is one and the heck of it is that each affects the other and that what you are striving after or should strive after is complete balance. And it is he who most closely attains complete balance who has the most rounded out and interesting life to himself and others. The question I would like to have you ask now is where reason comes in."

"What is the distinction between reason, intellect and thought?" This from Harwood.

"Reason -- suppose you define it, Emmet," replied White.

"Such words as reason, intellect and understanding run so close together in ordinary parlance that it is hard to distinguish them in extraordinary parlance," said Emmet. "Reason of course is logical thinking. You reason when you start from a premise and from that premise think logically to a conclusion."

"Where do you get your premise?" asked White.

"From a variety of things," said Emmet. "It may be from intellect itself. It may be from simply the data of sense impressions. However, it is very likely to be more that mere perception. For instance -- I am going along the street and I meet a young man who has only one leg. He is wearing the remnants of a soldier's uniform. Reasoning from these facts, I draw the conclusion that he is a wounded veteran. I may be all wrong but I draw that conclusion logically from the premises presented."

"Look at your mobile," White directed. (The group had been instructed by the Invisibles to make a mobile out of the ABC triangle.) "At what three points does the arc of reason open into something else?"

"It opens into subconscious, perception and thought," replied Emmet.

"O.K.," said White.

"Well," continued Emmet, "it is tinged with all those things and yet it is something different."

"I asked where did you get your premise," White persisted. "You get your premise for all your reasoning in one of three places: out of thought direct from Monas, out of perception or it is possible to get it out of your subconscious, and if you do the latter, it is something you have placed there for future reference which you have now pulled out, reasoned, considered and intellectually come to a conclusion about."

This conversation took place in 1947. Without intruding too much into the conversation, I would like to point out that White has just supplied an operational definition of something that has more recently occupied philosophers -- the question of whether objectivity can be achieved by eliminating non-rational sources of things to think about. Theologian John B. Cobb, Jr., discussed this effort in Christ in a Pluralistic Age. " . . . the course of modern thought," wrote Cobb, "has increasingly shown that reason ... can generate no content ...

philosophy is dependent on what is nonrationally given and can do nothing more than clarify this." [3]

The question I would like to pose to the reader is this: Hasn't White anticipated this line of philosophical inquiry? And if so, doesn't this amount to circumstantial evidence in support of the notion of his colleagues that all major thought originates with them, not with us?

Now to return to the Finleys' drawing room. White has just said that the premise for reason may come from the subconscious. But if so, "it is something you have placed there for future reference which you have now pulled out, reasoned, considered and intellectually come to a conclusion about."

"Rationally come to a conclusion," added Emmet.

"But you cannot do it without the use of your intellect," said White.

"That depends on how you define your terms," rejoined Emmet. "You might say that reason is an intellectual process."

"Let's see," Harwood interposed. "Reason is a mechanism which is actuated by intellect. Reason is just a --"

"Reason is more than a mechanism," interrupted his brother, "and it is actuated by thought. You cannot reason without thought. A cat can reason a little and it has not much intellect."

"Or very much reason." This from Emmet.

"Quite a little if you watch them," said White. "They do a pretty good job for little folks. They do not have much understanding either. They have a

---

3. The Westminster Press, 1975, pages 89 and 90. Cobb cites P.F. Strawson, Wilfrid Sellars, and "other analytical philosophers" in support of these notions.

little bit, and they don't have a whole lot of subconscious."

He now directed the group's attention away from reason and the "B" arc to the arc at the apex of the ABC triangle. "One of the things I called your attention to," he said, "was that, looking down the thought line or the inspiration line or the instinct line, you saw there two tertiary triangles. On the OA line you see to the right conscience and to the left wisdom. Now just as I told you (with respect to) intellect in the case of intellect and understanding, man understands one of those (conscience and wisdom) and its use better than the other."

"Which does he understand better?" This from Emmet.

"Conscience," said White, "because that is closest to his own endowment and because it has been trained. It is something that civilization forced upon man more or less and he has used it, and you both know what I mean. So I need not discuss it further. Wisdom, on the other hand, is something that men aspire to. All would like to be wise and many are. Also there are degrees and steps, heights and depths of understanding. And the other thing I want to call to your attention in connection with this is that wisdom, like understanding, is connected with the subconscious at one side and that the flow over the arc of the secondary triangle AOB is back and forth between understanding and wisdom. Man must have understanding before he can possess wisdom. Now do you wish to discuss this?"

"Why are these two, wisdom and conscience, associated with free will?" asked Emmet.

"Because conscience," replied White, "is the peculiar qualitative gift that is granted to the highest manifestation of consciousness, together with free will -- these two. They are placed at the norm high apex. Wisdom is the thing that men for earth use aspire to most. If a man is truly wise, he will make few mistakes."

"But," persisted Emmet, "why is wisdom peculiarly associated with free will?"

"Because," replied White, "it is the use to which man puts his free will that develops his conscience that, in turn flowing over to the subconscious, takes something of the supraconscious with it, that draws out of the subconscious such of his empirical knowledge as is worth feeding into wisdom and because free will goes through the AOB secondary triangle. These are the places where you get direct contact, and at the apex, from the supraconscious to the subconscious. Now a man who has a highly usable free will can draw, not only down to his Monas much, or something at least, of his supraconscious gift, but he can also draw it across to his subconscious for his daily use."

"Why the association of inspiration with free will?", Harwood asked.

"Because," replied White, "a man can get an inspired thought and if he is too darn lazy to do anything about it, doesn't use his free will to operate upon it, it might just as well not have happened. You get many ideas that you day dream about. They seem to be quite unusual and wonderful. Sometimes they are and sometimes they are not. But if you don't put them into action, if you just let them float around, they do not amount to much."

"Yes," replied Emmet. "But couldn't that be equally said of any apex? If down here on the perception line you got a bad smell, you certainly would be free to do nothing about it if you want to do nothing. On the other hand, you could run it down -- deodorize it as it were."

"Instinct would take you away from it," suggested Harwood.

"That is true," replied White. "But the thing I told you in the beginning of this discussion about the "A" arc hinge or the free will arc, was that they were put at the peak of the norm."

"Yes, but we are trying to ascertain why volition is associated with wisdom and conscience." This from Emmet.

"I gave you one reason," replied White, "which was that it made it possible for you to draw from your supraconscious into your subconscious for daily use."

"'It' means what?" said Emmet, the trained lawyer.

"The operation of your free will in coincidence with your conscience," replied White. "Now the man who balances his conscience and his free will will get wisdom. Wisdom like understanding is a gift that is a result of something that Monas has operated. You do not get understanding unless you definitely operate your thought, your reason and your intellect. And you do not get wisdom unless you definitely operate your free will, inspiration and conscience. And if you do, you are bound to get wisdom."

Good for a high-level specification. What is left is to reduce it to working computer code. Emmet continues the conversation.

"Can you get conscience without operating free will?"

"Well, it can at least hurt," replied White.

This reminded Harwood of the story about an old Scotsman who was very proud of his conscience. Finally one of his friends asked him whether it kept him from sinning. "No, indeed, it does not," he replied with dignity. "But it keeps me from enjoying of it".

There now followed an active interchange that illustrates the advantage of "conceiving" stations in these sessions. (As opposed to the "receiving" station, or medium.) The interchange starts with Harwood speaking.

"Just there," he began, "it seems to me -- check me on this -- in just thinking about the three corners just now, it seems to me that each corner has a power factor. Free will, emotion, reason -- each corner has a source factor -- conscience, feeling, intellect -- and each has a resultant factor -- wisdom, intuition, understanding."

"Each corner has a --," Emmet tried.

"A resultant factor, a depository," replied Harwood.

Emmet tried again. "First you said each corner had --"

"A power factor," supplied White.

"Will has a power factor," continued Harwood. "Emotion is a power factor."

"And reason is a power factor," said White.

"I don't quite see the last," said Harwood.

"I do," said Emmet. "You have excellent reasons for doing things. If that is not a power factor, I don't know one."

"Sure, I see now, of course," said Harwood. "Isn't that funny? You present a little different slant and then you get it."

"Just as your conscience can be active with your free will doing nothing about it, so your intellect can be active with your reason doing nothing about it," said Emmet.

"Right you are," concurred White. "Now for the benefit of the station, please name the secondary triangles."

Now occurred the part of the conversation where the model calls for a distinct portion of the mind to deal with the subconscious. White has asked for names of secondary triangles and Emmet is replying.

"On the left is recall or memory."

"It is not memory," said White sharply. "It is recall. Here is something you have got to clear up. Memory and recall are two different things. Memory is a deposit in the subconscious and recall is an act of Monas. The recall secondary triangle is a very important operation of the mind."

"Well, it does not seem that one can do anything about anything without the use of it," said Emmet.

"No, you cannot," replied White. "It is as you develop that triangle that you get the full benefit of your subconscious. Because it is bounded by thought and by inspiration and by the subconscious, and wisdom touches it and understanding touches it."

"There is your picture, Emmet," concluded White, thus rounding out a conversation that occupies several sheets in the sitting notes. (Sheets 260-267)

The reason subprocessor is assigned in the ABC triangle to the arc that connects the subconscious with consciousness. It is fed by the thought line from Monas, and it bounds the areas assigned to understanding and intellect. But the exercise of reason involves the entire triangle, and the free will processor is sometimes invoked in the process.

In an early discussion an Invisible has just told Emmet Finley that his reaction to a bee sting has nothing to do with real choice. There followed an extended discussion.

"That is right," agreed Emmet. "Let's take a case of that kind. I meet a girl as a young man, and I am tempted to say to her, 'Let's get married'. And I think it over for a long period of time and I decide either to do it or not to do it. This is something that is going to affect my future happiness. When the choice is made, of course, obviously the necessity for making the choice arose in the conscious mind. But when the choice is made, is it made in the conscious mind or is it made in the super and the subconscious?"

"In the super and the subconscious mind," replied the Invisible. "Now listen, Emmet, when it comes into the conscious mind, a choice of that kind has both a time and motion element in it, actual time and motion. Both receptivity and frequency go into making that choice. That choice comes down into your free will, flowing in from both sides from the top of the triangle, and then it comes down that dotted line" (described below) "and comes out in your conscious mind, and you conduct it out and impinge it upon somebody else. Because you see, the content of consciousness operates both ways."

"I do not mean to be facetious," said Emmet, "but they say that marriages are a result of proximity which gives them a very spatial consideration."

"That makes it all subconscious," interposed Harwood.

"No, not all subconscious," the Invisible insisted.

At this point Emmet tried a different tack. "Now this is what is meant, I assume, by the school of psychology: if you want to do a difficult thing, do not will to do it, wish to do it, if you want to do what is difficult for you to do. Willing to do it will just block the very old devil out it."

"Of course it will," the Invisible agreed.

"Then where does this willing thing come in, this duty and willing to do the thing that you do not want to do?" Harwood wanted to know.

"It comes into the picture at the apex of the triangle, where the free will in this little loop that we are talking about, is attached to the supraconscious and is also attached to the subconscious and digs down toward the conscious", replied the Invisible.[4]

"You see, we are doing this in the diagram. In the first place, you must remember that the supraconscious and the subconscious are attached to each other; they are actually attached. There is no break in the triangle. It is like a circle. Only it is shaped; we shaped it like a triangle because plane surfaces are easier to deal with than curved surfaces.

"Now you see, when you get down to B, the subconscious and the conscious are attached. There is no break and you run along the conscious and it, too, is attached to the supraconscious and there is no break. You see the whole thing is really a circle. But these straight lines are more easily visualized. Now back up here is your free will. Your judgment too, is up there, and your judgment is back of the free will."

"I am going to make a suggestion in here just to interrupt," said Emmet. "I would suggest that the little circles be called B prime and C prime, so that we won't have to continue this repetition. Now you want to know, what is in the area, A prime, B prime, C prime?"

"Yes, what do you think?" the Invisible replied.

---

4. In the phrase "digs down toward the conscious" the Invisible is alluding to the attention line that hangs from the arc of free will and searches along the BC line.

"I would say that it would be the ego, the eternal self," said Emmet.

"Yes, you would be pretty nearly right," said the Invisible. "It is your sitter behind your judgment that is in there; and it is the thing that operates this free will in conjunction with the supraconscious and the subconscious. Because you control the whole business. You see, well, let me repeat, that the gift of God to man is the free will."

"He didn't give us very much," Emmet grumbled.

"You are given as much as your degree of quality vouchsafed to you," the Invisible rejoined, "plus the quantitative development that you put into that free will."

"Well, two percent," said Harwood, backing Emmet.

"More than that," the Invisible insisted. "So you see, when you make a judgment, such as the fact whether or not you are going to marry a certain individual, a serious judgment of that kind, there is quite a process goes on in the subconscious which, since it is a serious thing, calls upon the supraconscious for aid in the decision."

But Emmet was not convinced. "Yes," he retorted, "but may I point out some other factors. A man can consider a problem from the point of view that you are speaking of, where you would have to call upon the deeper layers of his consciousness, but you can say now, this girl, she is good-looking, that is one reason for me to marry her, she comes from a good family, she has good social position, she has savvy and by gosh, she has money, here are some splendid reasons for me marrying this young lady. By golly, I do not see that the super and the sub have a darn thing to do with it."

"That is what I want to know," said Harwood, now a witness for the defense. "Now, if a person does a thing on the basis of purely reasoned judgment and does not depend on the basis of anything sub or super, so far as he is able to rule it out -- I mean he is an intellectual and he is going to decide entirely by intellectual tabulatable reasons. If he makes his free will choice on the basis of that, where does this thing reside, this intellectual thing, that says A, B, C, D and 1,2,3,4?"

But the Invisible was a determined tormentor. "You cannot decide anything, you cannot think a thought without calling on your sub and your super," he maintained. "You call upon your whole mind. Every doggone impingement that comes into you starts activating your whole mind, just as surely as you drop a pebble in the water and every little particle that touches it goes out in circles."

"You did not answer Harwood's question," needled Emmet. "What he wants to know is, where is the seat of the intellect?"

"Yes, where in this picture do you put that?" asked Harwood. "May I give an answer?"

"Yes, do," said the Invisible.

"That would depend," said Harwood, "upon where your dotted line goes from the hammock down to the BC line. If the dotted line goes down to that portion of the BC line, which represents reason, then, well, you would get a purely reasoned judgment. That is what the person would think."

Harwood's terminology anticipates the discussion of types of attention in a later chapter. His "hammock" is the arc of free will. The dotted line is an attention line that drops down from the arc of free will to the BC line, and cuts it here or there (left toward reason or right toward emotion) depending on the individual case.

But the Invisible was adamant. "You see, you cannot get a purely reasoned judgment after maturity," he said.

"Well, it would look like a purely reasoned judgment," Harwood whined.

"Two plus two equals four," Emmet bristled. "Now that is a purely reasoned judgment. What are you going to do about it?"

"Two plus two equals four is in your subconscious," the Invisible retorted. "It has been there ever since you have been in the second grade."

"That is right, Emmet, she has got you there," said Harwood.

"You make a purely reasoned judgment, which you think is a purely reasoned judgment," the Invisible continued, "that is the one time in God's green earth that you tap your supraconscious deliberately."

But Harwood is not convinced. "For a purely reasoned judgment?" he asked.

"For a purely reasoned judgment, what you think is a purely reasoned judgment," the Invisible replied.

"How do you figure that?" said Emmet.

"Because man's supraconscious is a part of his mind, it is a part of his brain, it is a part of his mechanism that he operates and it is there that he uses the self to get what he wants to operate on the BC line," said the Invisible. "It is there that he gets what he wants, that will flow down into the will, to make the will power operate on the BC line. The BC line is your contact with the outer world. It is not your supraconscious or your subconscious that ever contacts the outside world. That is you. That is the thing that you use."

"I think I could think of an instance which would be purely reasoned," said Emmet the attorney. "Take a court of law. Take evidence. This man is charged with having stolen a dozen eggs from the grocery. Now certain witnesses are brought in to testify to certain things, including the fact that the man had a dozen eggs in his pocket that he could not account for. The court of law would be very remiss and the cause of justice would miscarry if the verdict was based too much on the color of the man's hair, on his previous history, on the hunches that the jurymen might have as to who was telling the truth or not telling the truth. Of course all those things do enter into the verdict. But ideally, it should be rendered according to the evidence and that seems to me a purely rational proposition. When it ceases to be rational, you are likely to get bum justice."

"The verdict is rendered on the evidence," replied the Invisible. "The evidence is safely in the mind of each individual juror, in his reasoning mind. Now what is his reasoning mind made up of? His reasoning mind is made up of his God-given quality and his subconscious empirical knowledge."

"Then the reason is an activity of all sides?" queried Emmet.

"You are darn right it is," said the Invisible. "The reason is an activity of all three sides of the triangle and a baby cannot reason." (Sheets 98 through 104)

The reason subprocessor got its initial definition on Sheets 130 and 131. Ruth Finley had been carrying on an extended conversation with White, only one side of which was audible. Finally she explained to the others.

"The emotions flow out of the supraconscious into the conscious and there they are acted upon and judged," she explained. "So -- they get into the mind, don't they? Stewart says that this arc joining the AB and BC lines is judgment, consideration.

"How does judgment differ from thought?" Harwood wanted to know.

"Judgment differs from thought because it is conclusive so far as the Monas is concerned," said White. "Thought is the road to judgment, is the balancing of possibly more than one idea in connection with any given problem. You judge a thing. You make your decision about it. You may change it. Nevertheless, at the time, the judgment is made by the conscious and subconscious minds."

"I should think a better word would be 'reason'," suggested Emmet, at the top of his form.

"All right," agreed White. "Yes, you see, it is your instantaneous experience, the thing that has impinged the thought on your mind, the consideration that you have given it and in order to do so, you must draw out of your subconscious mind or memory, your empirical knowledge concerning it, and it may be ultimately that you will draw on your supraconscious mind before you come to a final conclusion. But the reason, the judgment, the operation, goes on between the conscious and subconscious phases. Don't forget that. When you drop that decision into your subconscious--"

"It runs up then, ultimately needing another judgment up at the top," interrupted Emmet. "But that is another story. Another kind of judge."

"Yes," said White. "That is the supraconscious."

"It is a moral judge, maybe, as distinct from a rational judge," suggested Emmet.

"The idea is there and we can tidy it up later," concluded White. "You have gone quite a long way this evening."

But free will is not always invoked. Frequently when we think we exercise our free will we in fact don't. The subconscious has handled the entire transaction. Emmet was fishing for this difference when he said:

"Now I will take a little illustration. I can or cannot, as I choose, lift my hand, that is certainly a fact known to my conscious mind. I do lift my hand. Now you mean to say that I lifted my hand because there has been an impingement on my conscious mind. But the actual lifting of the hand, the actual exercise of the choice to lift the hand, was an operation that went on in the super and the sub."

"It went on in the subconscious mind in that particular instance," said the Invisible.

"In the subconscious mind?" said an unbelieving Emmet.

"Because," continued the Invisible, "it is in your subconscious mind that you have trained your muscles to lift the hand."

"I will take another little illustration of the same kind, continued Emmet. "It has not occurred to me lift my hand or to do anything about it at all. But if a bee comes along and stings it, then I lift it darn quick."

"Well, you have an impingement upon your consciousness there; upon your tactile --" the Invisible started to answer.

"But the question is, have I made a choice?" interrupted Emmet.

"You have made an instantaneous choice," the Invisible agreed.

"Where did I make it?" Emmet wanted to know.

"You made it in the subconscious; it was a reflex action," the Invisible replied.

"So that the bee stimulating a reflex action better illustrates the freedom of choice than my just saying consciously that I will lift my hand and then lifting it," said Emmet.

"In that particular illustration, it does," agreed the Invisible. "But it has nothing whatever to do with where you have to make a real choice, where it is going to affect your future life, or that is going to affect your happiness."

Problem Solving

Problem solving uses the subconscious, but in a rather complex interaction with other parts of the model. Consider this long interchange that starts on Sheet 125. The session is from May 19, 1947. I have edited out portions to facilitate the presentation.

"The job tonight is to name the OA line," commenced White. "I think you have all been considering this, as we have. We want a term that is simple and plain. The word I wish to give you to consider is inspiration. It is not completely satisfactory. I ask your aid in getting something that will connote that idea plus.

"We have Monas as the center of the triangle, he continued. "It is obvious that the OB line, dipping into the hinge of the subconscious and the conscious, should be thought. The other line OC, dipping into the hinge of the conscious and the supraconscious, obviously must be instinct and all that appertains thereto. Now, the nearest word I can suggest to you for the line from Monas to the hinge of the supraconscious and the subconscious, is inspiration. Over this line, if you can term it such, will come genius, flashes of instinct, and in reverse, would come the asking-for by the Monas."

Here the kitten in the kitchen did so much meowing that the station was seriously disturbed. Emmet got the cat and tried to hold it, but it wiggled so much that he finally had to take it to the basement. After that, Harwood and Emmet consulted the dictionary and the Thesaurus for a better word than inspiration but did not succeed in finding it.

"I suggest we use the word 'inspiration' until we get an inspiration," Emmet finally said.

"What do you think comes over the OA line to the Monas?" White asked. "You understand that these diagrams are supposed to represent functions."

"Well, we don't know much about it," Emmet parried. "I guess you had better tell us."

"It is over this line that Monas, well, just to use the term, is inspired," White replied. "It is over this line that you have the feeling from the supraconscious to the Monas that amounts to genius. Here are those problems solved that you wrestle with and cannot conquer yourself. They drop from your thought into the subconscious. There they contact the supraconscious and the next day, by means of the supraconscious, you become aware of a solution.

"Now we learned when we were studying for the Unobstructed Universe that all conductivity operates in two ways, he continued. "It can go forward or it can go back. So it is possible for the Monas to contact the supraconscious over the OA line, but this is a road that has become almost obliterated in modern man, due to his mechanical education. Are you interested?"

"Following you with great interest," said Harwood.

"I think you must discuss the matter," replied White.

"Well," said Emmet, "I think that this line has been more or less obliterated, not only in consequence of modern education, and perhaps not primarily so, but also in consequence of the evolution that has carried man out of his sub-human degree into his present development."

"But if that is true," replied White, "why is the OC line more in use than the OA line? OC is the instinct line. The OA line is more a psychological line and the OC line is more a physical line."

"I withdraw my question," said Emmet.

"Certain people do use the OA line," continued White. "Some have developed it consciously. Some are born out of a degree that makes it operable, even as the OC line is operable in the definitely lower degrees, that is, animals. But when the OA line is highly operable in a man, he is almost invariably of an exceedingly high degree of evolution and his accompanying faculties, his methods of the use of thought, his method of operating his mind, will be on a par with his evolution.

"I am trying to make some sort of a route for the process," said Harwood. "If I sit down, for instance, to write a story, and I want to draw inspiration, the place where I want that inspiration to register, is in my thinking mind, which has been placed in this diagram on the OB line. The supraconscious resides on the AC line. The material I want must come from the AC line through the OA line to the OB line."

"You, Monas, decide to write a story," replied White. "You have the general plot, a generalization of the characters, but either you have to laboriously figure out the consummation of the plot and the characters with all the ramifications of both, or you are going to have to get help. The help you want for the purpose of this illustration, is in the AC line, the supraconscious.

"Just for your information, it probably is not there," he said surprisingly. "It probably is in the AB line or your own empirical knowledge, but for the purpose of argument, we will say that it is in this AC line.

"So you, Monas, have decided to use your mind to produce this story," he continued. "You start thinking about it over the OB line -- all you think about it, drops into the subconscious or the AB line. You don't finish the story in one fell swoop. It cooks, as you say, in your subconscious, and you go back to your desk the next day and you have the story.

"How did you get it?" he asked. "In the particular case, the wish for help from the supraconscious, generated in the Monas, traveled down the thought line into the subconscious, like the marble, up the subconscious to the hinge where the solution, which was always in the supraconscious, comes along and tinges it. Now if your story is a big story, if it goes beyond your own empirical knowledge, if it goes beyond your own interpretative thinking, the inspiration will be inspiration. It will come down to Monas over the OA line, the way most music, for instance, comes."

"Which direction does it travel, up hill or down?" Harwood wanted to know.

"Down your Monas, in the middle," replied White.

"Does it come from O down to A, or from A up to O?" asked Harwood. He was thinking not of the plane, but of a pyramid.

"It comes from A down to O," replied White.

"How does it get over into thought?" asked Harwood.

"You put it there because your thought line is in Monas," said White. "It originates in Monas. It hooks Monas, the circle, in the triangle, to the awareness mechanism and the subconscious hinge or B."

A Flood of Memories

"People speak of having sometimes a flood of memories, which sweep over them and are based upon some thought that occurs to them or some incident," Emmet began. "Here is involved the opposite of dropping things into the subconscious. The flood comes rushing out of the subconscious into the BOC pie. These memories often have considerable emotion attached to them."

"Very simple," replied White. "The first thing that happens is an impingement on the BC line. The field BOC is put in flux and motion and Monas gets the reaction. Then the flood of memory occurs, not only over the mind field, but also there is a direct impact that runs around and touches at the hinge of your whole subconscious line. This is something that has to do with the emotions. So it goes to C as well and picks up an emotion that in the original was exceedingly strong. At C it is mingled with race experience and emotion and degree emotion. It goes back to the subconscious.

"Now the subconscious wants to be in use," he continued. "It must be released. Some time or other everything in the subconscious must be released. It has to be put to some kind of use. If you don't put it to use in your XYZ span, it will have to be accounted for in the 1-2-3 triangle, which is the Orthic triangle. So when a man says he is flooded with memory, that memory is something he has deliberately hidden as deeply as possible in his subconscious. Being deeply hidden, it is of itself seeking release. It floods over the AOB triangle to Monas, it slops over into the BOC triangle. It then runs around and gets into the AOC triangle."

"Does the flood of memory come directly into Monas or does it first flood into the BOC pie?" Emmet wanted to know. "Or does it come directly out of its own pie?"

"Out of its own pie, directly," said White. "But it floods over into the pie where Monas does most of his thinking, most of his emoting, as it were, which is the BOC pie. However, a great many people do not do it this way. A lot of them do it over in the AOC triangle and some do it in the AOB triangle. When you get an upheaval, an upsurge of all dead emotion which you think you have conquered, it is going to concentrate over in the "C" hinge."

"How does it get over there?" asked Emmet.

"By the process of attraction," said White. "You must remember that the entire surrounding field of Monas is a magnetic field and that any magnetic field is made up of particles that are attracted to each other."

The Subconscious in Sickness and Health

In discussing the pathology of the subconscious, two principles were insisted on. First, most memories have an emotional tinge, and consequently may be subject to intentional or even unconscious repression by Monas. Second, the subconscious always attempts to resurface any repressed memory. These concerns are dealt with at length in the chapter on dreams.

At one point the group discussed a case history presented in the chapter on dreams, about a woman who unwillingly stayed home for 20 years to care for her parents -- creating a mountain-sized repression smoldering in her subconscious.

"The therapeutics of the situation would be this," said Emmet. "If your reason induces you to do a thing, then you should cut loose from the emotional drag in the opposite direction. If you do not, you will get in trouble."

"And right there," rejoined White, "is where you can expect help from the AC line. Not through the emotional arc, but through the will arc and that is where you can train yourself to get it."

Harwood objected at this point that the individual would find it impossible to eliminate the emotions. White and Emmet conceded that perhaps one could not accomplish this fully, but that still the cutting off of emotions in such a case was the ideal, that one could minimize the emotional drag and so approximate the ideal.

"Still," continued Harwood, "it seems to me that when these things go into the subconscious as a suppressed wish, the thing that holds them suppressed, must be an emotion of some kind."

"What you say, Beese, is true," said Emmet. "But there is another category of repressions. We have been discussing the case of a person who consciously represses. Now there are cases where things are unconsciously repressed."

"Give an example," suggested White.

"Well, take the case of a small boy who goes into a new school and is picked on by the older pupils," replied Harwood. "He has an impulse to get back at them, but he is scared to do it, because he is too little."

"The too little is important," said White. "All his life he is always too little to overcome the other fellow."

"But I want the mechanism," replied Harwood. "Does he have one emotion suppressed by another emotion, fear?"

"Childhood fear at first," said White. "Ultimately a habit of fear is formed. It could be eliminated if brought into the AOB triangle and submitted to the arc of reason. Because it was a childish affair, he can get away from it."

"But thoughts are associative," said Emmet. "One thought leads to another. A man has an experience. It is in his subconscious. Then he has another experience and this latter experience sets up a train of thoughts and recalls the first experience."

"The first step, replied White, "is for a man to recognize the association. A bygone happening can only be learned from. You have an experience, unpleasant and unhappy. You try to stop thinking about it and it drops into your subconscious. It gets into the subconscious and travels along and hits another subconscious experience, which has had a like effect upon you, maybe 20 years ago. The two fuse together and in consequence you may have an obsession."

"Or perhaps," said White, "you have this accumulation of unpleasant experiences in your subconscious that takes on the color, not only of the later experience, but say of two previous experiences of similar type. Of course this, without your knowing it, will intensify your last experience. How are you going to handle these memories? They will well up out of the subconscious into your activated mind. It is here that this teaching must be made clear, because the only way that a thing can be controlled is up over the OA line through the free will into the supraconscious. You must call on the supraconscious to operate the free will to the degree necessary to pull down the intensity of this triple experience in the subconscious."

"What is the difference between this process and one that causes a neurosis?" This from Harwood.

"The man who truly uses his free will, plus the reason, and knows he is controlling his mind with wisdom, will have no neurosis, because he decides," replied White. "Monas is at the wheel. Neuroses are the result of emotions suppressed, because there is probably shame on the part of Monas or some other opposing emotion."

"The flow is two ways," he continued. "Monas not only receives, particularly over the OA line, but also projects over that line. Monas also projects into the supraconscious through the subconscious. He can create in his subconscious a wish pattern, a habit, that will stimulate in his supraconscious a response that will come to him in one of two ways. Either through the subconscious or direct over the OA line."

Further Thoughts on Mental Health

"While both negative and positive emotion are inherent in the supraconscious, the earth activities as the result of impingement, occur in the subconscious," said White one day. "The reason for this being that as soon as either of these emotions is entertained by an individual, the thought that it engenders is dropped into the subconscious. The strength of that thought will draw out of the subconscious something in addition to the original thought dropped into the subconscious. Or something may be drawn on, that submerges the original thought.

"You will recall that when I first talked to you, I said that the triangle was like a neon sign, that there was an intermingling, an interflow of points of contact, that a thought dropped into the subconscious was run along the AB line like a marble and that it either took on additional coloring from the interflow of the supraconscious or it was sort of whitened out, eliminated by the supraconscious, or at least a start was made toward elimination. If a man is born with a supraconscious, the original degree of which had a large portion of love and understanding, wrong thoughts that come into the subconscious are faded by the supraconscious. There is a judge at the apex."

"I told you that the mind of genius is fed by the supraconscious over the OA line," he said on another occasion. "Now the thing that man needs to get back to and to understand, is that it is over this line that he can contact his supraconscious and draw out of it the super needs, the super food -- something above or beyond the ordinary living."

"How shall he do this contacting?" Emmet wanted to know.

"That is the whole question," said White. "It starts, I think, with a conviction. Conviction is followed by a desire. Desire is followed by a subconscious wish-establishment.

"Once the subconscious wish is established, Monas, reflecting the desired thought, can get a message over the OA line. Some people call it prayer, some call it meditation, some call it contemplation, but it is the ridding by the Monas of the mind of those concepts or things that Monas decides are not what the individual wants his mind to consider or to put into the subconscious.

"Thought creates habit. It is about all that does create habit. There are of course physical habits and there is physical training, as when a pianist trains his fingers. But there has to be first a decision made -- a desire -- a wish -- before even the training of your fingers can be accomplished. If a person is of the cast of mind who is always looking for -- the words do not come tonight -- insults is too strong."

"Rebuffs?" suggested Emmet.

"Thank you," replied White. "If a person is always expecting rebuffs, he will strengthen that idea in his subconscious to a point of almost creating the condition for himself. Your psychologists have termed this an inferiority complex. It is a thought habit."

"How can we get assistance in doing the right thing?" Emmet wanted to know.

"All right," said White. "You wish to have a normally happy frame of mind. Then you must deliberately cultivate that attitude of mind. The best way to do that is, at a time when you have impingements that may worry you, to continually set up the counter action that will create for you the most stability, contentment.

"You cannot control all events, but you can control what you think about events. And it is the repetitious dropping into the subconscious, the wish, the thought, that makes an accumulated response. In addition to that, Monas can reach along his OA line for help."

"How?" This from Emmet.

"That is an active thought also," said White. "It starts with thought. It is a volitional wish that knows it is going to be answered. We are trying to show you how to push a button inside your consciousness to get a desired result. The button in all cases is thought. It is the kind of thought, persistence, faith in your thought, that will produce the result."

"But," said Emmet, "aren't there some devices by which one could accomplish this purpose?"

"If you start from scratch," White replied, "you have got to first establish a habit of surety from Monas. If you can realize that this Monas, this you, is part of the whole -- part of all there is -- and that you have a right to trust this whole, then you will get the help. It is rather like quicksilver. If you break quicksilver in drops, these drops immediately tend to move back and recreate the whole. Now Monas can contact the whole. But so far as the BC line is concerned, all Monas gets there is earth experience."

Chapter 5. Dreams

WHITE proposed a simple classification of dreams based on the parts of the mind as described by the ABC triangle. To understand the system, you need to read his description of sleep, presented below, and the discussion of types of awareness and attention, discussed in a separate chapter. The material below is presented as it occurred. The reader can turn it into textbook style as desired.

"Suppose we discuss sleep," he said one day by way of introduction.

"What is sleep?" he continued. "It is the switching off of the BOC triangle. That does not mean that the individual is anything but fundamentally conscious. Man never loses his consciousness after he has been differentiated as man. That is a big statement. His consciousness is immortal.

"Sleep being the switch-off of the BOC triangle, what is switched on then during sleep? Naturally the AOB triangle. This triangle is always used by Monas even when the BOC triangle is in major operation. It has for its long leg the AB line, which is the actual subconscious or the AB band if you prefer that. And this wells into the operating mind of Monas, which surrounds Monas in his triangle.

"This fact accounts for a number of things. If this AOB triangle is the sleep triangle, then that means the attention line (once again anticipating the chapter on types of attention) is coming down from the emotion arc, which touches the AB line in two ways. "A" is the hinge attached to the supraconscious. Suppose you have some XYZ disorder. People frequently say they won't eat this or that at night because it makes them sleepless, or a heavy meal with some people at night gives them, as they say, bad dreams. Out of this AC line where you have all your qualitative inheritance, which includes the operation of your XYZ triangle pretty much, at least the organs of it, and where you have knowledge that you are unaware of, where you tap a knowledge that you are unaware of, you get a double dipping into the subconscious, when the triangle is flipped over for sleep.

"Now this too is why frequently when in your focused attention day you have been studying a problem you cannot solve, you will wake up in the morning with the clear answer. You have put the question into the subconscious. It is there. And it has run along the subconscious band and in sleep the attention from the emotional arc will pick it up and get your solution."

"Do you mean that there is a better contact between the subconscious and the supraconscious in sleep than there is in waking moments?" Emmet wanted to know.

"Yes," said White; "unless there is a very special stimulation. Now that is not always true but it is normally true. Men can re-establish contact with the supraconscious in their waking moments and that is the desire of men and the need of men. But what I am trying to get to you now is that you actually have that contact and it operates. It operates particularly in sleep."

"Let's picture this on the triangle," suggested Harwood. "You go to sleep. Would that turn the triangle over?"

"It doesn't turn the triangle completely over unless it is complete anesthesia," replied White. "Any strong impingement such as a loud sound, or perhaps the odor of fire, that would touch on the BC line would awaken you. You see there is an alertness in sleep that there is not in anesthesia."

White introduced the classification of dreams in a different session.

"All right, boys, let's take sleep," he began. "This is not, Emmet, a position in the book structure, but the discussion of sleep will appear.

"What is sleep? Sleep as you experience it is a cessation of cognizance, or surrounding or impinging occurrences. One of them may be so strong as to wake you up, but for the normal duration of sleep, it is a cessation of cognizance. That makes the BC line of the triangle dormant for a period. Now you may have sleep with dreams or without dreams that you are conscious of after waking. The mind which only registers cognition through the nervous system, by way of the brain, is asleep. What do you suppose -- in other words, is the AB line dormant in sleep, as is the BC line?"

"I should say not," said Harwood.

"Why not?" asked White.

"Because of dreams," Harwood replied.

"Suppose you don't remember your dreams. You do have dreamless sleep," White suggested.

"The psychologists go on the theory that everybody always dreams, whether they remember or not," said Harwood. "The only failure is in recollection."

"What do you think, Emmet?," said White, determined to get the conceiving stations into the act.

"I don't know," Emmet replied. "I dream very little. That may mean only that I fail to recollect. But if the psychologists say that you dream constantly, then they have conducted experiments and made observations that have led them to that conclusion."

"I cite my own experience," said Harwood, "which is that before I turned my attention to dreams, especially my own, I was under exactly the same impression that Emmet is under, namely that I dreamed rather seldom. But after I turned my attention to it, I found that every single time I woke up, I had a dream on hand. Now that might have been that I dropped a suggestion into my mind, that I would have a dream."

"How many classes of dreams are you familiar with?" asked White, finally broaching the subject that was on his mind. "There are dreams suggested by each happenstance of the day, or a concern of the day. Are you familiar with that type of dream?"

"That is the kind Freud would call all dreams," said Harwood. "He says all dreams deal with material from the previous 24 hours."

"That is not true," said White. "That is, it is not true as far as a day's experience of the mind is concerned. It may be true so far as the day's experience of some disturbed organ of the physical entity is concerned. There is a fine distinction there and one that should be made and understood. Frequently such dreams, as far as the mind is concerned, presage effects -- they foretell. Please discuss that."

"There is a book called *An Experiment with Time*, in which the author tried to pin down definitely prophetic dreams," said Harwood. "And he made a pretty good case of it. Then the Jung School of Psychology, contrary to the Freudian, is based on the general assumption that all dreams are in a sense prophetic; that they show the drift of mental and emotional imputations."

"I want to establish the number of types of dream," persisted White. "That is the afternoon's job. We have the dream set up by the immediate experience of the waking day. It doesn't even need to be the preceding waking day. It can be any day that has enough of shock or emotion in it to make an impact, a rather deep coloration, as it were, on the mind, which drops same into the subconscious. Now that can produce a dream immediately or it can travel along in the subconscious until it meets an analogous experience that is translated into the mundane experience and produces a dream.

"Another kind has not much to do with events or even highly stimulated emotions, but has to do with an imbedded wish in the subconscious itself, something that the dreamer has established as a goal for himself."

"Will you include under wish all sorts of needs which may be really subconscious?" asked Harwood.

"No, not actual needs," replied White. "Perhaps that classification should come before the wish classification, but the wish classification is the aspirational type. It is a dream that results from day dreaming. Day dreaming can degenerate into a subconscious habit. Even after a person has cured himself of day dreaming, thinks no more about this thing, it can come back to bedevil him. I realize as well as anyone that accomplishment, work, comes only after the idea, the aspiration, the dream, the conscious dream that you call day dreaming. I am not talking about the day dreaming that becomes so intense, as to produce a real work. I am talking about the day dreaming that gets no further than repeated wishful thinking without acting."

"All right," said Emmet. "You have two classifications. Of course, Freud puts those all under one heading. That is, I mean to say, that Freud says that every dream is the wishful fulfillment precipitated by any event or occurrence or thought in the 24 preceding hours, as I recall it."

"Can't you see that that's wrong?" said White.

"No," said Emmet, refusing to be railroaded. "I can't see that it is wrong, any more than I can see that it is right. I am just telling you what Mr. Freud says."

"Well, from experience in looking at my own dreams, I would say that I had already decided that Freud was wrong about that," contributed Harwood. "This all makes sense to me."

"Is there a third classification?" This from Emmet.

"Oh yes, there are several," replied White. "Beese brought out the necessity or need dream. The mind is aware through the Monas and the race experience of the supraconscious of many things that it does not so recognize and that are not called into being by an impingement on the BC line. There is that class of dream.

"Let's see if we can produce a good simple example of that kind of dream. One would be -- well, you had a story told you here in this room yesterday evening about a little girl who always has a dollar tucked away some place. She never spends that last dollar. That is a very crude example, but it is quite apt.

"She is less than 14 years old," he continued. "She has always lived in entire comfort and has had few restrictions or refusals of her ordinary desires. Coming out through that child already (and if you could examine her dreams, you probably would find a more extensive application) are race experiences and it comes down along the OC line to her Monas.

"*Instinct*," he emphasized. "That tells her that in her old age she must, as the squirrels take care of food for the winter by storing nuts in the holes of trees, store for her protection. Now dreams of that kind can occur, dreams of accumulation, of safety, of a protective type, where the dreamers set up protection for themselves. Can you, Emmet, see the difference between that kind of a dream and the wishful dream?"

But Emmet wasn't having any. He replied that dreams were a matter of symbolism and that anyway, there were as many types of dreams as there were experiences.

"All right," replied White unabashed. "But what do they symbolize? Back of the interpretation of the psychiatrists or psychologists of the dream is a very simple classification. A great deal of what Dick called hypotheses has been wound around this new science. You take the dream of nakedness. What is that supposed to mean?"

"I don't know." One imagines that Emmet is considering a sulk at this point.

"Well, it goes back to your OC line," supplied White. "It goes straight back to the need for protection covering your body, fear of loss, the racial feeling. Those are fundamentals. Your experience over the years may have intensified that, but surely no mind can be born with racial experience who has not something in his AC line of that type. You see the point of all this is, that by your dreams you can tell the intensity of the type of racial experience impingement content of the AC line."

"Not only the AC line, also the AB line," replied Emmet, awake at last.

"Yes," pursued White, "but if a man's dreams turn one way, then that means that he has had in his degree of quality the racial experience that has come out of one place more than it has come out of another place. That is the reason for this sub-stratum analysis of the origin of dreams. What they spring back to. We have the type of mind that has dreams of ecstasy, of happiness. Those dreams are not unpleasant, but on the contrary, take the dreamer out of his ordinary humdrum existence into something very pleasant."

To place this conversation in context it is necessary to go back to the First Divulgence and its teaching that each of us is born out of a particular degree of quality. This is a basic evolutionary doctrine. What is suggested above is that the details of this heritage can be explored through an analysis of dreams. This is as close as this teaching gets to the Bridey Murphy phenomenon, which White disavows, saying elsewhere that we bring no specific memories with us, only general coloration, with the very rare exception of an individual born out of an exceedingly high degree.

A racial dream can be strong enough to wake the dreamer up. White described this in a different session, one concerned with describing sleep itself. The discussion begins by noting that in sleep the ABC triangle is tilted, so that both lines BC and AB point in the sensitive downward direction.

"When the "B" hinge is down," he began, "your AC line, which represents the supraconscious, is up, directed toward what we call Orthos. Consequently you have your AB and BC lines at an angle for impingement from earth.

"You can be wakened in two ways," he continued -- "by a sensory impingement of bed clothing, for instance, or by the ringing of a bell, these impingements occurring on your BC line. Or you can be awakened by a subconscious call such as occurs when you say to yourself before going to sleep, I want to waken up at 7 o'clock. Some people can do this.

"Or you can be awakened in another way. When the supraconscious is towards Orthos, you have a diffused impression from Orthos. You have two like areas. Your AC line contains in its normal position your race and degree experience. When this face is up and flat, impingement on it can be and is straight. Sometimes you use such impingements and sometimes you don't. You get your rest. Why do you sleep? For refreshment not only to have your body rested but you need also rest for your mind -- for Monas himself.

"Now you have a racial dream. It runs around and gets into your subconscious. You can have degree dreams that will do the same thing. Or you can have dreams that go into the subconscious and are not strong enough to wake you up and you will half remember them the next morning when you do wake up."

"I think the main point has been made," said Emmet, perhaps tiredly.

"Certain types of minds solve problems in sleep," said White, still fresh. "You see, the subconscious can reach up into the supraconscious just as the supraconscious can reach down. You have your open tubes and when we watched her (Ruth) draw the first mobile, the tubes were left open for access to each other."

The team also discussed dreams resulting from repressed material in the subconscious. Harwood White broached this subject one day. "Take the tendency of the subconscious to seek release," he began. "Is this synonymous with the Freudian wish?"

"Freud was on the right track," his brother answered. "But he attributed too much of the content of dreams to sex repression or sex wish."

He followed this remark with an extended speech.

"It is true," he continued, "that one of the driving forces in the physical body in the obstructed universe is reproduction. It is one of the things man has been taught to control. Fundamentally it is biological.

"The upsurging dream up of the subconscious does not necessarily have anything to do with that. It is primarily the thought operation on an experience which Monas performs before it goes into the subconscious -- the depth with which Monas tries to repress this particular thought, the recurrence of it, the sharpness of its original impression, the emotional content with which it was dropped into the subconscious.

"All these things may have nothing whatever to with sex. The eternal fundamental characteristic of the subconscious, which is to release itself, is what brings these dreams into the attention of Monas again."

But Harwood was not so easily satisfied.

"What my question meant was this. Is the tendency of the subconscious to release itself synonymous with an urge to fulfill a wish of any kind?"

"Well, suppose we take an example," his brother replied. He then recited Ruth Finley's overwhelming desire to write books. (This wish was part of her fundamental makeup, and had not been satisfied even by the fact that she had written books. The creative desire continued to upsurge, and though she had written, she felt that she did not have the complete faculty. Hence a certain degree of repression.)

"In the AC line?", rejoined Harwood.

"No," his brother replied. "The repression is in the entire mind, particularly in her BOC triangle."

"Take another example," he continued. "Let us suppose a Mrs. Jones, who was born into a family of children of which she was about in the middle of the stepped down ages. She was, as a child, without the first interest of her parents, or without their last interest, she being the middle child. She was rather a nonentity, but she got along with her family. Yet she was suppressed by the more adult opinions of the older children and she had to give in to the younger children.

"She envied her older brothers and sisters and at the same time was not permitted any authority over her younger brothers and sisters. Still she happened to be born with a great desire to make friends. She married happily but as that worked out, it didn't give her the scope or position she desired. So inasmuch as her overall childhood experience had gone into her subconscious, it colored in later years all her contacts and friendships.

"The result was an inferiority complex. This was only an emotion. If it had been dealt with reasonably, handled with wisdom, it would not have become a complex. But as it worked out in her subconscious, you had a seething cauldron of social desires, all unsatisfied.

"Now let us say she has a dream. A person comes to her exquisitely dressed or she dreams that she was traveling or doing anything that had to do with a general realization of her wish for scope and position. Of course she never dreams definitely about her actual inferiority complex. She dreams only of her release, and she does this symbolically."

But why dream at all?

"The reason for the dream," said White, "is that the supraconscious, the wisdom which she has inhibited, is trying very hard to get this suppressed, unhappy thing out of her subconscious."

"Suppose," said Harwood, "that a person is born with a special potentiality on the AC line?"

"That is a talent, perhaps small," replied White dryly.

In his answer we see his disapproval of mystic withdrawal from active living. But his brother was not easily rebuffed.

"In the course of the person's early life," continued Harwood, "this tendency or bent is repeatedly brought into the BOC triangle by circumstances, and if the circumstances contain a frustrating element so that the tendency is not satisfied and developed, then it drops into the subconscious with repressed emotion attached. When you get enough experiences of this kind piled up and added together in the subconscious, or even if you get one sufficiently drastic experience early in the game, then you would have the condition spoken of as a suppressed wish which tries to free itself and express itself in action. And when it cannot do that, it appears in dreams."

"It will appear symbolically in dreams," replied White. "Why do you suppose that is?"

"Pride, I suppose," replied Harwood. "Or it might be fear that holds it back. Some such emotion."

"It can be emotion," replied White. "But it can also be reason. Also it can be will. Any one of the three arcs can hold it back."

"Suppose," he continued, "a woman who wants to go out into the world and earn her own living. But she has an old father or mother whom she feels needs her service, and so she remains in the home.

Two things decide her: reason and her will, but she does not control the emotional angle of it. The conflict remains in the emotions: she wants to go but instead she stays. And so the thing, having gone into the subconscious, stays there for, say 20 years."

White's group apparently had a body of material prepared to describe dreams encountered while a patient is under anesthesia. It seemed important to them. But the conceiving stations were uncooperative and so most of the material is lost to us. The four abortive attempts I found are presented below.

"I am anxious for a clue as to how the will operates under anesthesia," Harwood began one day.

"During anesthesia," replied White, "you have the "C" hinge at the top. That brings your "A" hinge over here (left) and your "B" hinge over here (right.) That is complete anesthesia, and you have the emotional arc attention line dropped straight down. During that period, if the anesthesia is complete, the attention line is straight. You see it doesn't swing."

"Doesn't swing?" queried Harwood.

"Which attention line -- the emotional?" This from Emmet.

"The emotional attention," supplied Harwood.

"And yet you have very vivid dreams under anesthesia," said Emmet.

"You may," said White. "But such dreams will be a welling up through the AOB triangle and the very fact that the emotional attention does not swing, though it may deviate a little bit --"

"That gives me a big idea," said Harwood, off on a tangent.

"Let's take it up at the next session," replied White dryly.

A second unsuccessful attempt occurred during the conversation reported above that had Ruth drawing a mobile of the triangles. "At this point the communication skidded on the subject of anesthesia dreams," the record reads. "Particularly the anesthesia dreams of Alex. We did not transcribe this matter from the Sound record."

"Alex" was Mrs. Harwood White. One suspects some sensitivity here. Had the recorded record been transcribed we could have drawn our own conclusions. But it was not, and the recordings are all missing.

However, White was not yet beaten. "The first thing this morning," he began another session, "is to get into your minds quite definitely that for the present situation Orthos is fixed."

So far so good. He has them out in the back forty and plans to broach the subject while they are unawares.

"The 1-2-3 triangle is fixed," he continued, obviously on the subject of tipping the triangles. "You have reference to it, yes, both in your ABC and XYZ triangles. The ABC triangle more particularly than the XYZ triangle. Keep these fundamentals in mind, not only in the questions you ask so as not to confuse the station, but also so that you do not confuse your own minds. All of the many questions that I hope you are going to ask, base them on that premise.

"Now let's go back to the subject of anesthesia," he continued without a break.

Nice try but no cigar. "Again there was a skid," the record reads, "and the record was not taken off the Sound Mirror".

There was one more try, likewise unsuccessful.

"Now to finish this question of the type of dreams that come in anesthesia," White began. "You must remember that the impulse of the ABC triangle, as in the case of the XYZ triangle, is to return to norm."

To this brave start the record replies laconically, "Again a discussion of anesthesia was undertaken but again it skidded, and no record was made from the Sound Mirror."

So much for what might have been.

The remaining material on dreams was dictated not by White but by his wife Betty. She was good at this job. The reader will remember that she dictated virtually all of The Unobstructed Universe. The subject matter asks of the reader that he or she have mastered the discussion of types of attention and awareness, which are the most advanced of the areas of the model.

"Now we will go back to the amplified plane of the AOB secondary triangle of recall and operate it in conjunction with the three types of attention -- focused, diffused and background," Betty began. "The first thing to consider is that this line of attention drops from the "C" hinge. It is colored by the arc of emotion, the cones of feeling and intuition and by the band of instinct leading direct to Monas.

"When focused attention is directed to amplified recall," she continued, "you get dreams in sleep. These dreams are fairly well focused. They are frequently remembered and in the remembering you can almost always trace their outer dress to some recent happening. They are rather intuitive dreams -- dreams that have to do with matters not too deeply imbedded in the subconscious, which matters the dreamer can frequently ferret out for himself. Not always, but frequently depending upon the use to which he has put his intellect and reason.

"These dreams are useful to physicians only when a patient is convalescing after a long acute imbalance between his XYZ and ABC triangles. They do not indicate any abnormal mental condition, but rather a tired mental condition or a worried mental condition. Before we proceed with examining diffused attention on amplified recall, are there questions?"

"Let's go on with the discussion," said Harwood.

"First one question." This from Emmet. "Why are these particular dreams rather intuitive, as you said they were?"

"I suppose I used the word intuitive in its less scientific sense," she replied.

"Did you use it in the sense of the use made of it in this divulgence?" pursued Emmet.

"No," confessed Betty. "Let me say just one more thing. These focused dreams deal with matters very close to the surface of the needs of the dreamer. Now we will go on to diffused attention and amplified recall.

"This is a type of subconscious knowledge that may or may not be formulated as a dream. Under certain stresses a person by the use of diffused attention in the subconscious can recall to his awareness things that he has willed to forget. These matters are usually regretful to him -- something that he has put aside in many cases successfully.

"But if he has not been completely successful in putting them aside and if they have not been handled by the quality of his supraconscious flowing over the "A" hinge, they can create a subconscious disturbance that may manifest itself in a restless sleep of unremembered dreams. Here is where the physician can sometimes advantageously step in, and by the use of methods lately developed, and which the doctor can discuss with you, aid the patient in uncovering this subtle and to him unknown and unconnected disturbance.

"Now the third type of attention, background attention on amplified recall, is rarely if ever recognized by the dreamer without specific aid," she continued. "Usually it boils and moils in the subconscious without even formulating itself into the shape of a dream. This happens when individual experiences are accentuated in the subconscious band by racial or degree experiences from the supraconscious. They can be of two types -- a racial knowledge that is below the quality of the individual and so disturbing to him and antagonizing to him, or the opposite, that is, race knowledge awakened in the subconscious so far beyond the qualitative ability of the individual as to upset him.

"Now these things that I have said to you about the three types of attention directed at amplified recall of the subconscious are the barest outline," she continued. "They are suggestive only and are intended to provoke questions and discussion.

"I wish to say that this is a new and enormous field," she emphasized. "It is not your province or ours to go into it too deeply. But it must be recognized and enough must be said for the specialist to be given a new key for analysis. We would like to clear this before we discuss the AOC secondary triangle."

"Why is the word "amplified" used in this secondary triangle or in any secondary triangle?" Emmet wanted to know. "What is the special significance of the word in this connection?"

"The term amplified means pretty much what it says in your ordinary definition of the word. Beese gave Ruth an example of an application of it this morning that is pat. The active part of a radio is the input from the antenna to the grid. The passive part of the radio equals the B Battery. The output or audio circuit equals amplification. In other words, amplification is the result of the other two.

"I am not quite satisfied yet," said Emmet, who was frequently not quite satisfied. "What is the point of similarity between amplified awareness and amplified recall?"

"Similar in intensity," replied Betty. "The 'C' hinge is conditioned by two bands that meet -- perception and supraconscious."

"Suppose we take a concrete example that Beese has been dealing with -- his friend Hooge," she continued. "It is not possible to get the attention line from the "C" hinge as deep in the recall secondary triangle as the amplification plane without a tilt.

"Now it is at this hinge, the 'C' hinge, that the closest connection is made with the XYZ triangle. Imbalance of either triangle puts a stress on the other. Hooge started out with a fairly normal dream difficulty, an adolescent dream difficulty. Certain impingements were made on his perception band and carried into his awareness that were of a highly emotional nature. He had had a bad home experience and was unlucky in love. Both dealing directly as far as he was concerned with his sex instinct. His quality was not of the type to will this out. So the background attention of the supraconscious, which is quite directly connected with race experience and racial instinct, got to operating in his amplified subconscious, where all this stuff had naturally gone.

"Now from here you can take up the doctor's diagnosis. All I have done, and what he could not do at the time because we had not then created the mechanism of the triangles, is to tell you the operation of the resulting fact or condition diagramatically."

"It seems to me the amplification always come from the outside," attempted Harwood.

"You mean that amplification is the result of both active and passive attention," supplied Betty. "Consequently it is a direct impingement from, now get this, the XYZ triangle or the BC line. What does this mean? We are talking, remember, of the subconscious. You can get a subconscious reaction from any internal bodily disturbance or in prolonged awareness disturbance.

"What I was going to say was that in no other of the secondary triangles save that of recall is amplification affected in the same way. It is true, however, that the body and its functions do affect all three secondary triangles and their functions. But the one most affected is the AOB secondary triangle, because the attention line operating through it drops from the "C" hinge, which is the closest connection with the XYZ triangle."

"Is an amplified memory caused by a stimulated emotion?" This from Harwood.

"It could be," replied Betty. "It could also be caused by the type of memory it is, being strengthened or enhanced by direct supraconscious contact over the "A" hinge."

That completes the report on dreams. The reader may have wanted technical detail, but that was not the point of the model. The point is to supply the expert with a framework that reflects the Invisibles' notion of how the pieces work together. The technical details can be elaborated on this underlying framework.

Chapter 6. Diabolism

S*INCE you are so hell-bent on this diabolism*, the doctor said one day, *let's get it out of the way. I want to take up for you two or three of my own cases which I treated on earth.*

Diabolism? It's what the doctor said. We usually call it "possession". It is an unsettling notion for the modern mind neatly sanitized with respect to such possibilities. Anne says that mental unbalance is often caused by obsession. You will find her statement on an unnumbered sheet following Sheet 84 of the records. The doctor's cases follow. They start on Sheet 77 in the records. I have not edited them, except to cast the interchange between the doctor and Emmet as a conversation (which it was in any case); to undo Emmet's identification of himself and Ruth as Darby and Joan; and to use standard terminology.

Case No. 1

This was an unmarried woman who at the age of about 40 became intermittently insane. I did not have her put away. She lived on Market Street and I had been her family doctor for some 20 years. This intermittent insanity started with the first signs of menopause. This is always a drain on the nervous system. The form it took was that she would go into the basement, wrap her arms and legs around an iron pillar there and become almost co-matose.

It took me a couple of years to find out why she did this. The explanation is so simple as to seem almost silly. Her father had had a habit of playing with her from babyhood and swinging her with her head down. The child's auditory nerves were not too stable and this had produced seasickness. When it came along to the time that she had the same type of seasickness produced by an interior physical re-adjustment, she went to the place that seemed to her most stable, though there was now no chance of her being turned upside down.

Case No. 2

This will be cited to call attention to the borderline. It is the case of a woman who lived in the country. You know that more isolated women go insane than any others. Loneliness does it. This woman lived out near Springfield. She had a large family of children, and seemed perfectly normal in most ways. But suddenly she decided that she was Mrs. X, we will say. Now, Mrs. X stood in Akron for what Mrs. John Jacob Astor stood for in New York. She was rich, enjoyed travel, had great beauty and was a social center. She had died when the farmer's wife was a school-girl, several years before her marriage.

Now we are getting to the difference between real obsession and an actual hallucination. You see, the farmer's wife had always wanted the life represented by Mrs. X, so when she had a physical breakdown of her nervous system, her wish desire came to the surface and dominated her thought. Now Mrs. X was dead, but she did not obsess the farmer's wife. It was purely the coming up through the subconscious, to occupy a soft spot, of the wish desire the girl had had all her life.

Case No. 3

This was a man and a paranoiac. He was a German by descent and fixed on a historical character he admired. This was not a desire, but an over-estimated valuation of character. He thought that Bismarck was a kind of God.

In all three of these cases, there was a physical breakdown which weakened causation and permitted these abnormal misconceptions. The first case I cured. The second and third went from bad to worse, and both died in asylums.

Case No. 4

This was the case of a young woman, a very pretty girl, more highly sensitized than any of the other three examples, who had had an unhappy love affair. Her name was Grace and Ruth knew her. The man in the case was not to blame. She fell in love and he did not. This set up a high degree of emotional frustration in Grace. It was an English family, and her father was the John Bull type. He ruled the household. Then he died, and Grace, who had always been gentle and submissive, began to take on the character of her father. She started to drink, smashed and banged and deliberately terrified the people in her house to get her own way. Finally her mother called me in.

It was a case of semi-obsession. This girl's disappointment had weakened her will, wracked her body and scarred her nerves. Then the dominating influence of her father was suddenly removed. In his attempt to console his daughter in her legitimate grief over his loss, he impressed his personality on her to such a degree that she used it as a defense mechanism. The father could not entirely control her. If so, he could have helped her. But as it was, she only made a translation of his earth personality.

Case No. 5

Now we can go into the case of R, which you and Emmet have diagnosed pretty accurately. Your friend was a psychic, a sensitive. He was born with a bad set of nerves and bad coordination -- which was why he never completely accomplished the music he dreamed. He had a horrible sense of frustration. Also he had many things in life which upset him.

R was born out of a degree of quality that his environment and physical body did not permit him to fulfill quantitatively. And this is always bad. He became interested in psychics. In the meantime he had built up in his quantitative thought a defense, a sort of excuse mechanism, for not having been able to fulfill his quality. He was so much a psychic that had he been able to handle it rationally, he would have been able to let through valuable communications.

But there was always war within him. For one thing, he was oversexed and never satisfied. Consequently when the poor old Negro came over here and tried to get in touch with those who meant his stability, R was the only one he could affect. And R did not give him what he really wanted -- love and affection. Rufus succeeded only in translating his horror story of suffering and death through R's soft spot of frustration.

Now after you had got rid of Rufus, you had a number of other personalities to get rid of. Why did these have possession of R? For two reasons. First, because for the time being it was easier for R, not having completed or educated his own ego to develop quantity according to his qualitative degree, to let somebody else run him than to run himself. That is his side of it.

Now the side over here is that the personal characteristics are somewhat slow in changing. Vision is wider; understanding is deeper; will power and selectivity, these being evolution's gift to the individual, are greater. But they are not perfect. The door was open. The ego was attracting to itself a great deal of attention -- undivided and concentrated attention which, had he received it on the concert platform, would never have been sought elsewhere. And so these entities came in. He permitted the lower degrees to rule.

This is not the whole story. Much of the story comes technically at the apex of the triangle. Each experience is like a marble dropped into the subconscious. No marble is ever dropped into the subconscious that does not get a reflex from the supraconscious. In the apex of the triangle, is the power to modify the marble which is a new habit of the individual, and either increase it or diminish it. Take the example of the hereditary drunkard. He can either discard this hereditary influence -- the color flowing in from the supraconscious -- or he can intensify it. In the first case, he will be only a periodic drunk. He will still go on bats, but they will be only occasional.

There is just as much a mechanical framework to the content of consciousness as to the respiratory system. What you think about each marble calls down from the supraconscious the coloration which the marble will have in the subconscious. If you repeat a kind of thinking which you in the apex disapprove, you strengthen by so much a habit which later will hit you in the face.

"Then," interposed Emmet, "you concede the reality of obsession?"

"Yes," replied the doctor.

"Is the obsessor actually malevolent or the station translating erroneously?" Emmet wanted to know. "What is the source of the badness?"

"The source of badness," the doctor replied, "is this: Insanity is negative. It overstresses negative things in the personality of the insane. You will once in a while find a case where the person believes himself to be truly gentle and you will then get a superior type of reflection. But for the most part the negative, or the lower emotional, or more physical qualities of the insane person will call to what were the lower or more physical qualities of the entity communicating. And this is what brings the bad influence. In other words, the selectivity of the mind of the insane person has been so weakened that it is the lower emotions that well up and call to the like of the obsessor.

"Why does the other fellow respond?" asked Emmet.

"Because he is still human and is trying to get rid of the things he has found out he does not want," the doctor replied.

"So he hangs them on his victim?" This from Emmet.

"Let's go back to Rufus," suggested the doctor. "Rufus died of cancer of the intestine. He went to R because R was the one of the boys he could contact most easily. Certainly Rufus did go over with cancer and maybe sometimes he thought of the pain and terror of his illness. Now he did not want to give this pain and terror to R, but he did want to get from R the understanding and sympathy he would have received -- could R have visited him in his last month or two and heard all about it. And R's ego translated Rufus' physical difficulty into an analogous difficulty for himself."

"Did Rufus know the damage he was doing?" Emmet wanted to know.

"No," replied the doctor.

"Why not?" From Emmet.

"Because Rufus was not of a degree high enough to project his intelligence through R to the facts of what R was doing," replied the doctor.

"Why did Rufus do something he would not do on this side?" asked Emmet.

"Because Rufus could not understand that the mere telling of his tale to R would so translate itself," the doctor replied.

"Why didn't the Invisibles help Rufus," Emmet wanted to know. "Why was he cut off?"

"That was Rufus' desire," replied the doctor. "We can no more ram conversion down the throats of ourselves than we can down yours. And we would not do it if we could."

These records are the more surprising when one remembers that Ruth Finley's relationship to her communicators was always a beneficent one. You will find other cases of like disturbances recounted in the books White wrote after his wife died. How widespread this type of phenomenon is, the doctors will have to tell us.

Chapter 7. Tipping the Triangles

IN order to introduce the subject of triangle tipping it is necessary to peek ahead at a subject developed more fully in the chapter on lines of attention. I refer to the so-called "arrows of attention." (There is a diagram of one such arrow at the end of the chapter on the model's diagrams.)

There are three such arrows, one for each of the three arcs. Monas uses them to direct its attention. Just as there are three compartments of the mind -- awareness, recall and aspiration -- so there are three corresponding attention arrows.

The arrows emanate from the arcs and terminate at an arrow head pointing to a particular spot on the opposite side of the ABC triangle. The attention of Monas is thereby directed to the point where the arrow head strikes the opposite side.

Thus the attention line from hinge "A" (the ABC triangle's apex) falls through the middle of the triangle, passing through Monas and striking line BC, the line of perception of the outside world. The arrow is not stationary, but instead hunts along the line BC (perception, or consciousness), from intellect on the left to intuition on the right, depending on the immediate interest of Monas.

Similarly, an attention line drops from the "C" hinge and directs the attention of Monas along the subconscious; and an attention line drops from the "B" hinge and directs the attention of Monas along the supraconscious line.

Only one attention line is active at a time. The others go on "alert" but are otherwise quiescent. This statement holds whether you are awake or asleep. There is never a time in the existence of Monas on the earth plane when one of the attention lines is not focusing.

With that brief introduction to the subject of how Monas directs its attention, we turn our own attention to the subject of triangle tipping. Please use your attention line hanging from apex "A" as you read this section. You need it there at any rate just to read; it picks up the printed word that way, bundles it up, rolls any inflammatory material along the BC line to the "C" hinge and the arc of emotion, then up to Monas, who runs it down the thought line to the arc of reason to see if any of this makes sense.

While reason and the intellect are examining a particular thought, please observe that your attention line has wandered away from the printed page and with it the middle of the line, and gone to the left and is currently directing the attention of Monas to the arc of reason. Thus the attention arrow hunts continuously along the awareness band.

It can also happen that your mind slips spontaneously into a controlled day dream, where the intellect has been upgraded to understanding, and understanding perhaps to wisdom. When this happens, the interest of Monas has passed to the attention arrow arising from the "C" hinge and directing the attention of Monas to the AB line of the subconscious, vibrating as it does so between the sub arcs of understanding and wisdom, and using the recall mind to probe the subconscious store for any relevant information.

Although it is unlikely, still for some this material may awaken their aspiration, thus activating the attention arrow arising from the "B" hinge and hunting along the supraconscious band; directed, surprisingly, by the reason arc with its intellect and understanding subprocessors, but vibrating between conscience and feeling.

But not too long please. We have the current chapter to attend to. There will be much more on this subject in the chapter on types of awareness.

The Normal Positions and Their Meaning

Prior to addressing the subject of tipping, White undertook a review of the triangles in their normal positions. A couple of points stand out. First off, the positions of the triangles have to do with their sensitivity to outside impingement. That is to say, in the standard position each triangle side presents its surface to its impingement environment at a certain angle, and that angle determines the sensitivity of that side to impingements.

The other point is that the three triangles -- ABC, XYZ, and 1-2-3 -- have a standard effect on each other in the normal position. When a triangle twists with respect to the others, that effect changes. For example, the BC line is expected to be parallel to the YZ line. If it is not, the other lines of the XYZ triangle start exerting their influence on the BC line, with strange effects. These off norm positions have curious results and are the things the world has long sought to understand. These details were discussed by the group in some detail.

White broached this subject one day with an extended speech. "The Orthic triangle which we gave you is in a degree a frame of reference," he began. "But it is not your habitual day by day impingement. It is out of what you came and toward which you return. On these two counts it must be taken into consideration, but the thing that is important is the operation of the ABC triangle and the load it carries in the shape of the XYZ triangle. Because after all you are more definitely yourself in the ABC triangle than in the XYZ.

"There is no portion of the ABC triangle per se that can be eliminated without changing the power or the earth evolutionary quality of Monas. You can eliminate certain things of the XYZ triangle and not change the earth evolutionary power of Monas. In fact sometimes a bodily incapacity or handicap or limitation accentuates the operation of Monas.

"For Monas in reality dwells in the ABC triangle alone. The phrase that you have a material body and a spiritual body is true. Monas is the spiritual body. He only inhabits the physical body. The ABC triangle is more of a monistic unit than the XYZ triangle which is made up of innumerable individual unit cells, which in turn constitute the various bodily organs. It is a little like a person inhabiting an entire apartment house instead of only one suite of rooms."

"Are the impingements always on the face, or primarily on the face?" Emmet wanted to know.

"From anything that is outside of Monas himself," said White "-- and you must understand that Monas himself is a little universe, which contains much, and that much of what he contains is in flux, in evolution -- outside impingements, whether perception, subconscious or supraconscious, are primarily on the faces of the triangles."

"You say that anything that is not in Monas, that is to say, anything that impinges from the outside, impinges primarily on the face?" replied Emmet.

"Primarily," said White.

"Now that means that the things that are outside Monas are as follows," said Emmet. "The outside earth world of perception, the outside world of the body of subconscious thought that is not the subconscious thought of the individual Monas particularly, but is rather the subconscious thought of other Monases."

"Mass thought," supplied White.

"Yes," said Emmet. "And on the other side the mass thought, as it were, of Orthic supraconscious. I take that back. It is the mass thought of degree and race experience."

"Right," agreed White.

"Now the question," pursued Emmet. "We know that the outside material world impinges on the BC line -- perception. Does the world of mass thought impinge upon the line AB -- subconsciousness?"

"Yes," agreed White.

"Does degree and race experience impinge upon the line AC -- the supraconscious?" asked Emmet.

"Yes," said White.

"Where does Orthos impinge?" asked Emmet.

"Orthos is all around you," replied White. "We postulated Orthos, however, as being over you, that is, above you for the exigencies of the diagrammatic presentation, and the earth as being below you. Every apex when it is at the top of the triangle is an antenna towards Orthos. In other words, we said, for instance, that when you had complete anesthesia your 'C' apex was at the top. When that is true for your body, for your material existence, your 'C' apex is being fed by Orthos. It takes in the little life line, the little stream of sustenance that keeps these earth deadened nerves and earth deadened consciousness going. Is that clear?"

For readers who think they may have missed something, the above description seems to expect us to be using the mobile of the triangles rather than the printed page. Mobiles hang, through the force of gravity, with the BC line facing the earth and the "A" apex pointing towards the heavens.

The other difficulty is the premature mention of anesthesia. It is presented below in the present chapter; the readers are encouraged to hold their interest in abeyance until then.

The ensuing discussion finds Emmet struggling with the difficulties of this aspect of the model.

"Might I restate it?" he began.

"Yes," said White.

"Then there are two types of impingements," Emmet summarized. "One which we might call primary or the norm. These are the impingements on the three faces. They have nothing to do particularly with Orthos."

"Well---" began White, clearly unconvinced.

"Well they are floating in Orthos of course as is everything else," pursued Emmet. "But we have defined them primarily as perception from the earth plane, perception from the mass subconsciousness which is not Orthos particularly and perception from the race and degree experience which is not Orthos particularly. It is a specialization in each case. These we will call in the earth existence the primary impingements. We are not using the word primary now in the sense of what is more important or what is less important.

"The secondary impingements are Orthic," he continued. "I take it that the Orthic impingements come from whatever apex is at any given time at the top of the triangle. For instance, you use anesthesia as an illustration, with 'C' at the top. Now we will put 'A' at the top. There you have the diluted Orthic content of the normal mind. Put 'B' at the top and what have you got?"

"You have thought reaching out into the universe," said White.

"Toward Orthos?" asked Emmet.

"Yes," replied White.

"In other words, it is at this point, at the apex, at the top apex, whatever it is, that you contact your degree, which is your main approach towards Orthos," summarized Emmet. "All right then, if you agree with what I have said that settles my questions."

"I have another question I want to ask," said Harwood. "Suppose there is no apex pointing toward the top. Suppose there is an apex straight down. Suppose 'B' is down. Then you get the line AC facing straight up."

"That is sleep," said White.

"Now you have got AC facing Orthos," said Harwood. "Give us the implications of that."

"Why not?" replied White. "You are getting rest. Where do you get rest? You have stopped your BC line for impingement purposes. That doesn't mean it is not getting a type of impingement this way." Here the station gave a gesture indicating 'obliquely'. "You could be wakened at any moment by a crash or by a call. Such impingements can awaken you."

"With AC straight across -- asleep -- there is a temptation to think you are exposed terrifically to the Orthic world." This from Emmet. "You are not at all in the position you are when your apex is pointing to Orthos."

"By Jiminy, Beese, he has got it!" ejaculated White.

"Let's explore," said Harwood, taking up the argument. "When you have an apex up. you are extended further into Orthos. So you would get a more direct, a less diluted impingement with your apex up. Now you have got your AC line facing up -- a big wide area, facing up, but it is lower down from Orthos.

"It is a diffused area," said White.

"That's good -- very important," said Harwood.

"But why do you get the diffusion?" This from Emmet.

"You got a big area facing up," said Harwood.

"But why that particular area -- why AC?" Emmet persisted. "It is the supraconscious: the more sensitive face, facing to Orthic impressions. You have turned it toward degree."

"I wouldn't say it was more sensitive to Orthic impressions," said Harwood. "Its receptivity is a special kind. Isn't it?"

"When the supraconscious is towards Orthos you have a diffused impression from Orthos," said White in a speech used elsewhere in this book but repeated here for clarity. "You have two like areas. Your AC line contains in its normal position your race and degree experience. When this face is up and flat, impingement on it can be and is straight. Sometimes you use such impingements and sometimes you don't.

"You get your rest," he continued. "Why do you sleep? For refreshment not only to have your body rested but you need also rest for your mind -- for Monas himself. Now you have a racial dream. It runs around and gets into your subconscious. You can have degree dreams that will do the same thing. Or you can have dreams that go into the subconscious and are not strong enough to wake you up and you will half remember them the next morning when you do wake up."

In another session White called the attention of the group to the second frame of reference -- the XYZ triangle.

"You live in a world of time, space and motion," he began. "You operate in such a world. Your body is obstructed by time, by space and by motion. Your body is your XYZ triangle and time, space and motion constitute the frame of reference for it.

"Your ABC triangle is something else again. It is not obstructed by material time, space and motion. On the contrary, it is only obstructed -- only operated in reference to -- receptivity, conductivity and frequency, which are the co-existents of consciousness in Orthos. The co-existents of consciousness in the material world are time, space and motion. Now have you any questions?

"I have not been thinking of the ABC triangle as Orthic," said Emmet.

"It is not Orthic," replied White. "Its frame of reference is Orthic. Just as the frame of reference of the XYZ triangle is what you know as matter. Now this you certainly must realize and understand. I told you in the beginning that you were working far more in the Orthic than you realize. True you are bound by your BC line. But surely your AB line is not bound by time."

"On the other hand I do not conceive it to be Orthic either," complained Emmet.

"I didn't say it was Orthic," said White. "I said your frame of reference is Orthic for the ABC triangle."

"Why isn't it just as accurate to say the XYZ triangle is the frame of reference for the ABC triangle?" said a skeptical Emmet.

"Because it does not happen to be true," replied White. "The frame of reference for the XYZ triangle is time, space and motion just as they are the frame of reference for all material things. It is the frame of reference for the obstructed universe. Now it is true that you are living in your body. Also that your body is obstructed by all these material co-existents. But this afternoon I want you to get very definitely the difference between the XYZ triangle and the ABC triangle."

"That is perfectly clear," replied Emmet. "However, the ABC triangle is certainly obstructed on the BC line by the possibilities of sense perception. It is obstructed on the AB line by the fact that there is nothing in that line that has not been first received on the BC line -- assimilated and cogitated perhaps but put in via the BC line. So there is limitation. The AC line, on the other hand, might by some stretch be described as framed in Orthos, as having Orthos as its frame of reference. But it seems to me that, in general, ABC is an obstructed universe triangle."

In this speech you can observe a conceiving station doing its homework.

"It is both an obstructed universe triangle and an unobstructed," replied White. "There is much of the ABC triangle that you take with you into the unobstructed universe. There is nothing of the XYZ triangle that you take with you into the unobstructed universe."

"It seems to me that in order to make that perfectly clear, we would have to have our fourth triangle as a frame of reference. Isn't that true?" This from Harwood in one of his unsuccessful attempts to get White to extend the triangles.

"No," said White. "It is absolutely impossible for you to operate your body other than in the obstructed universe. The co-existents of consciousness in the obstructed universe are time, space and motion. Your body has to endure time, go through space in some fashion if it gets from here to there, and the only way it can go through space is by the use of some type of motion.

"Now we went all through this psychological idea of time, space and motion when we got The Unobstructed Universe. We had to postulate Orthos in order to understand it at all. Now it ought not to be so difficult for you to realize that, if your material world is obstructed, as it is, and your psychological world is semi-obstructed, as it is -- and you know it is -- when you get your pluralistic monism set up, as an individual earth unit of consciousness, you must have two frames of reference. You have got to have your obstructed frame, or the material frame, the form frame, and you have got to have the unobstructed frame, the Orthic frame, or if you wish, the spiritual frame. Now if that weren't true, all of the accepted material that we struggled over in The Unobstructed Universe would be false.

"Now I haven't said that the only frame of reference for the ABC triangle is the Orthic frame. Ultimately it will be, when you take a portion of the ABC triangle into the unobstructed universe.

"But even where you are, there are things about the ABC triangle that are unobstructed. That is what makes it possible for you to understand that there is such a thing as Orthos. It is on these facts that are in you that we have been able to postulate this whole idea of Orthos.

"Now this has to be very thoroughly understood by both of you before we can start twisting the triangles, because you have got to remember that your body is obstructed, that you yourself, that your Monas, is obstructed only so far as it is occupying, for the experience of earth -- for the gaining of quantity -- this body of yours.

"That is not to deny that all consciousness has form. We have form here. You cannot see it yet. You have form on earth that you cannot see. But you know it is there."

Triangle Tipping in Daily Living

Managing the triangles is the job of daily living. It is like surfing. You want the three triangles always to be in balance. But their normal action is to wobble as their faces are impinged upon, or on input from their fellow triangles, just as their normal proclivity is to return to a balanced position. This does not necessarily happen automatically. If the wobble is large enough to attract the conscious attention of Monas -- that is to say, to engage the BOC secondary triangle, otherwise known as the awareness mind -- then Monas will want to make a conscious effort to redress the imbalance.

"For the purposes of the divulgence of the Content of Consciousness, which is your earth existence, the Orthic or 1-2-3 triangle is stationary," said White one day. "The 1-2-3 triangle is fixed. You have reference to it, yes, both in your ABC and XYZ triangles. The ABC triangle more particularly than the XYZ triangle. Keep these fundamentals in mind, not only in the questions you ask so as not to confuse the station, but also so that you do not confuse your own minds. All of the many questions that I hope you are going to ask, base them on that premise.

"I think we had better give you a little talk on the wholeness of the triangles," he continued. "They are correctly named, that is, all of the areas, and you have done a wonderful job with it all. The thing I want to impress upon you next is that these positions of the triangle in their norms (are important): just the position retains something of its color, of its adaptability, of its capability, of its kind. For instance, the AC band, having a background of the Orthic triangle as frequency, is fairly constant as to its character. That is, you have got that as its fundamental quality. And if you tip the XZ line away from its position that ordinarily corresponds to the 1-3 line of the Orthic triangle, the line that comes up (the YZ line) gets a little of that color.

"The same thing is true about yourselves. You have an emotion. You get an impingement through the YZ line that is transferred to the BC line. That is what happens, you know. You get an emotion as a result of this impingement. Well, you cannot get anything of that sort happening that you don't get a little twisting and wobbling of your triangles. The very stable person, the person who has a very strong will, can keep his triangle with all of its impingements pretty much in the norm, so that he can handle most of the resulting action in the ABC triangle, or even a pain resulting in the XYZ triangle impinged upon the brain. He can keep himself pretty normal. But all of these slight tiltings out of the norm that are not as great as sleep or anesthesia, or as a profound illness perhaps, are the daily action of the balance. That is what we mean: that you want your triangle balanced.

"Now as to the turning of the triangles, we gave you these triangles to turn because an impingement on the XYZ triangle usually throws it a little off norm. The same is true, as you well know, of your ABC triangle.

"These off norm positions have curious results and are the things you have long sought -- and the world has long sought -- to understand. The juxtaposition of the off norms are the interest points.

"You also had a phrase that was caught in one of our former dictations concerning the 'face'. Now, though it is perfectly true that Monas is impinged upon on all sides at all times, that the universe is a whole, that it is all around you and that its influences are all around you, it is also true that your impingements are most acute on the BC line. That is just a fact that you accept. If you are blind to earth, to matter, that does not mean necessarily that you are blind to the subconscious band or the supraconscious band. In fact it usually intensifies them.

"Now for the purpose of the diagrams and to make all this more plain, let us assume that Orthos is above, as indeed it is in the solar system around the planets. In other words earth is earth; earth is material; you are living on earth, and it is the earth impingement that you have to deal with every day and that we want to show you, we hope, how to handle more efficiently and more satisfactorily to yourselves.

"So we have the norm line at the base which is toward earth, with your feet on the ground as they say, and the apex pointing up, and we will call that toward Orthos. At least it is not the material thing that you deal with daily. Now all the time that your norm BC is toward the base, and receiving earth impingements, you have two sides of your triangle with their apex into Orthos, which means that impingements from Orthos on the subconscious and the supraconscious are oblique. They are always there. Everybody has them. The apex reaching up into Orthos is sort of like a lightning rod feeling for the lightning -- a -- how shall I say it -- a sensitive --"

"An antenna," supplied Harwood, ever the engineer.

"Antenna, as it were, which is better than lightning rod," continued White. "Now the tipping -- these sides of the triangle we can know will be easy to understand if we just call them faces. So you see that as you tip your triangle you get less impingement on certain faces and more impingement on others.

"It is seldom that an individual is at norm. There are various people who depend a great deal on their subconscious. You may be at norm at ten o'clock in the morning and then you become engrossed in some deep study in which you are fishing in your subconscious for memory, for empirical knowledge, perhaps to write a book from, perhaps to do something else with, and you will get a slight tilt. So that instead of your subconscious coming at its normal angle, you just get a little tilt so that you get a little more impingement on the face.

Case History No. 1: the Furious Man

By way of illustration, or perhaps as a boon to the programmer who has to develop files to exercise the system, White described a small number of concrete case histories.

"Well now suppose there was a man -- this is a hypothetical case -- who got angry quite easy, and something happens in the outside world that makes him perfectly furious," he began. "Place that impingement first on the XYZ triangle and then on the ABC triangle using the Orthic triangle as your stationary frame of reference."

"Well, there would be a sensory impingement on the YZ line, which would then impinge on the BC line." This was Harwood's interpretation.

"Try to see first what the effect would be on the XYZ triangle," prompted White.

"Well," attempted Harwood, "on the XYZ triangle, it would travel along the YZ line toward 'Z' --"

"Well, what is at 'Z'?" White interrupted.

"The endocrine glands and digestion," said Harwood.

"And what would happen?" White parried.

"There would be a sudden discharge of adrenaline," said Emmet, getting into the conversation.

"And your digestion would quit," said Harwood.

"All right," approved White. "What would happen to the triangle? Where would the weight be? What adjustment of balance --" White began.

"The 'Z' hinge would drop down,' said Harwood, firing on all cylinders.

"All right," said White. "Now drop your 'Z' corner just a little. We have got the adrenaline gland working. Now what happens?"

"Now it gets into the theater of emotion, into the 'C' arc," interposed Emmet. "Then what happens?"

"It depends on the man," said White. "It depends on the quality of the individual. He can let his ABC triangle be pulled into exact juxtaposition with his

XYZ triangle or he can keep it in balance. Now suppose it is pulled down."

"Then he wants to go into action and hit somebody," said Emmet.

"All right," said White. "Now what happens? You have got the adrenaline glands working. Now what is the other stunt?"

"Now he has got free will deflected off of '1,'" said Emmet.

"You are right," said White.

"And he has got his intellect and his understanding and his reason deflected off of '2,'" said Emmet.

"You bet," said White.

"He is out of focus," continued Emmet. "So he becomes a creature of impulse."

"He is deflected from contact with Orthos and isolated as an individual," Harwood contributed. "He is all by himself, and there is no more Orthic support. Meanwhile he is projecting himself into the world more prominently on the emotion end of his two triangles."

"Now listen a minute," said White, warming up to his point. "You have got the whole thing deflected and your AC line, instead of being at norm, is turned more toward the vertical. All of your race inheritance, everything you ever had, is rolling right straight down to the 'Z' hinge."

"Down hill," said Harwood. "It has got a steep drop."

"You see what you are up against," said White.

"Cave man, animal inheritance," said Harwood.

"Sure," agreed White.

"That's interesting," said Harwood approvingly. "Good stuff. That is logging in the tall timber."

"That is one of the great simplicities," said White.

The group returned to this case history on the following day. "Let's go back to our furious man of yesterday," said Harwood. "Your 'C' hinge being down drags your thought downhill too, doesn't it?"

"When your 'C' hinge is down, where does your 'B' hinge go?" replied White. "Why, it goes up toward the subconscious. And that brings into play all the subconscious resentments you have kept piled up since you were a kid. But if the tilt of your furious man could have been handled quickly enough by will, then he would not have socked the other fellow."

"His ABC triangle would have bounced back pretty fast," suggested Harwood.

"It would have bounced back and quieted him down and he would have had a minute or two of clenching his fist and maybe cursing a bit, and that would have been that," said White.

"And by that time his XYZ triangle would have gone back up," concluded Harwood.

Case History No. 2: an Artist

"Now what would you like to discuss next?" began White on a subsequent occasion.

"Well, let's talk about some pleasant emotion," interposed Emmet. "We have talked about a disagreeable emotion. Can anyone figure out something that is pleasant?"

"Suppose we took the triangle the other way," said White. "Much depends on which triangle tilts first. In the case of the angry man, the XYZ triangle tilted first. But what of the lift you get out of anything that is so-called artistic -- a beautiful building, music, a good play or movie, anything of the sort? What would happen first in such a case, do you think?"

"Impingement on the YZ line," suggested Harwood.

"Would it tilt the YZ line?" asked White.

"I wouldn't think so, no," replied Harwood.

"It might or it might not," White continued with his illustration. "It would depend on the intensity of the thrill."

"I don't think it would tilt the YZ line first," said Harwood. "I think it would go to the BC line next."

"All right, and what would happen there?" White queried.

"Then it would travel over to the 'B' corner and the 'C' corner," said Harwood.

"You can't have it go both ways," White objected.

"Why not?" said Harwood.

"It might go preponderantly one way," said Emmet. "But one's appreciation of a great work of art might be both intellectual and emotional."

"It might give you the thrill and arouse thoughts," Harwood replied. "But it seems to me the thrill would come first. Let's say it would go the 'C' corner first."

"No, it would go the 'B' corner first," White corrected.

"Why?" Harwood wanted to know.

"Because at the 'B' corner you have your intellect," said White, "and it is your intellect that is aroused first. Now you may get an emotion out of it but first you have got to have an intellectual appreciation of the thing. So here you get a tilt of your ABC triangle. Now it may be so great a tilt that it will pull your XYZ triangle down too. But would it? Wouldn't it have to be quite a jolt to do that?"

"Yes, that's true," Harwood agreed. "But after it went down to the 'B' corner it might go to the 'C' corner and arouse emotion."

"But would it travel over the BC line?" asked White.

"No," said Harwood. "It would travel across the BOC secondary triangle."

"Sure," agreed White. "Now you see you have a new picture."

Case History No. 3: the Intellectual Man

"Now suppose a person who is so fascinated with intellectual pursuits that his ABC triangle is completely out of focus," said White by way of introduction. "What is going to happen to his XYZ triangle? Look around you in the world."

"It would be pulled down to the 'Y' corner," suggested Harwood.

"Well, what is at the 'Y' corner?" queried White.

"The excretory glands and the respiratory system," said Harwood.

"You would break out in a cold sweat," contributed Emmet.

"The digesting thing would lift up in the air and you would get a skinny guy," suggested Harwood. "It would put the emotions up out of focus with earth experience and the intellect down into it too much."

"Wait a minute," said White. "You are going a little too fast. Suppose the ABC triangle tipped down with all this intellectual thrill that you get and your XYZ triangle stays stationary."

"With your 'B' hinge tilted down and your 'Y' hinge not, all of your foci would be out of register," replied Harwood.

"They would not be out of register," corrected White. "They would be out of norm but --"

"I mean that A would not be on 'X' and so on," said Harwood.

"Well," said White, "one thing you would get if you overbalanced intellect without trying to keep your XYZ triangle in position, would be an emotional reaction -- usually not eating enough because your digestive system is over there. That is the thing that feeds the XYZ triangle. Either you wouldn't eat enough or you would eat too much. This is one of the reasons doctors always advise people who have desk jobs, who use their minds to the exclusion of their bodies, to have some special exercise or play or something that keeps the balance in trim. It can stay out of balance for a while, but the minute you begin using your XYZ triangle, you pull it back into place with your ABC triangle.

"Now Beese," he continued, "you have taught tennis and you know that the game is a very keen employment of both the ABC and the XYZ triangles -- that it is not only a game of the XYZ triangle but it is the man who thinks quickly, who has quick perception, whose BC line is very sharp watching the frame of reference of his XYZ triangle that wins.

"Well, now, one of the uses of the 'B' hinge is to sharpen the BC line. You see, you have got to have a sharp BC line to get ahead of the other fellow, don't you? It is the YZ line, too, of course. But it is the taking in and assimilating of the sensory perceptions that has to be really sharp. If you don't deal with them quickly, you might just as well not have them so far as result is concerned."

"But do you sharpen them by tilting the BC line?" This from Emmet.

"Yes," said White. "You do sharpen them in that way."

"You bring your intellect closer to the field of sense perception," suggested Emmet.

"Yes, you do," White agreed. "Now in your mobile keep your YZ line straight and bring down the 'B' hinge until it is touching the line. Now you see in the segment of intellect, you have a focused impingement of Monas himself down into the sensory region seeking reception."

"Are we talking about a work of art of a game of tennis?" asked Emmet.

"It doesn't make any difference," said White.

"Yes," Harwood agreed. "Anything you use your brain on, your intellect."

"That takes care of that hinge," Emmet concluded. "Now you have got your emotions, which are involved in a work of art, if not a game of tennis."

"Well, if you lose in tennis, they are, and also if you win," said White.

"Yes," agreed Emmet. "They probably are involved even during the game. But in any event you have your emotions now move up. What does that mean? In other words, what is the difference between moving them down to YZ and up to XZ?"

"Well, for one thing," White suggested, "it is possible that they might stimulate the autonomic nerves so that you would get some help from there."

"Yes," Emmet agreed. "Now what if I turned the 'C' hinge down toward the sensory perceptions?"

"As I see it," Harwood responded, "if the 'B' hinge is dropped, that tends to raise the 'C' hinge toward the reservoir of racial experience which then pours content into that corner and so tends to weight it down. Isn't that the way equilibrium tends to reestablish itself?"

"It does two things," said White. "It pours content down toward the 'B' hinge, without having it necessary to run around through the emotions --"

"Wait a minute --" Harwood interrupted.

"All right," resumed White impatiently. "Your 'C' is up here pointing into the supraconscious. Now it is an open line right straight down to 'B' at an angle. Now what would the --"

"Gee whiz!" interrupted Harwood again. "I am stuck now. Let me see. You tilt the triangle and 'C' approaches quality. Then the AB line is more nearly vertical, so that the contents in that tend to all slide down hill, you said."

"You have your 'B' hinge seeking a sharper sensory perception," said White. "Your BC line, therefore, is tilted up toward the right so that it goes to the autonomic nervous system, which in turn, in your frame of reference, is frequency, quality. Now certainly your quality, if it can run down hill toward your intellect, is going to give a different slant to whatever perception you have sharpened than it would to someone else's perception which has been sharpened at the same point, isn't it?"

"It is not quite clear to me how it runs down hill," said a pragmatic Emmet.

"It runs down the BC line," supplied White.

"I have the diagram before me," said Emmet. "May I state what it says to me?"

"Please do," said White.

"Hinge 'B' containing intellect is down toward YZ which represents the sensory and motor nerves causing them to be perceptionally sharpened," said

Emmet. "If you are looking at a stage play or movie, you see better. If it is a case of a movie, your hearing is better; you pick up more. 'C' is raised in the direction of the autonomic nervous system, the cerebellum, frequency and quality. So the feelings are increased, and the resulting emotions are exalted into the qualitative side of things, with a nervous system intervening which is more or less automatic. You don't have to do anything about it -- it just flows. That is what the mobile would show."

"Then how does the quality get over to the intellect?" White wanted to know. "You see that is why we have all these open spaces. It is so that the stuff can flow around."

"It doesn't seem to me it could go down to the BC line," said Emmet. "That represents the senses."

"But it does go down to the BC line," said White. "It goes straight down to the focused sense perception. And it may be that it enhances other sense perceptions on the way. Just as a person bereft of a given sense perception finds his other sense perceptions enhanced.

"Now that doesn't mean that it cannot come to intellect in two ways. It does. It goes down the BC line to enhance the senses for your further appreciation and enjoyment. Also if this works at all, it must go down through the emotional arc because the emotions are very closely tied to your quality. There you get your emotional arc working too. It may even get away from you a bit, the way it does sometimes at a movie. When this happens, it is perhaps because your quality is overly sympathetic. Then the emotion goes up the instinct line to yourself and you begin to think about it, and then it goes down to your intellectual perception where you are seeing all this. Do you understand that?"

"Not exactly," said Emmet. "It doesn't seem to me that the intellect is involved there at all. If your emotions are disturbed, your intellect can tell you it is all darn nonsense, but the emotions go right on working."

"Why, yes, your emotions go right on working but your intellect has been involved to the extent that it is telling you it is darn nonsense," replied White.

"Well, what happens is, you see something," said Emmet. "It awakens a thought. The thought goes up to Monas. Then if it is going to awaken emotion it has to go down the instinct line."

"Then the emotions are stirred," White agreed. "You see, the thing runs two ways. You get your highly perceptive focus concentrated on the YZ line. You understand that, don't you?"

"I get it that something is happening on the YZ and BC lines, and this goes into my thought," said Emmet.

"And it may go in the other direction across the secondary triangle," said White.

"Yes," said Emmet, "it may flood the entire secondary triangle arousing all its functions at one and the same time."

"And the returning flood may gravitate across the secondary triangle too," said Harwood. "It is not confined to the BC line."

"But it does go down the BC line as well," said White.

"Intensifying your perceptions," supplied Harwood.

"Those perceptions in use at the time," corrected White. "Now suppose you very much enjoy eating -- that taste means a great deal to you. In this case your sense of taste would be stimulated, also your sense of smell. You realize, don't you, that you cannot have any one sense stimulated without having at least one other stimulated at the same time?"

"Well," said Emmet, "that seems to be a bypath."

"No," said White, "it is not."

"Well, now suppose you tilt your triangle down at 'B', suggested Harwood. "This also makes the AB line more vertical so that things run down it faster and everything piles up in that corner from your subconscious."

"Yes, you get quick reactions from your subconscious," agreed White. "The man who tilts his ABC triangle toward his intellect, has a great power over his subconscious."

"Those are the good effects," agreed Harwood. "But suppose you have a guy who does this all the time and when --"

"And never gets back into focus with his XYZ triangle?" interrupted White.

"Yes," said Harwood. "Then what?"

"Well, then you got a guy who has a neurosis or nervous prostration or something," said White. "You see, you have to take into consideration this lesser triangle which you have to live in, just as you have to consider a house you live in. If you let a house go to ruin, pretty soon you just can't live in it."

Extreme Tipping

Three modes of extreme tipping are described in the sitting notes. These modes are sleep, anesthesia and mediumistic communication.

In sleep the ABC triangle rotates counterclockwise and attempts to move the "C" apex toward the top, with the AB line or subconscious attempting to become the base.

In communication the ABC triangle rotates clockwise and attempts to move the "B" apex toward the top with the AC line attempting to become the base.

In anesthesia, complete anesthesia, one has apex "C" at the top and the AB line perfectly horizontal and at the bottom.

A side positioned at the bottom and parallel to it gets its impingements normal (at right angles) to its surface and has its impingement sensitivity enhanced. The remaining two sides face upwards at an angle and receive impingements obliquely, lessening their force. Bear these basics in mind in the following material taken from the sitting notes, in which the various points relating to extreme modes of tipping are developed little by little over many conversations.

In all the discussions the BC line is normally the base of the ABC triangle. White notes that this is not an absolute requirement, but rather a historical peculiarity which has implications for cultural development. The conversation opens with a reference to the attention lines described briefly at the beginning of this chapter.

"The dotted line in the triangle that appeared early in this divulgence and which you were again discussing last evening, does swing from the various arcs," he began. "It is there attached. It is controlled, as is all else in the triangle, by Monas. But it is freer, more flexible and is always the line of focused attention.

"Do not confuse this dotted line of focused attention leading from the arcs with another type of attention that has been developed in the past few centuries by man along the BC line. The second type of attention, which has become acute in the mechanistic age, is known as diffused attention. It is important and has much to do with the lack of concentration and contact with the arc swinging from the AB and AC lines. The reason for this is that in the present day the normal position of the triangle is with the BC line as its base.

"Of course that is always true when Monas is developing all the earth plane, but the triangle is malleable. You discovered last evening that it could be tipped.

"For instance, when you are under the control of an anesthetic, the whole point of that is to tip your triangle. The thing that happens is that your triangle is thrown over and the base of your triangle becomes the AB line. That is anesthesia. There are people who, through self-training or certain inherited qualities or because they were born out of an infinitely high degree, can tip their triangle, so that the AC line becomes the base. When this occurs, you have completely self-induced anesthesia or concentration to the nth degree."

"When the triangle is tipped, what is BC doing?" Emmet asked.

"It is still a side of the triangle and can be impinged upon through the senses," White replied. "Some people under the influence of an anesthetic can bring back memories of what happened in the operating room."

"Why is the tipping of the triangle a better symbol for anesthesia than simple collapsing of the lines AB and AC?" Emmet wanted to know.

"I never said that collapsing of the two lines occurred except when Monas is ready to be transferred from the obstructed to the unobstructed universe," White replied.

"Turning the triangle around gives a picture that depicts a condition existing when the bottom part of the triangle represents the major awareness," said Harwood, warming to the task. "When the BC line is at the base, you are aware in that department. When the AB line is at the base, you are aware in that other department."

"This is too advanced," said White. "Let it go for now."

"I want to go on a little farther about the tipping of the triangle," he began on another occasion. "Monas of course has to stay put. The ordinary position of his triangle, particularly when he is awake, is with Apex 'A' at the top.

"What is sleep? Sleep is a tilt of the triangle with the apex 'C' approaching the top. What is total anesthesia? It is the complete tilt of the triangle with apex 'C' temporarily definitely at the top. You see the triangle does not have to go clear over, but a deep sleep will put it clear over. Complete anesthesia naturally dissociates focused attention and you do get the triangle clear over."

The discussion then turned to the subject of Ruth's communicating mind. Emmet thought Ruth picked up messages on AC, that they were then transferred to her OA line. But also Emmet thought she continued to register on the BC line though without later memory of such registration.

"She is still functioning on the BC line," said White. "You see, in order to have the OA line operate, we have to tilt her triangle so that the AC line base is just over the border."

* * *

"A new member of the party," said Emmet one day, noting the announced presence of White's wife Betty, an unusual occurrence.

"Are there any questions?" asked White.

"No pressing questions," rejoined Harwood.

"Then suppose we discuss sleep," began White. There followed an extended discussion already used in the chapter on the subconscious. I extract here those parts necessary for the discussion on tipping.

"What is sleep? Sleep being the switch-off of the BOC triangle, what is switched on then during sleep? Naturally the AOB triangle. It has for its long leg the AB line, which is the actual subconscious. And this wells into the operating mind of Monas, which surrounds Monas in his triangle.

"This fact accounts for a number of things. If this AOB triangle is the sleep triangle, then that means the attention line is coming down from the emotion arc, which touches the AB line in two ways. 'A' is the hinge attached to the supraconscious. Suppose you have some XYZ disorder. People frequently say they won't eat this or that at night because it makes them sleepless, or a heavy meal with some people at night gives them, as they say, bad dreams. Out of this AC line where you have all your qualitative inheritance, which includes the operation of your XYZ triangle pretty much, at least the organs of it, and where you have knowledge that you are unaware of, where you tap a knowledge that you are unaware of, you get a double dipping into the subconscious, when the triangle is flipped over for sleep."

"Do you mean that there is a better contact between the subconscious and the supraconscious in sleep than there is in waking moments?" Emmet wanted to know.

"Yes, unless there is a very special stimulation," said White.

"Let's picture this on the triangle," said Harwood. "You go to sleep. Would that turn the triangle over?"

"It doesn't turn the triangle completely over unless it is complete anesthesia," replied White. "Any strong impingement, such as a loud sound or perhaps the odor of fire, that would touch on the BC line would awaken you. You see there is an alertness in sleep that there is not in anesthesia."

"Right," said Harwood. "So it is turned part way over. Now that would put the attention line from 'C' in operation."

"Yes," agreed White.

"Now, if before you go to sleep, you set your will in motion --" Harwood began.

"No, that is just why you must not try to will to do things," rejoined White.

"Well," replied Harwood, "if you activate your will before you go to sleep in the direction of the solution of your problem, then when you go to sleep you might say that your will retains a glow of activation so to speak and draws the attention line to that end. This would emphasize the connection between the AC and AB lines by having the attention line pulled over there."

"Yes," replied White. "But suppose ABC with its BC line down. Now you go to sleep. 'C' comes up a little bit and you get a tilt. And you see 'A' tilts down toward the thought arc, and you don't get a complete tilt of 'C'. You have put in your mind this problem and it is a little bit of an emotional problem with you. You want to solve it. Consequently you get two pulls on the AC line. You get it at the 'A' arc and you get it through the attention line. The 'guardian of the threshold' as it were, in sleep is the attention line from the arc of emotion at the 'C' hinge, does that mean anything?"

"What do you mean by the 'guardian of the threshold'?" Harwood wanted to know.

"It is the guardian of the connection between the ABC triangle and the XYZ triangle," said White.

"Please say it over again," prompted Harwood.

"There is never a time in the existence of Monas on the earth plane when one of the attention lines is not focusing," said White. "That is what I mean."

"Then during sleep, the C' (the C attention line) is doing the focusing?" asked Harwood.

"Yes," said White. "But suppose you have a loud crash in the next room. Then flop goes the triangle and you get your other attention line in operation."

"Here is a hypothetical case," proposed Harwood. "You have a problem. Just as you are drowsing off you say to yourself, 'I want a solution'. Then when you go to sleep, your attention line, C', goes to work to find the solution. It would have to swing down to the 'A' hinge to find it because there is where the AB line contacts the supraconscious."

"No, it would not," White replied. "For this reason. The area of the "C" hinge is already hung from one side on the AC line. You see one thing you have not completely realized is that these arcs are actual connections. Let's take ABC again. You have the arc of free will up here. It connects your subconscious and your supraconscious."

"What does that connection mean?" Harwood asked. "What function does it illustrate?"

"It illustrates first the gift of the free will," said White.

"It illustrates the existence of the free will," Harwood repeated. "What does the connection illustrate?"

"The connection illustrates that if you permit, if you will, you can get a constant flow from the supraconscious into the subconscious," replied White.

"Over the will line?" asked Harwood.

"Over the will line as well as at the hinge," replied White. "And you can stop it."

"Over the will line?" asked Harwood.

"Over the will line," replied White.

"You might not be able to stop it over the hinge," supplied Emmet.

"You never can stop it over the hinge," replied White. "You see that is what modern education and modern life has done."

"Let's not repeat that one," said Harwood. "We know that."

"But here is where it has done it," insisted White. "It has not done it with the emotion arc. The emotion arc is also attached to the AC line but it is not attached to the subconscious line. And there you use it. You get it with emotions, with race emotions, with intuition.

"Suppose you have a sudden fright -- you will get it then as a reflex out of that line, and the reflex may be muscular from XYZ or it may be the result of an act or a thought on your part that you had never had before or that you picked out of the air, as you think, to correct something. These connections of these arcs to the various lines are of very great importance. Think that out and you will see why it is important and why the arc from the AC line to the BC line is called emotion. You can see the inevitability, can you not, of the conscious line being joined to the subconscious line by the arc of reason?"

"One has hardly questioned that, inasmuch as you reason from the data of sensation plus the recallable items that are in the subconscious," said Emmet.

"Let's get back to sleep," prompted White.

"Let's get to sleep again," said Emmet, willing to let the conversation turn facetious.

"You are asleep," said White, obviously game. "Sleep occurs with different people, at different angles of the tip. This is hard to say."

"At different degrees of the tipping," suggested Emmet.

"Yes, the same as bellboys," Harwood chimed in.

"Some are 10 cents, some 5 cents and some aren't worth anything," said White. "When it isn't worth anything, that means insomnia. The darn thing won't tip."

"Or get tipped," said Harwood. "I have a question. In the daytime the A' line of attention is activated mostly by will, but can be attracted by either emotion on the one side or thought on the other. Now when you are asleep, you have the C' line of attention operating, pointing toward the AB line, and it moves back and forth on the AB line."

"A little lopsided," said White.

"That line, namely C', is controlled largely by emotion," said Harwood. "But you have will on one side and reason on the other, which can pull it to some extent. How can the will, when you are asleep, pull the line over in that direction? That is what interests me."

"It cannot pull it as easily as thought, because the tip of the triangle is this way (to the right)," said White. "Consequently your will is very much in abeyance. That is one reason why it is so hard to give some people an anesthetic. They will not take it and you can't get the triangle completely tipped, and yet when the triangle is completely tipped, the attention line from the arc of emotion can go clear over to will. Just as the attention line from the arc of will can go clear over to emotion when 'A' is straight up and the BC line is flat, that is during waking moments."

"One point you just touched on," said Emmet. "You spoke of conditioning yourself to solve a problem with a wish in the emotion arc, rather than through a volition in the will arc."

"I said something like that," said White.

"You didn't get it quite over?" asked Emmet.

"Don't will a thing," said White. "Emotionally wish it. Desire it."

"Desire power," supplied Harwood.

"Desire power will go further that way than will power," said White, "because the will power is iron, rigid, not flexible like emotion."

"I am anxious for a clue as to how the will operates under anesthesia," said Harwood.

"During anesthesia you have the 'C' hinge at the top," said White. "That brings your 'A' hinge over here (left) and your 'B' hinge over here (right.) That is complete anesthesia, and you have the emotional arc attention line dropped straight down. During that period, if the anesthesia is complete, the attention line is straight. You see it doesn't swing."

"Doesn't swing?" asked Harwood.

"Which attention line," asked Emmet. "The emotional?"

"The emotional attention," said Harwood.

"And yet you have very vivid dreams under anesthesia," said Emmet.

"You may," said White. "But such dreams will be a welling up through the AOB triangle and the very fact that the emotional attention does not swing, though it may deviate a little bit --"

"That gives me a big idea," said Harwood.

"Let's take it up at the next session," said White.

There was considerable discussion about the art of communication -- that is to say, about how White was able to use Ruth to say what he wanted to say. There was much of the same in White's earlier work, but it was of a different sort, based on different premises. The discussion in these sittings is in terms of triangles, and it is all new.

"It is on this triangle and through it that you get communication as you have it right now," said White at one point. "This is a high degree of use in your day and age of this triangle. This triangle, to be used as it is now being used by Ruth, has to be tipped. It has to come over through the -- that's funny --"

There followed a long pause and a struggle as White attempted to reassert his control over the communications channel.

"When you have sleep, the idea is to get the 'C' apex put toward the top," he said when communication resumed. "In communication you want to get the 'B' apex toward the top."

In the course of ruminating about the triangle as used in communication, Ruth put it this way: "It, the 'B' apex, is the one that is uplifted, that turns up to be impinged upon, instead of down."

"When you go to sleep," White continued, "the triangle tips and the 'C' apex goes towards the top.

If it went completely to the top and you got a perfectly horizontal AB line, you would have complete anesthesia. Now if the triangle kept on turning that same way, with the AB line here, you would ultimately get 'B' at the top and the AC line at the bottom.

"Then you see the triangle would turn the other way -- one way for sleep (counter-clockwise) and this way (clock-wise) for communication."

"I don't see that," said Emmet.

"I should think that if the AC line were to be impinged upon by the world, it would be turned down," said Harwood.

"The bottom for all material world contact, and you have a world subconscious," White replied. "You don't contact the supraconscious from the world as you know the world."

At this point Ruth joined the conversation. She apparently was able to do this without leaving the trance condition.

"The supraconscious is your universe contact," she began, "and it seems to me from what they have told me that the AC line should go up this way and go flat across the top for the stuff to pour on to, for the impingements to hit.

"Now of course, if you had it perfectly horizontal, with the 'B' hinge down here, that would be death so far as the world is concerned, just as when the AB line is completely horizontal, you have complete anesthesia.

"Now you don't tip the triangle that much. People with a high degree of contact can be so in tune with the degree source that they can induce a sort of simulation of death that is not actual, and in trance they can go out and have experiences without loosening the cord of the Monas to the XYZ triangle.

"There is a peculiar counter rotary motion of the two triangles during this type of communication, and that seems to be why it was so important for me to try to get the XYZ triangle straightened out. So that we could go on and understand something specific about the secondary AOC triangle and its use, because it is there, on the AC line, that all supraconscious impingements from the unobstructed universe are made.

"That doesn't mean that the supraconscious band contains other than what we have already outlined, namely, degree experience, race experience, control of the body functions, and so on. But it does mean that there has to be a peculiar adjustment of the XYZ triangle to the ABC triangle to permit this impingement in a very high degree, such as direct voice, and not have it tipped too far. I cannot straighten out for you which way the ABC triangle goes, whether it continues in one motion or whether it goes back. It is difficult to see."

After a long pause, the communication continued.

"When Monas' triangle is in normal use," said White picking up the thread of the conversation, "the BC line is at the base. When sleep is induced, the AB line or the subconscious attempts to become the base and goes from left to right. When the AC line is put into extraordinary use, like trance, it attempts to become the base, which is always the best point of impingement and it moves from right to left. In other words, the subconscious and supraconscious move in opposite directions in attempts to become the base of focus."

"In the instance of sleep and trance?" asked Emmet.

"Yes," said White. "But that is when they become the basis of focus."

"That is when their movement is in opposite directions," said Emmet.

"Yes," said White.

"I don't see what the directions mean," said Emmet, perplexed. "Do you know, Beese?"

"Not the slightest idea," said Harwood.

"Now both triangles turn in two ways," explained White. "You had a long discussion of the differentiation between the position of the ABC triangle in sleep and in trance. It is obvious to you that sleep and trance are two very different things. It must also be obvious to you that to attain trance, the individual does not go through sleep. Consequently to attain these positions immediately, you have to turn your triangles two ways, clockwise and counterclockwise."

Chapter 8. The Types of Awareness and Attention

THIS chapter explores the furthest limits of the model, namely, how Monas controls its attention and how this interacts with three basic divisions of the mind.

To review, the divisions of the mind are three: awareness mind, recall mind and aspiration mind. Each of these divisions operates at a particular moment in time in one of three energy levels or planes. The planes of the mind's divisions are called active, passive and amplified. Monas directs its attention to each plane in turn through the attention arrows introduced in the chapter on tipping. There are then three types of attention, and an active arrow assumes, at a particular moment in time, one of these types. They are known as focused attention, diffused attention, and background attention.

The total number of combinations of these -- mind division versus plane versus attention type -- is twenty-seven. These combinations are captured in the accompanying diagram. In the right-hand portion of the figure below, under "Types of Attention," you can discern twenty-seven cubes. To select a particular cube, we will first pick a division of the mind -- either awareness, recall, or aspiration -- and denote this selection by shading in the appropriate column on the diagram's far right. After that, a check mark on the face will indicate the selection both of a plane of this division and of a type of attention.

Table 1. Types of awareness and attention

The divisions of the mind are:

. awareness
. recall
. aspiration

The planes of the mind's divisions are:

. active
. passive
. amplified

The types of attention are:

. focused
. diffused
. background

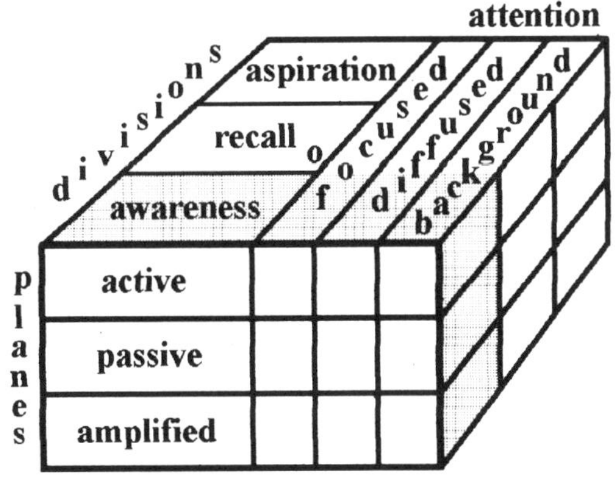

Figure 11. States of the mind

To further simplify the treatment of this topic, we will number each of twenty-seven possible states of the mind. This scheme is as follows.

Table 2. The mind's divisions vs. planes vs. attention types

division	plane	attention
1. awareness	Active	focused
2. awareness	Active	diffused
3. awareness	Active	background
4. awareness	Passive	focused
5. awareness	Passive	diffused
6. awareness	Passive	background
7. awareness	Amplified	focused
8. awareness	Amplified	diffused
9. awareness	Amplified	background
10. recall	Active	focused
11. recall	Active	diffused
12. recall	Active	background
13. recall	Passive	focused
14. recall	Passive	diffused
15. recall	Passive	background
16. recall	Amplified	focused
17. recall	Amplified	diffused
18. recall	Amplified	background
19. aspiration	Active	focused
20. aspiration	Active	diffused
21. aspiration	Active	background
22. aspiration	Passive	focused
23. aspiration	Passive	diffused
24. aspiration	Passive	background
25. aspiration	Amplified	focused
26. aspiration	Amplified	diffused
27. aspiration	Amplified	background

Next we will provide a brief description of each state. This will serve as a reference for the more detailed discussions which follow.

The awareness mind

1. Awareness, active; focused attention

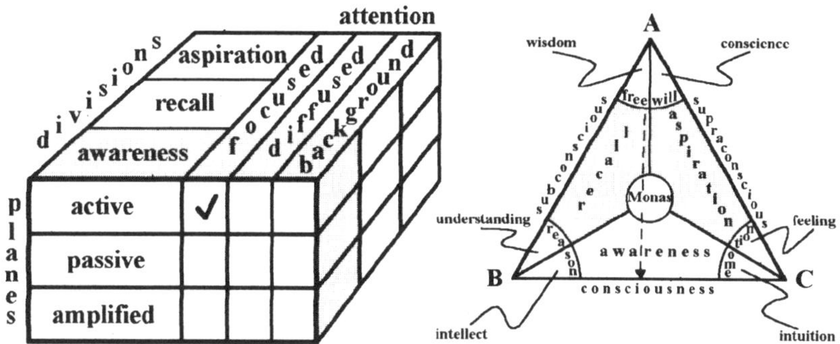

This equals concentration, with the use of intellect and reason.

2. Awareness, active; diffused attention

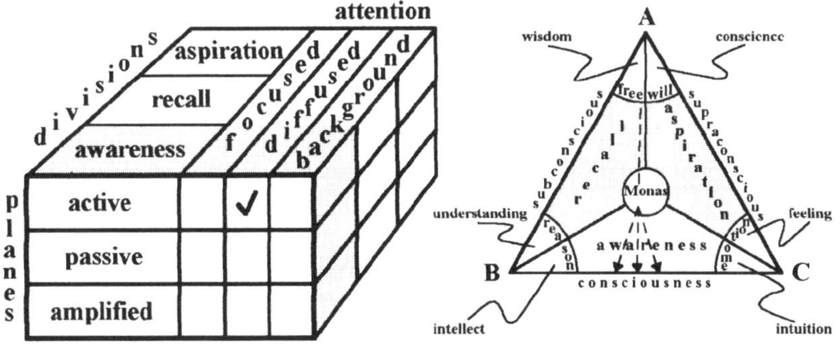

Characteristically accompanied by multiple impingements on the BC line.

3. Awareness, active; background attention

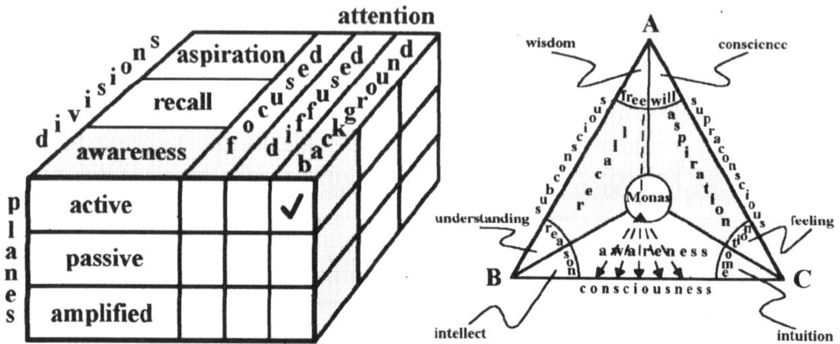

Suspended awareness, as when one lets a room impinge without focusing on it, keenly aware but not looking at anything in particular.

4. Awareness, passive; focused attention

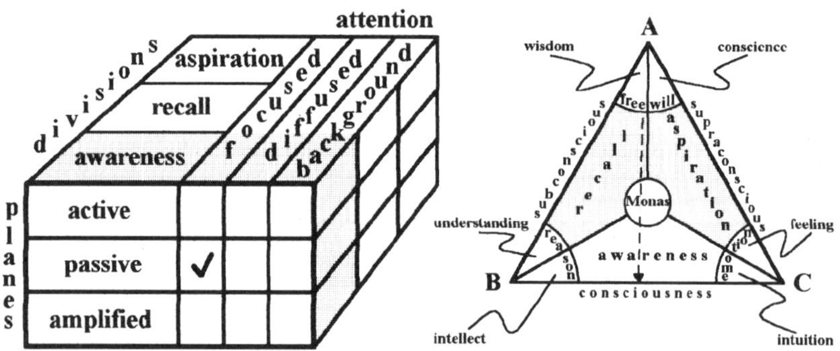

As when reading and enjoying a book. No action is involved, though your attention is focused on the book.

5. Awareness, passive; diffused attention

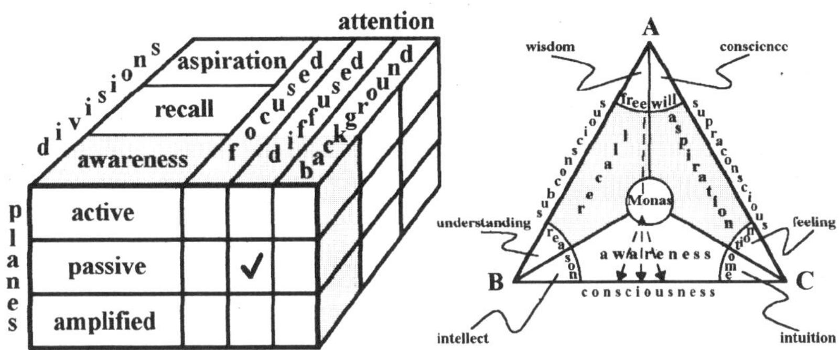

You're bored. You know what is going on all around you, but it is passive knowledge.

6. Awareness, passive; background attention

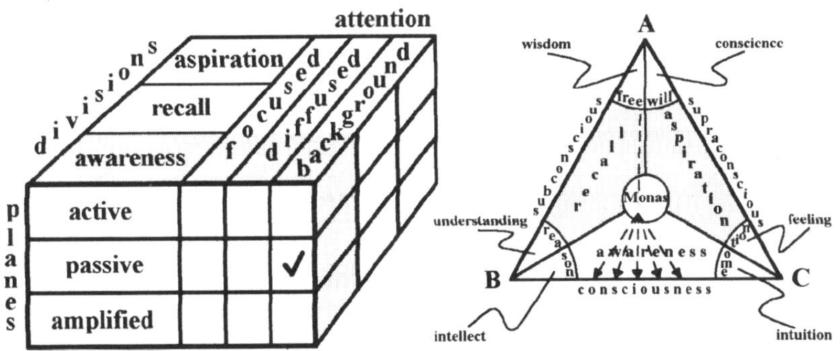

This is a species of day dreaming.

7. Awareness, amplified; focused attention

You are inventing something. You're wide awake and super-concentrated.

8. Awareness, amplified; diffused attention

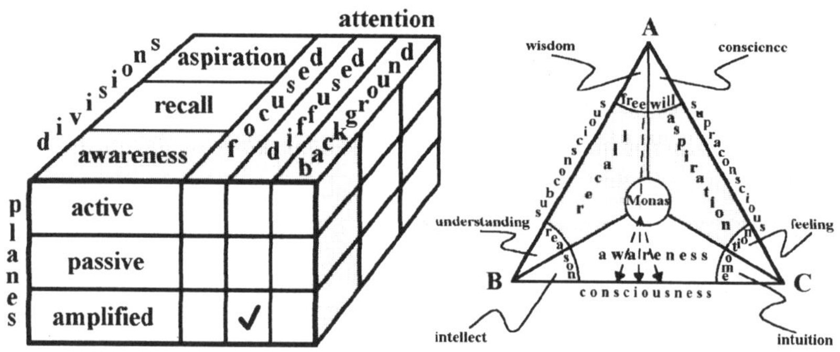

You're in a condition of shock. Something has happened that amplifies your awareness. Your attention is diffused so that you can take in a number of things and get a quick reaction.

9. Awareness, amplified; background attention

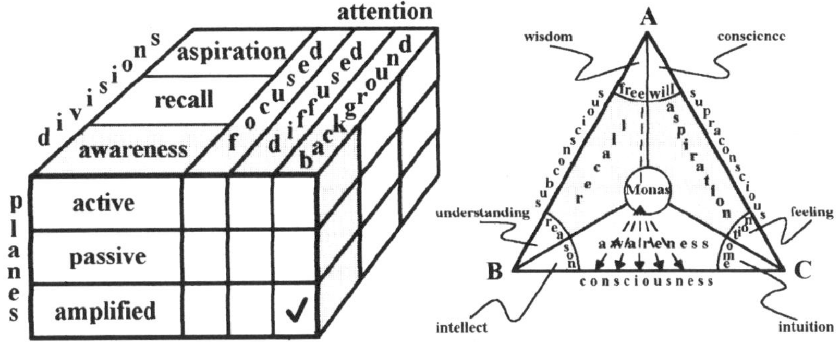

Your mind is giving acute consideration to a very broad field of awareness. This has to do with the emotion arc rather than the reason arc. It is not day dreaming.

<u>The Recall Mind</u>

10. Recall, active; focused attention

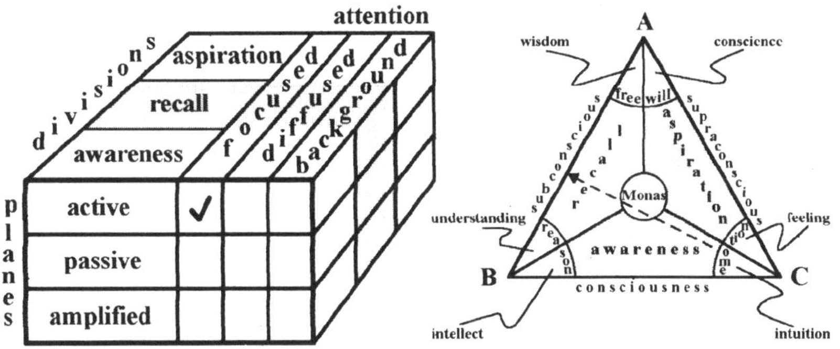

The simplest of memory seeking. No effort is involved; it happens automatically in conjunction with something Monas is doing. Examples: how to spell, how to throw the car in gear.

11. Recall, active; diffused attention

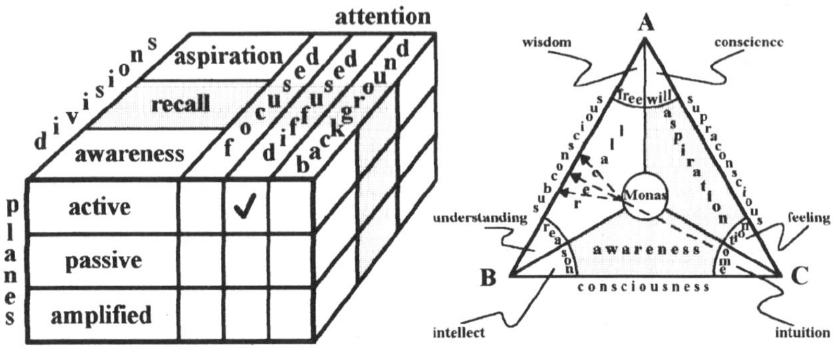

Here you get a quick emotional reaction out of the subconscious. It is a kind of shock recall.

12. Recall, active; background attention

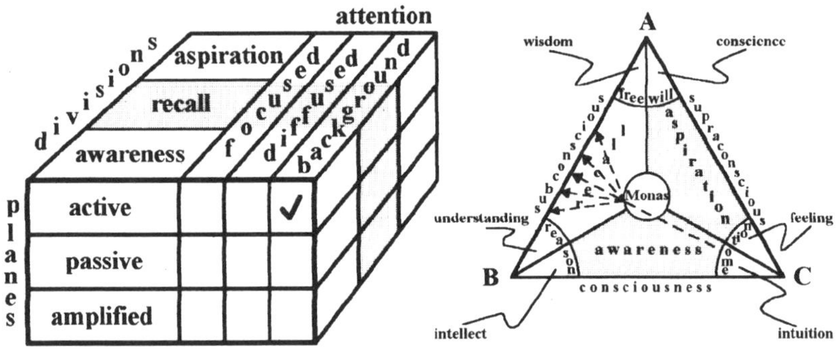

"And this background that is on the alert is just floating around of itself, very lazy like, half-thinking. It is suddenly attracted by an active recall and it comes into the recall mind and it may or may not be important. But it is there."

13. Recall, passive; focused attention

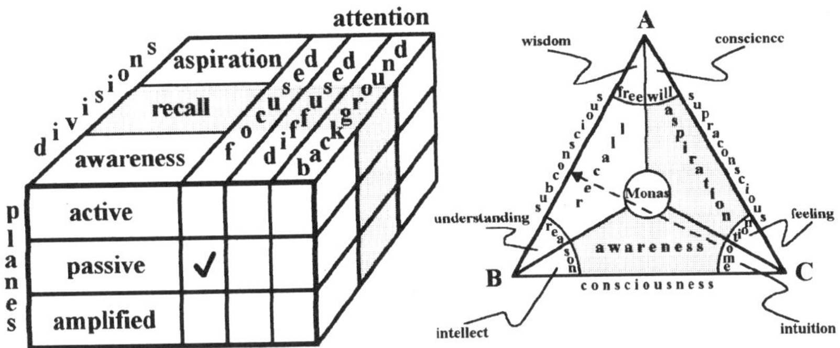

This is where you have to do quite a good deal of digging to remember something, like remembering what your license number was last year.

14. Recall, passive; diffused attention

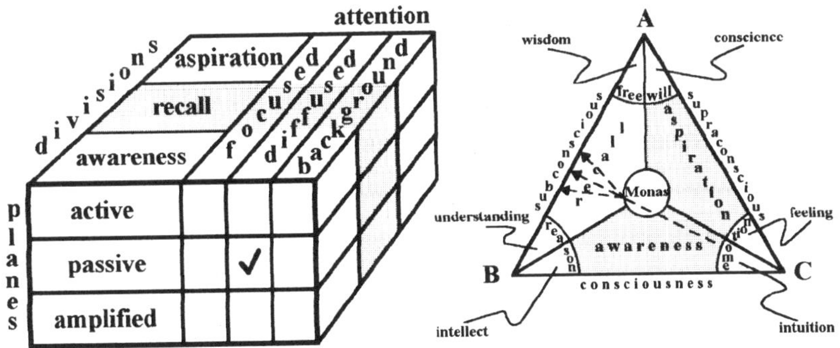

"You go in deeper, go through a longer period of -- well, fear, for instance. Or shock. And you get more out of your subconscious for protection or solution.

15. Recall, passive; background attention

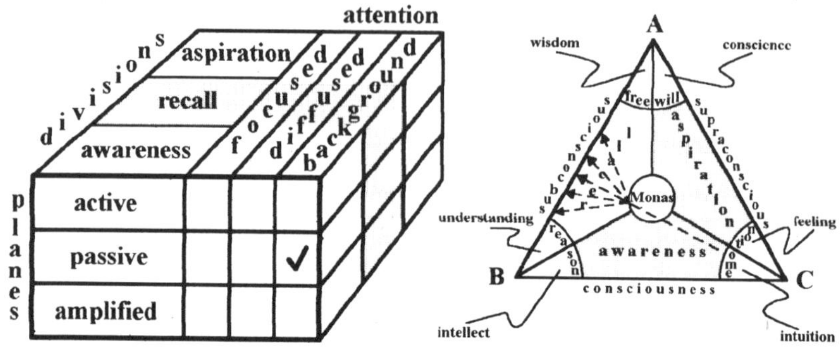

All background attention is more or less a dreamy state. You sense it as an influence upon yourself. It is a very delicate state of conscious subconscious. In the other two types of attention in the subconscious you get a net result in passive recall. But in this you just get the color -- a sort of feeling.

16. Recall, amplified; focused attention

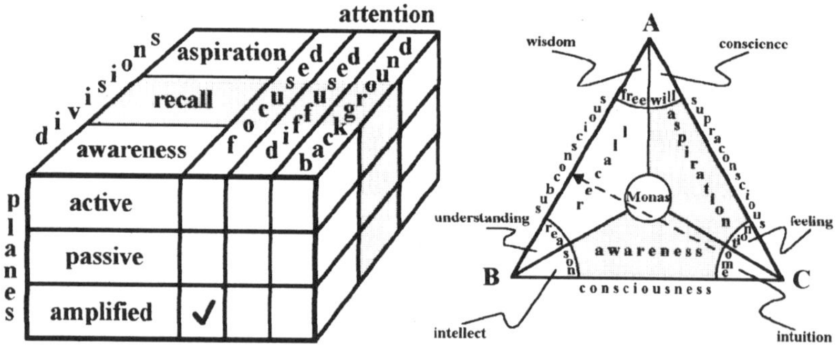

Touches on psychiatry. It is a deliberate suggestive recall. This type of recall causes dreams that deal with matters close to the surface of the dreamer's needs.

17. Recall, amplified; diffused attention

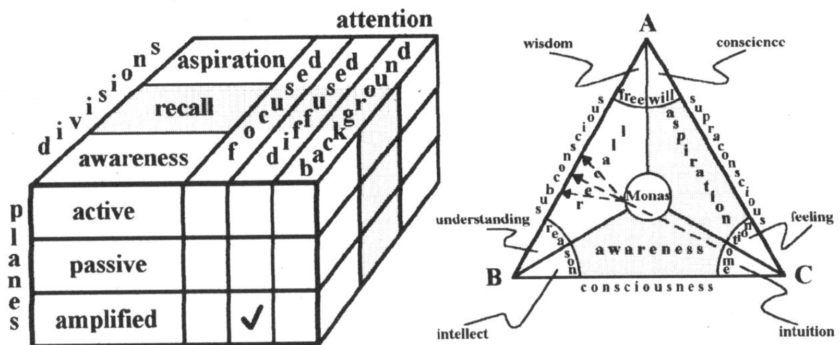

"All modern mental therapeutics are based on amplified recall and the use of the three types of attention on the same." This type of recall can create a restless sleep of unremembered dreams.

18. Recall, amplified; background attention

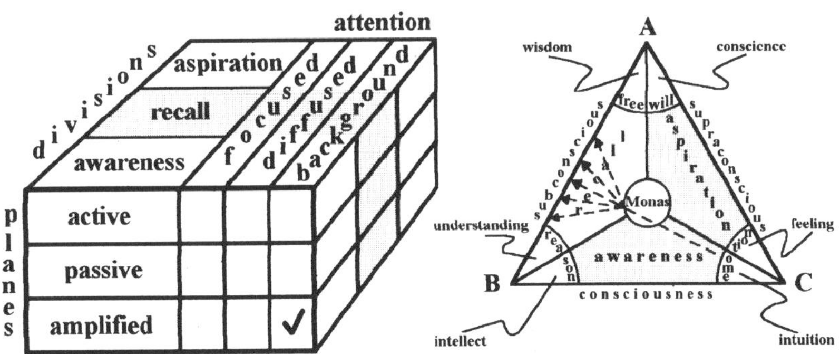

The amplified subconscious is the depths of the subconscious. You can go into this type from shock. Or in sleep it disturbs the individual without formulating itself into a dream.

19. Aspiration, active; focused attention

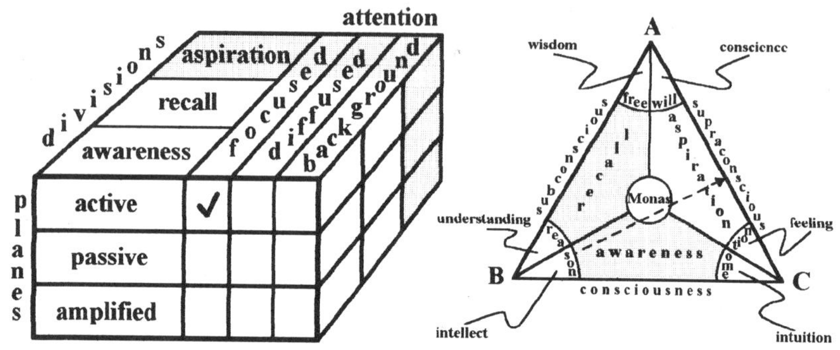

Active aspiration is some type of prayer. This type is a formulation of something that Monas has decided he wants.

20. Aspiration, active; diffused attention

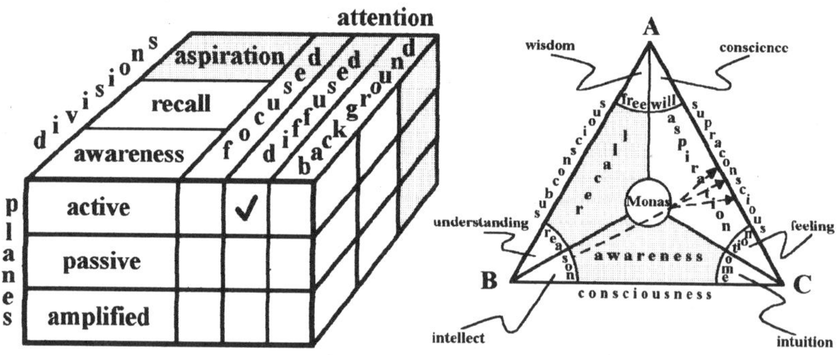

Monas has decided to do something about his aspiration. He tries to get something for himself out of the inspiration band (the OA line).

21. Aspiration, active; background attention

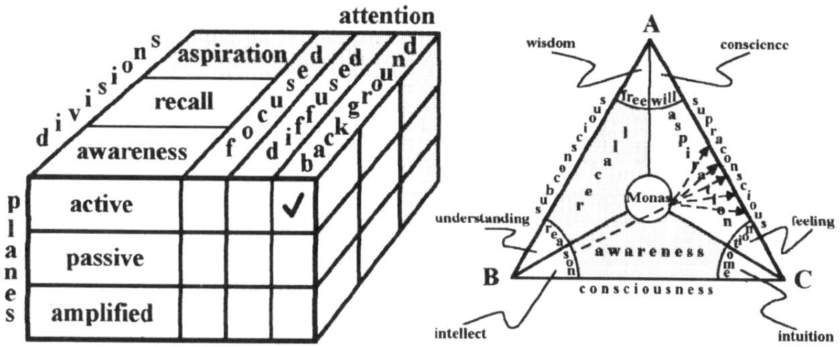

A mood of frustration. It is the wish that is never fulfilled.

22. Aspiration, passive; focused attention

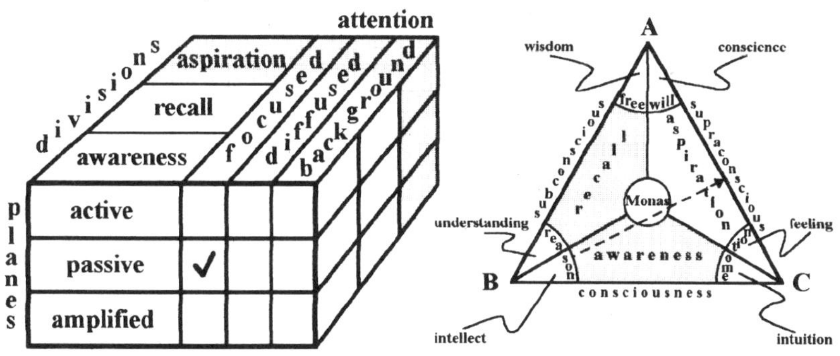

Beyond prayer. Focused, meditated thought concerning the wish previously formulated.

23. Aspiration, passive; diffused attention

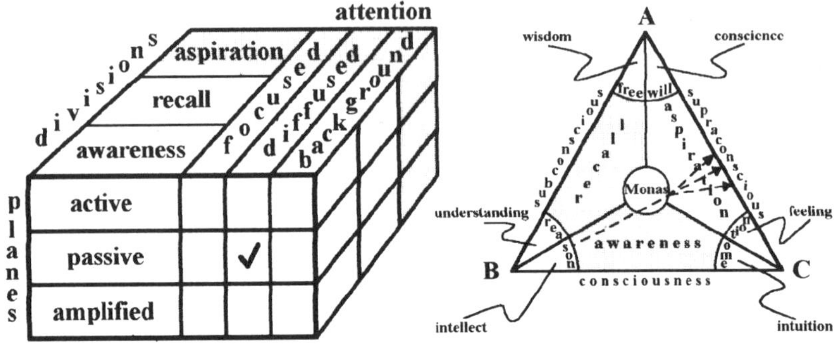

True meditation. No. 22 has gotten as far as diffused attention, which brings to bear on the wish a great deal of that which the individual has placed in his subconscious.

24. Aspiration, passive; background attention

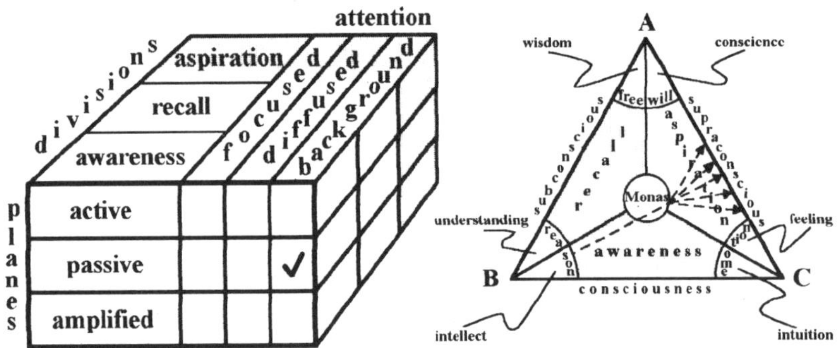

A follow-on from the meditation of No. 23. Provides the individual with a background attention that lives with him and is quite comforting to him. Getting very close now to faith.

25. Aspiration, amplified; focused attention

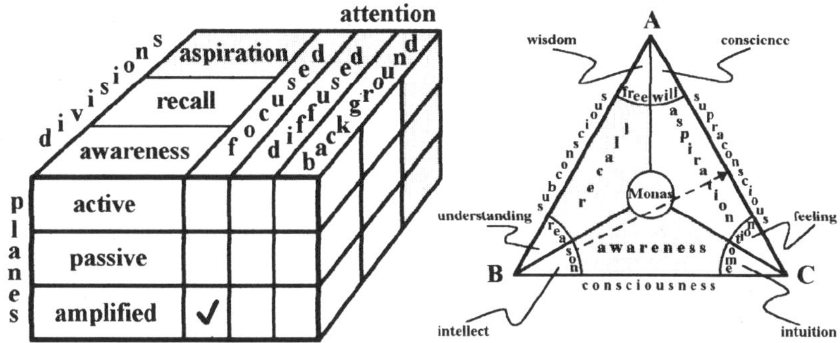

In this state Monas wants faith -- wants to know he is immortal, that he can draw out his own quality from his supraconscious, that he can touch his degree in emergencies. In the amplified plane there is always an augmentation from outside Monas.

26. Aspiration, amplified; diffused attention

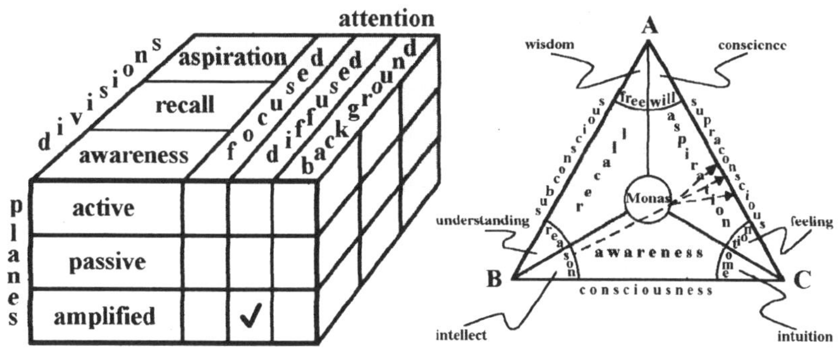

An augmentation of No. 25.

27. Aspiration, amplified; background attention

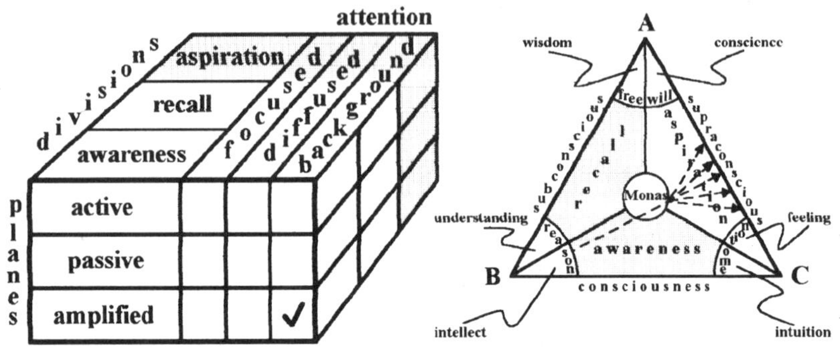

Faith in your background attention to live with.

Chapter 9. Lines of Attention

AS mentioned, this subject was introduced in the chapter on tipping. Here I will give some of the sitting conversations on which that description was based. The attention lines, three of them, each in three flavors, complicate the model. The following conversations show Emmet and Harwood trying to come to grips with this complexity, with White trying to keep the subject simple.

An Invisible had just explained to Emmet that there was a direct connection between the free will (the arc at the "A" apex) and the conscious mind, even though free will is not a conscious operation.

"What is the nature of the connection?" Emmet responded.

"Well, the easiest way for me to tell it to you," said the Invisible, "is (that) it is a picture. It is a dotted line that comes down from the middle of this little hanging thing that we have called free will, and it is a little fragmentary dotted line that comes down straight and it moves back and forth, sort of like a metronome, along the line of the conscious mind, and wherever the conscious mind is impinged upon, there it is."

At a later sitting, with White dictating, the subject was expanded upon.

"The dotted line in the triangle that appeared early in this divulgence," he began, "and which you were again discussing last evening, does swing from the various arcs. It is there attached. It is controlled, as is all else in the triangle, by Monas. But it is freer, more flexible and is always the line of focused attention.

"Do not confuse this dotted line of focused attention leading from the arcs with another type of attention that has been developed in the past few centuries by man along the BC line. The second type of attention, which has become acute in the mechanistic age, is known as diffused attention. It is important and has much to do with the lack of concentration and contact with the arc swinging from the AB and AC lines. The reason for this is that in the present day the normal position of the triangle is with the BC line as its base. Of course that is always true when Monas is developing all the earth plane, but the triangle is malleable."

Harwood introduced a long, confused discussion with one of his suggestions that the model be expanded. This passage is of interest also owing to an emotional clash between him and Emmet that was a recurring theme of the sittings.

"I have an inspiration," began Harwood. "It seems to me we are going to have to add another triangle to the series." He then proposed a triangle to represent the functions of the dotted lines.

"No," said White. "The swing of the pendulum can be indicated just as any swing of a pendulum can be indicated, by dotted lines. There will be times when the pendulum will swing across the static thought line and indeed all three lines from 'O' to apex, but it never will stay long in one place."

"You hope to indicate all that by a series of dotted lines?" This from Emmet.

"All you have to do," said White, "is to take the two dotted lines down on each side and say that they swing. And when you have perfect concentration, the attention line is stationary."

"This thing is not a pendulum," quibbled Emmet, "because the circle is in the middle."

"No, it is not a pendulum exactly," concurred White.

After setting up a second reel on the Sound Mirror, White continued.

"Monas is a circle," he began. "You have a dotted line coming down here from the center of the arc of will. And it drops through Monas down to the BC line. Now if that attention sways, pulled along this line by attraction, by an impingement of a sense, sound for instance, then it glides over to Monas. You see it cuts Monas in a different place. That does not mean anything of itself."

"Except that it does not move Monas," said Emmet.

"It doesn't move Monas?" said White, uncharacteristically puzzled.

"That is the reason why the pendulum idea is not quite right," rejoined Emmet.

"No, it is not quite right," agreed White.

"That is why 'they' are having this scramblation," interposed Ruth, stepping out of her role as receiving station. "They are having a convention on it."

"Look," said Harwood, his temperature starting to rise. "You have three kinds of attention control: will control of attention, ideational control of attention, and emotional control of attention. Now any one of them can take over, it seems to me."

"That is right," said Emmet, agreeing.

"Therefore, all those lines ought to be hooked up," Harwood exclaimed.

Here White started to interrupt.

"Now wait a minute!" Harwood burst out. "I will talk to your darn convention. Get your convention to listen in. Here is a guy that has got an idea. Suppose you have a line of attention going down from the will to the BC line."

At this point the sitting notes record that Emmet's attention had wandered and he went into the dining room.

"Lost my audience," said Harwood plaintively.

"Go ahead," said White. "You have my audience."

"I lost Emmet," said Harwood. "That confuses me."

Here the record notes that something happened to the Sound Mirror and there was a general disintegration both of it and Harwood. One presumes that this note was entered into the sitting record by Emmet.

Presently Harwood, having collected his thoughts (and his composure), proceeded.

"Ordinarily you have the line from will down to the BC line operating as your attention," he said. "Will is controlling it. Sometimes emotion pulls it to one side or ideas pull it to the other side."

"Pull what to the other side?" asked Emmet.

"The dotted line," said Harwood.

"No, you have three dotted lines," objected Emmet, himself confused for a change.

"I am talking about the one line now, see?" clarified Harwood. "The dotted line from 'A' down. Now that dotted line is your normal daily attention focused on sense perception in the outside world. For the most part that is controlled by will but it can be deflected by emotion or by ideas. Now how are you going to depict the deflection if you do not have dotted lines running over to those arcs, which pull on it so to speak? If you had the dotted line from arc 'B' going across, and a dotted line from arc 'C' going across, then they will all intersect in the middle, wouldn't they?

"Now, you will that attention and pull the whole complex over to one side or the other," he continued, "which is what you do in your normal daily living. You pull the whole complex to one side or the other. But suppose you get scared. Then the line to the 'C' corner takes over and pulls your line from the 'A' corner over to that side ('C'), or if ideas take over, then the line from 'B' pulls the whole complex over. The mere attachment to these other two lines would not destroy the mobility of the whole complex. It would simply mean that will would mobilize the whole complex."

During the discussion that was not on the record, Harwood and Emmet developed the idea that it is easier for the ordinary person to permit his attention to be deflected in the direction of reason than it is for him to permit it to be deflected in the direction of emotion. You can think a thought easier than you can voluntarily acquire an emotion. Yet the latter is exactly what the good actor does. He manufactures an emotion, allowing his line of attention to be pulled toward the emotional arc.

"Listen," interrupted White. "You are trying to get the whole thing too complicated."

"All right," said Harwood, "let your convention decide about this. I am just offering ideas to --"

"Before Stewart says anything, I would like to lay my ideas before the multitude," said Emmet. "Beese has been thinking of this in entirely different terms from me. It is true that the lines intersect, as I can see them, but that is only a diagrammatic necessity. It hasn't anything to do with the reality. To me there are actually three dotted lines, one running from will to BC, one from emotion to AB, one from reason to AC. Now they don't all function at one time, although they may sometimes function somewhat together, with confusion resulting. But diagramatically, I have conceived them in this way, which is not the way you have conceived them at all. And that is --"

"That is exactly the way I conceived them," said Harwood.

"The operation of the line from 'B' is not going to disturb the operation of the line from 'A'," continued Emmet. "This line, that is, the 'B' line, is not there when the 'A' line is operating. Only the potentiality of the 'B' line is there. When the will line is operating, then the emotional attention and the reason attention are in abeyance. They are dormant, they really are not there. But when you try to depict them all at once, you do get them all there."

"That is what I was trying to figure out," said Harwood.

"Well, it is awfully hard to depict," agreed Emmet.

"I would not worry about the depiction. We can make three separate triangles for that matter," said Harwood, back at his old stand.

"Are you thinking that emotion swings willed attention?" asked Emmet.

"Too fast," interposed White, with no one listening.

"Emotion obviously deflects --" started Harwood.

"No," said Emmet. "It interferes with it only. You can get a combination of attention, see?"

"Wait a minute," said Harwood. "Return again to a hypothetical case. You got willed attention operating on a study. You then get your explosion."

"Willed attention is then out of the picture," said Emmet.

"It vanishes," agreed Harwood. "Then emotion pulls that attention line, from your mundane attention line, clear over to that side of the picture."

"No!" said Emmet and White simultaneously.

"The thing you are depicting by a line, which of course is not a line -- the reality just ceases to exist, that is, goes out of function," said Emmet.

"For God's sake, how do you show the attention that turns itself to the explosion?" shouted an exasperated Harwood.

"You cannot depict the whole thing on the triangle," interposed Ruth. "The triangle is only symbolical. Do not scramble this up so much. At the time of the explosion, emotional attention takes over for a moment, but I must insist that willed attention is the king."

"I don't squawk about that," said Harwood. "Here you have a definite occurrence. Your explosion situation. We got to get that so it goes on the picture or the picture is not any good."

"If Monas releases his real attention to permit his emotional attention to take complete charge, you have an entirely different reaction," said White. "Panic, hysteria, maybe insanity. Maybe your XYZ triangle comes up and takes charge. You see you have your finger on a fact all right, but we are talking about the normal situation."

"Function is involved," said Emmet. "So you are really trying to depict motion. Cannot be done on a diagram."

"If you take your ABC triangle and put it on a drawing board," suggested White, "and then take three pieces of string and attach them by a thumb tack to the arc and then pull the string or move the string around or better still, attach narrow pieces of Bristol board so you could move them as the hands of a clock --"

"Even then in the instance of emotional disturbance, such as the explosion occasioned, you would have to lift the string or the cardboard strip from 'A' entirely out of the picture momentarily, because it would be out of the picture," objected Emmet. "It has ceased to function. It is there potentially, but it just is not functioning."

"It doesn't look that way to me," said Harwood. "Does it look that way to you, Stewart?"

"When you have a sudden reaction on the BC line strong enough to make the impingement on the BC line flow to the emotional arc, instead of going up in the normal fashion over the mind pie, you are going to have a momentary impingement on Monas direct of the emotional impact," replied White. "But unless you have panic, the loss of control by Monas, the willed attention will come in and take charge."

"When you have that momentary emotional attention, what becomes of willed attention?" Emmet wanted to know.

"Willed attention is static," replied White.

"What do you mean by static?" asked Emmet.

"Simply that it is still there, ready to operate, but not functioning for that single instant," said White. "It immediately goes into action, however. But you cannot depict this on a diagram any more than you can show a moving train on a map. You can only tell about it in words."

An argument that pleased attorney Finley, it seems. In the ensuing conversation you should imagine Harwood on the witness stand being cross examined by Emmet.

"Now (that) we have that point made with Beese," said Emmet, "let's hear what he has to say about it."

But Harwood wasn't having any.

"I might as well be perfectly frank and say that you haven't made any point at all," he stated tersely.

"Have we made a statement?" said Emmet, refusing to back off.

"Yes," grumbled Harwood.

"All right, what is your reaction, Beese, to the statement?" needled Emmet.

"Don't like it from any angle," grumbled Harwood.

"Well, why don't you like it?" said Emmet, playing to the jury. "What do you want to do?"

"I don't know," said Harwood. "I have an idea of what I want to do but I have to develop it at my leisure. This I will try to do and present it for consideration of the house later. But I am not satisfied with the solution of the problem."

"All right," said Emmet. "Let it cook."

It did not have to cook for long. In chambers the two adversaries quickly came to an amicable understanding.

"In conversation following this session, we straightened the whole matter out," reads a note inserted into the record by Emmet. "I had been talking about one aspect of attention and Harwood about another. If one undertook to represent all three types of attention at one and the same time on the triangle, of course the dotted lines would cross, but ordinarily only one type of attention operates at the given moment. So the question is whether it is best to show all lines of attention on one triangle or to draw up three triangles, each of which shows one of the three types of attention.

"Also after this session, Harwood and I discussed three types of reaction that might follow the explosion. One fellow would recover quickly. His attention had just suffered a temporary or momentary deflection to the emotional arc. A second fellow might go into panic for say, ten minutes. He would get a considerable deflection to the emotional arc and he would not recover from it instantly, but he would in the course of a short time. A third fellow, maybe the chap whose house was blown down by the explosion, might go off the beam completely, and in his case the triangle might be tipped with the consequence that his attention would tend to operate permanently from the emotional arc."

At this point Harwood also inserted a note into the record.

"While taking this session off the Sound Mirror," he wrote, "Emmet and I discussed the voluntary control of attention. Emmet remarked that he could see how attention could be voluntarily focused on reason, but the focusing on emotion looked to him almost impossible. 'How about the actor?' I asked. 'He wills his attention to emotion. If he is a good actor, he actually evokes it.'"

In discussing the explosion, the two of them identified three types of reactions. They also decided to call the attention lines the A', B', C' lines.

The descriptions of the reactions now follow.

Reaction No. 1: A' moves from the "B" arc to the BC line to the "C" arc and then, under control of the will, immediately back to the "B" arc. This illustrates the normal self-possessed and effective person.

Reaction No. 2: The A' line moves from the "B" arc to the BC line to the "C" arc and stays there a while. This illustrates the person who would go into a panic or hysterics and become helpless.

Reaction No. 3: The ABC triangle would be tipped up on its "C" angle. This person would have a psychotic attack.

Still later the group hit upon a pattern for diffused attention. In such a case, all three of the attention lines, A', B' and C' could be operating more or less at the same time. This would picture the state of the person driving an automobile, trying to remember something, and at the same time receiving an intuition of an impending danger.

Another aspect of diffused attention was pictured by using a dotted band instead of just a dotted line. This would illustrate a diffusion over visual, auditory and tactile sensations. Also a spreading of each sensory avenue to include a wide field. As for instance, watching the road ahead and the speedometer at the same time and also listening for horse and engine noises and feeling the skid of the wheels on wet pavement. And maybe thinking over some problem or carrying on a conversation -- and feeling sore about it. On the diagrams they decided to use a shaded cone to depict diffused attention.

The reader will notice from the above that Emmet and Harwood had by this point developed an effective partnership, despite conflicting temperaments, or perhaps even because of them. There is more to this partnership than meets the eye. The Invisibles had tried unsuccessfully for two decades to get this material through via Ruth and Emmet Finley. They were particularly active in the months just before Harwood paid his visit to the East Coast. Yet the only records necessary for this divulgence are those produced in conjunction with Harwood's visit. The earlier ones are not always transcribed and in any event are only marginally useful. Furthermore, the intended book never materialized. After Harwood left for the West Coast, the project sputtered, then died.

At one point Emmet expressed some confusion in his understanding of the attention line used when one is thinking. This brought out the following discussion.

"I don't think you are using the attention line from 'B' when you are thinking," Harwood said. "You are using the attention line from 'A' in the act of thinking."

"Surely," White concurred.

"What other attention line hangs from 'B'?" asked Emmet.

"It is not the attention that hangs from 'B' that operates on the elements of the 'B' hinge," said White. "You see you put the arrow on the end of the attention line and the attention line that operates down at that hinge hangs either from 'A' or 'C'. Now those two attention lines can operate very close together in that hinge, in the whole arc. It is where the arrow points that you get your attention -- where the arrow hits."

"It is the arrow that is doing the job, not the place where it starts from," summarized Harwood.

"It is the start of the thing that controls," said White, "but what it works on is at the point of the arrow."

"You do not use your 'B' attention line in the process of thinking?" interposed Emmet.

"Not unless you direct it to your supraconscious," said White. "Then it feeds your thinking."

"How shall we designate the types of attention on the diagram?" someone asked.

"The attention line is in three degrees," said White. "Focused, diffused and background."

"How would it be to show the attention line as a cone of varying width, so that when you had background attention it would fill the whole secondary triangle?" asked Harwood. "Diffused attention would occupy part of the triangle. Focused attention would be a line."

"You could have it like an electric eye," said White. "When you get the dial set correctly, it is very narrow. And when it is blurred, it widens out."

This completes the material on the attention arrows. We can now turn our attention to the twenty-seven states of consciousness. I will present them a division at a time -- awareness mind, recall mind, and aspiration mind -- dipping into the records as appropriate.

Chapter 10. The Awareness Mind

THE subject commences with a long, discursive conversation devoted to the divisions of the mind. White is dictating. He has already described the awareness mind as given in the table presented in an earlier chapter, material which we will repeat and amplify below. He begins then by reviewing the twenty-seven states as defined above.

"I would bring to your consideration at this point, again, the fact that consciousness is one, a unit -- the only reality," he said. "Where we got somewhat confused was in trying to over-elaborate the planes of the mind. We have awareness mind, recall mind and aspiration mind. Their planes are three: active, passive and amplified. Now the same three planes obtain throughout the mind. Consequently the planes of recall are active, passive and amplified. The planes of aspiration are active, passive and amplified. They are operated by three kinds of attention -- focused, diffused and background. The difference, the fine diamond-cut difference, is the arc from which your attention hangs. It does not hang from the arc exactly but the arc of the hinge has much to do with the attention. It colors it, just as will power colors the attention that seeks along the BC band."

Descriptions of the nine states of the awareness mind now follow. They are separated here for reasons of clarity. In the record, however, they occupy a single short session.

Awareness, active; focused attention (state No. 1)

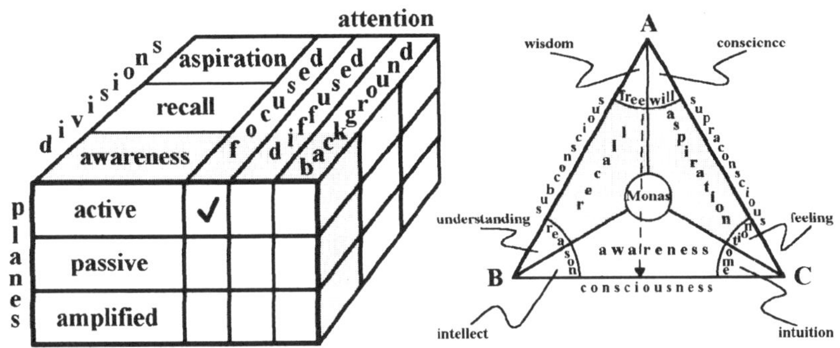

Figure 12

The record here is very short. White begins by saying, "Would it be worth while to examine the various kinds of attention in the field of awareness?"

"That would be very interesting," Harwood replied.

"We have three kinds of awareness," White continued, "-- active, passive and amplified. Attention is focused, diffused and background. Now let us take the focused attention when we have active awareness. This would equal concentration, with the use of intellect and reason."

Here Harwood in trying to kill a bug that had got into the room accidentally slammed the window screen and threw everything out of kilter -- providing as fine an example of focused attention as we would want.

Awareness, active;

diffused attention

(state No. 2)

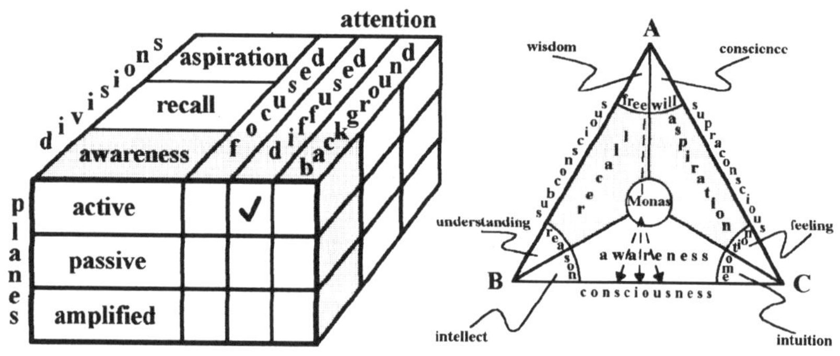

Figure 13

This description, also short, follows, in the record, immediately on the heels of the one above. White is dictating.

"Next we have active awareness and diffused attention," he continued. "This is not necessarily projected by Monas as is his active awareness and focused attention. Active awareness and diffused attention is usually projected by an impingement on the BC line, by more that one impingement probably. But it could be one large impingement. Or it could be a number of various impingements."

Awareness, active; background attention

(state No. 3)

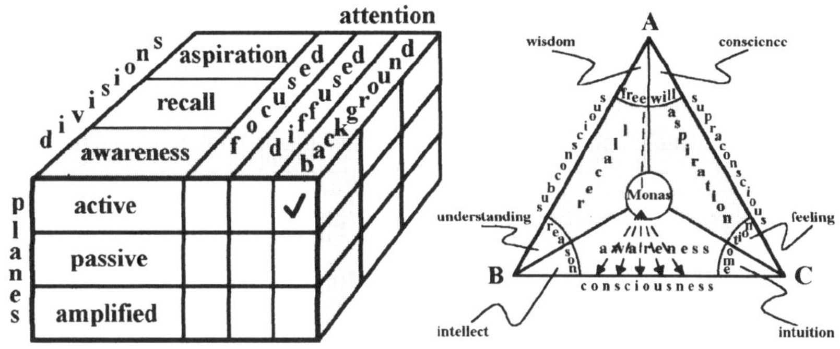

Figure 14

Again, the description in the record follows immediately on the heels of that above.

"We have now active awareness and background attention," White continued. "This is a sort of suspended awareness. It is potential. It has the potentiality of action suspended."

This evoked from Emmet the following: "As when one lets a room impinge without focusing on it, keenly aware but not looking at anything in particular. Yet you can focus definitely whenever you wish."

Awareness, passive;

focused attention

(state No. 4)

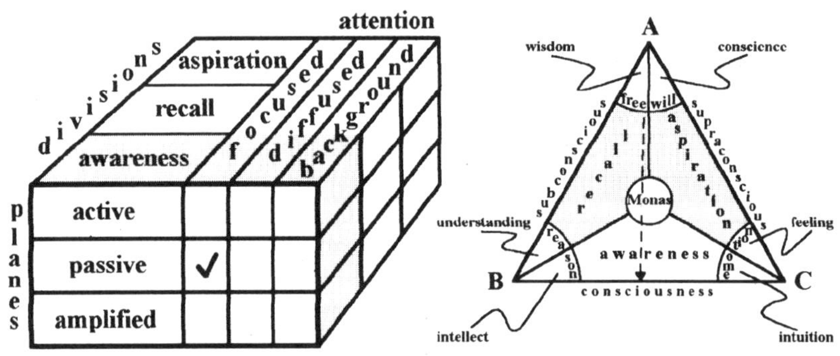

Figure 15

"Now we have passive awareness and focused attention," White said, "which is operated by Monas and is another type of concentration. It is when you are reading and enjoying something. You have a book, you enjoy it, you get the author's picture, but it is a case of passive awareness. There is no action in it, though your attention is focused on the book."

Awareness, passive;

diffused attention

(state No. 5)

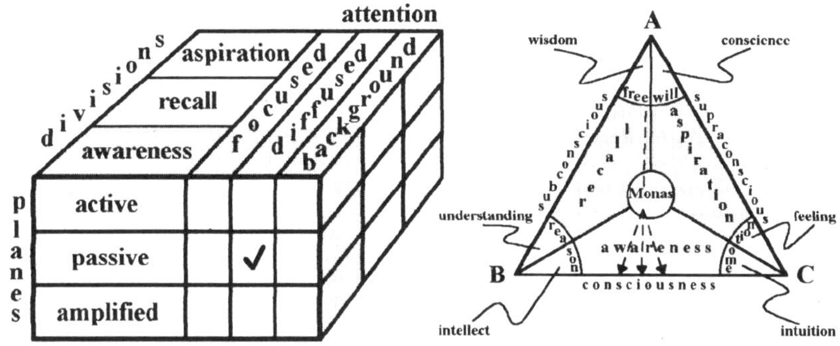

Figure 16

"In passive awareness and diffused attention," White said, "you are rather bored. You are all there and know what is going on in a room, let us say. You may even be listening or actually taking part in a somewhat stupid conversation -- various conversations. You know what is going on all around but it is a passive knowledge."

Awareness, passive; background attention (state No. 6)

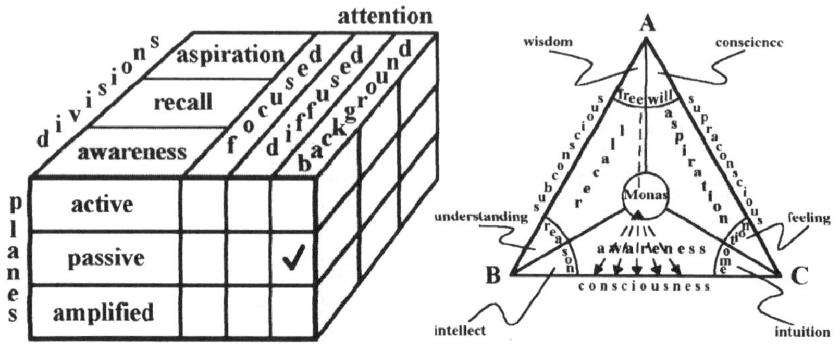

Figure 17

"Now passive awareness and background attention is a sort of day dreaming," said White. "You -- that is as good as I can do," he concluded, breaking off to start the next subject.

Awareness, amplified; focused attention (state No. 7)

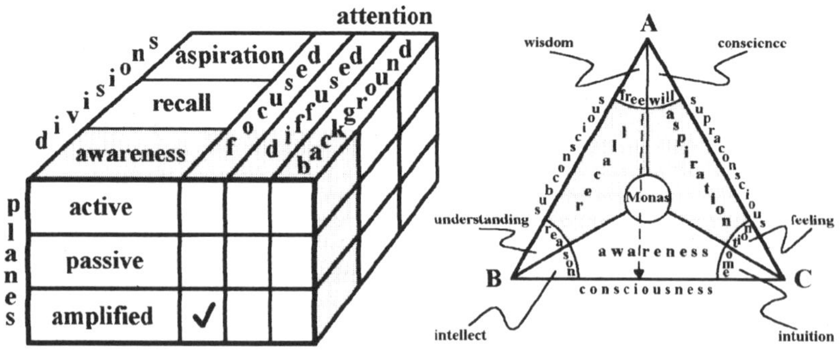

Figure 18

"Now you have amplified awareness and focused attention, which is very sharp," White continued. "It is directed by Monas and the attention is keen and the awareness is keen. It is the type of thing that occurs when somebody invents something -- like when you shut out everything else and try to super-concentrate on an invention. It is in your own mind. It is your work. You do not get inspiration about it at this point. You probably will later. But it is heightened awareness focused on some particular object that Monas is interested in."

Awareness, amplified; diffused attention (state No. 8)

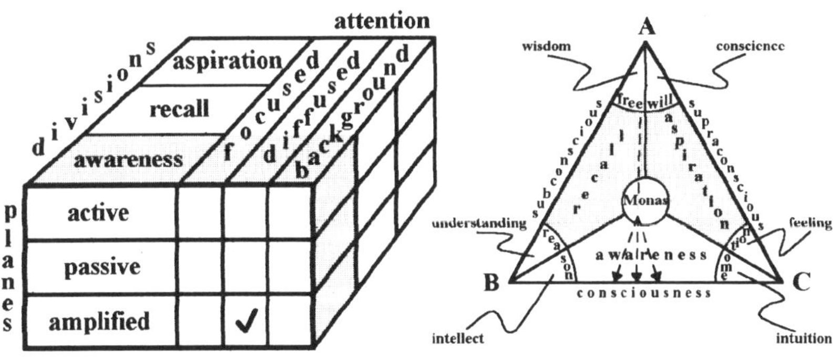

Figure 19

"Now amplified awareness with diffused attention is usually a shock condition," said White, "where you get an impingement from the outside world that amplifies your awareness and your attention is diffused so that you take in a number of things, and you get a quick act as a result."

Awareness, amplified;

background attention

(state No. 9)

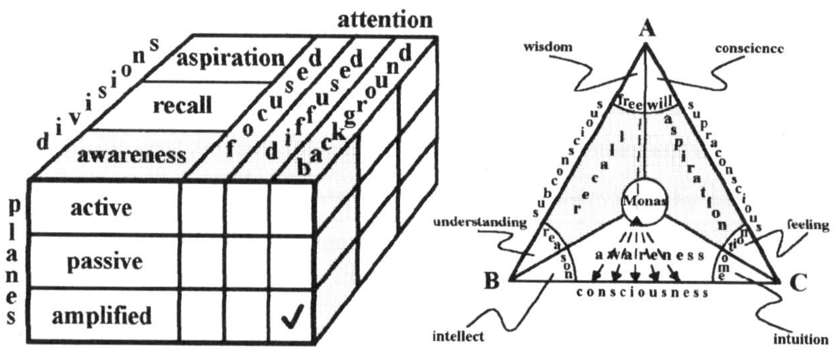

Figure 20

"Then you have amplified awareness and background attention, which is operated through Monas in the triangle," White continued. "It is not day dreaming. It is giving your mind in an acute state of consideration to a very broad field of awareness. Amplified awareness and background attention has to do with the emotion arc rather than the reason arc."

This completes the material from the record on the awareness mind.

Chapter 11. The Recall Mind

NEXT comes generic definitions of active, passive and amplified recall.

"We fairly well cleared up the awareness triangle," White began, "-- its planes of operation and its types of attention. We stated that there are only three types of attention. These types obtain on all three attention lines. We will now proceed to the AOB secondary triangle, which is known as recall, bounded by inspiration, thought and the subconscious.

"Now we will proceed," he continued. "The first plane of recall is active. That we will describe briefly as a deliberate act on the part of Monas to recall a memory or empirical experience, which also is a memory.

"The passive plane of recall is that in which Monas operates all the time without giving thought to it. In order to have active recall, he must will thought to activate memory. In passive recall, he does not need to will a thought to activate a memory. By that I do not mean the upsurging of the subconscious of which we have talked somewhat. I mean the very-close-to-the-surface subconscious that you use in a great many daily operations of working, playing, thinking. It is an association sort of thing. If you have placed in your subconscious a facility and you repeat that facility, say a muscular facility, you do not need to actively recall the subconscious facility. It combines with your present activity because it is just underneath the active surface of awareness. It is just way up at the hinge where you can get it quickly -- so quickly that you do not even need to call it.

"Now amplified recall is the upsurging that we were talking about. And that happens only in very special instances that we will discuss when we come to apply the three different types of attention to the three different places of recall."

Recall, active; focused attention (state No. 10)

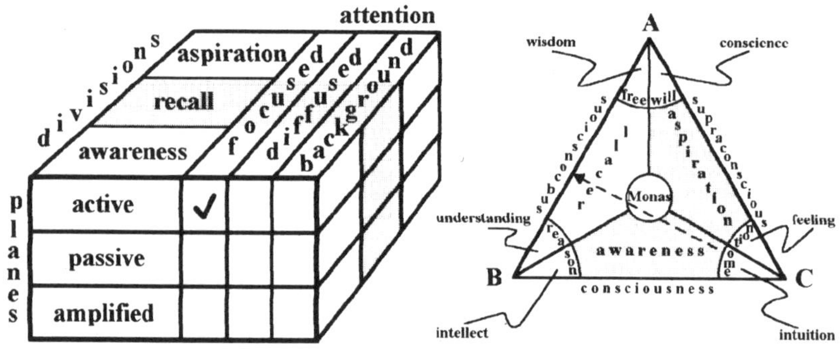

Figure 21

"Now let us take the first plane of recall and apply active recall, focused attention," White said, directing the group's attention to block No. ten in the list of twenty-seven. "That is the simplest of memory seeking. It is how to spell, which incidentally this station never accomplished. I am not going to be too profuse with illustrations. I am going to give you examples and you can supply more and come back to me for more if necessary. But we have our focused attention on active recall."

Recall, passive; focused attention (state No. 13)

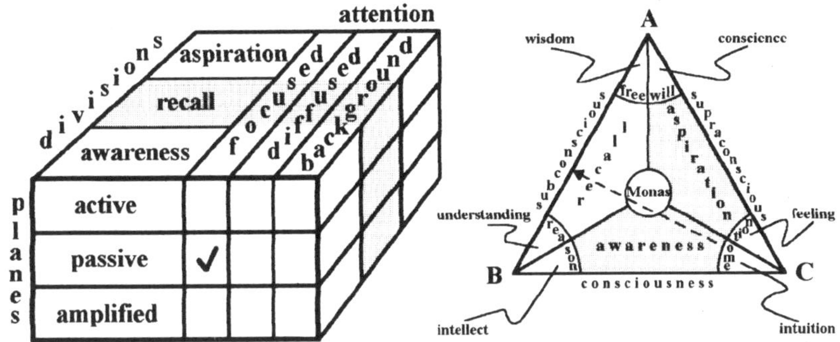

Figure 22

"This time I am going to do it a little differently because I think it would be easier for the station," White continued. "I am going to take each one of the attentions clear through the planes.

"We have had the focused attention on the active plane of recall. [Ed.: No. ten.] Now we pass to focused attention on the passive plane of recall. [Ed.: No. thirteen.] There is where you have to do quite a good deal of digging to remember something. It is in your mind all right and you understand it perfectly well, but maybe it is quite a long time ago that it happened or maybe it is a name that has eluded you and that you have to hunt, hunt, hunt. It is not active but you focused on it and you get it. Is that clear?"

"Perhaps I would like the word 'latent' better than passive," said Emmet. "Or possibly 'potential'. Suppose I am trying to recall something. It is active, like my telephone number."

"No, that is wrong," said White. "Your phone number is not an example of active recall. I told you that focused active recall was something that Monas did not even have to make an effort to think of, that it came up in conjunction with a present action or a present thought, that it was automatic."

"What are we talking about now?" said Emmet. He was evidently confused.

"We are talking about what you have to dig for," White replied. "You get gradations of passive recall from your present telephone number to your telephone number in Cleveland."

"Let me get this straightened out in my own mind," said Emmet. "Take passive recall. I start turning focused attention on passive recall and suppose I don't get an instantaneous result."

"You have to wait for it to come up," interposed Harwood. "It is down in storage somewhere."

"Listen," said White. "When you drive your car, and you stop, and then when you get ready to start again, you have so often started that car and made the motion to throw it into first so many times and thrown in the clutch so many times and gone through the whole motion of it so often that you don't have to think about any of it. And yet it is all very focused."

"Is that active or passive?" asked Emmet.

"That is a focused active recall," White replied.

"I am not arguing about the active," said Emmet. "I am talking about the passive."

"Focused passive recall is to remember what your license number was last year," replied White.

"You have to fish for it," suggested Harwood. "It won't hit you in the face."

"No," said White. "You have to actually make the effort."

Recall, amplified; focused attention (state No. 16)

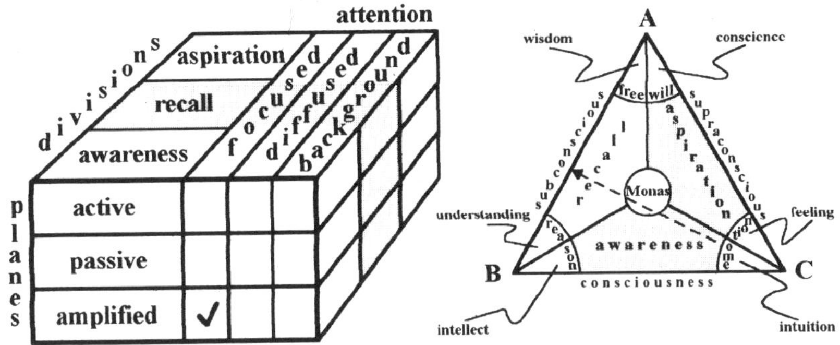

Figure 23

"Next you have focused amplified recall and here you get into psychiatry and I want to leave that for the moment," said White, continuing the conversation from the one immediately above.

"Well, just give us a tip-off so that we can be thinking about it," said Emmet.

"It is a suggestive, a deliberate suggestive recall," said White

"I have got it," said Harwood.

The subject was broached later in a passage dictated by Betty. The conversation was taken down by hand by Emmet.

"The same thing is happening here that happened when I gave you and Stewart The Unobstructed Universe," Betty began. "We have had to let you and Beese and Ruth too play with such terms as she could at first accept until the reality was conceived. It was easy enough to make her understand that there are only three types of attention. It was not so easy to make her understand that the mind, divided into the trilogy of the triangle, has only three types of activity -- active, passive and amplified. These three planes, let us call them, (Emmet suggests that fields would be better than planes) obtain in all three of the secondary triangles. The reason Ruth could not accept this fact at first was because of her complete realization and understanding of the motivation of the planes in the AOC triangle. Just to get the conception founded in her mind I want to name the motivation of the AOC triangle.

"The planes of the AOC secondary triangle are active, passive and amplified. They compare with the first terminology given as follows: The active equals prayer. The passive equals meditation. The amplified equals faith.

"Now we will go back to the amplified plane of the AOB secondary triangle of recall and operate it in conjunction with the three types of attention -- focused, diffused and background. The first thing to consider is that this line of attention drops from the 'C' hinge. It is colored by the arc of emotion, the cones of feeling and intuition and by the band of instinct leading direct to Monas. When focused attention is directed to amplified recall, you get dreams in sleep. These dreams are fairly well focused. They are frequently remembered and in the remembering you can almost always trace their outer dress to some recent happening.

"They are rather intuitive dreams -- dreams that have to do with matters not too deeply imbedded in the subconscious, which matters the dreamer can frequently ferret out for himself. Not always, but frequently depending upon the use to which he has put his intellect and reason. These dreams are useful to physicians only when a patient is convalescing after a long acute unbalance between his XYZ and ABC triangles. They do not indicate any abnormal mental condition, but rather a tired mental condition or a worried mental condition. Before we proceed with examining diffused attention on amplified recall, are there questions?"

"Let's go on with the discussion," said Harwood.

"First one question," said Emmet. "Why are these particular dreams rather intuitive, as you said they were?"

"I suppose I used the word intuitive in its less scientific sense," Betty replied.

"Did you use it in the sense of the use made of it in this divulgence?" asked Emmet.

"No," she replied. "Let me say just one more thing. These focused dreams deal with matters very close to the surface of the needs of the dreamer."

Recall, active; diffused attention (state No. 11)

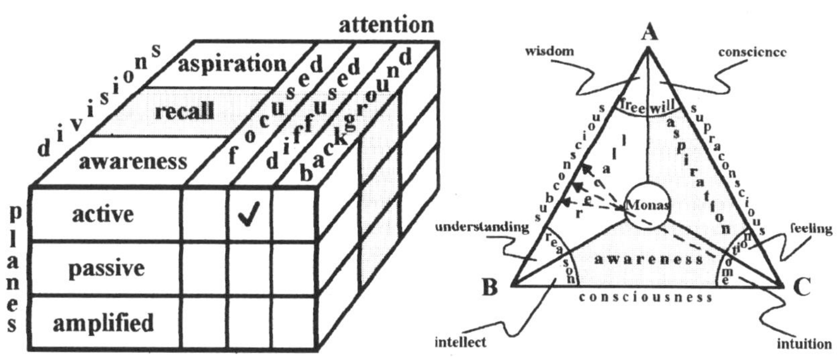

Figure 24

"Now let's go back and pick up your active recall with your diffused attention," said White, continuing an earlier conversation. "Here you get a quick emotional reaction out of the subconscious. You remember that this attention swings from the emotion arc. Something has happened to Monas in the way of perception or in his own thought that immediately arouses his emotions, so that he gets a diffused -- well it acts the same as it did in diffused awareness. It goes into the subconscious and all that is in the subconscious that can serve this need is actively recalled. It is a type of shock. It is a kind of shock recall."

Recall, passive; diffused attention (state No. 14)

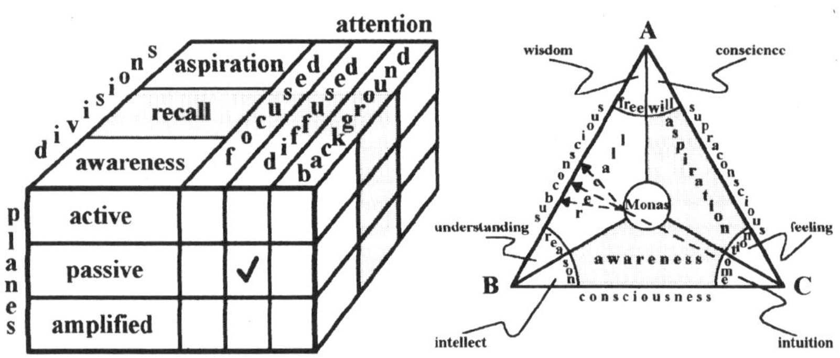

Figure 25

"Now we pass from the active to the passive," said White, "with diffused attention which means only that you go in deeper, that you go through a longer period of -- well, fear, for instance."

"Shock," suggested Emmet.

"Shock," agreed White. "And you get more out of your subconscious for protection or for solution. Frequently in this diffused passive recall you get solution of a large problem, something that has gone over a long period of time, something perhaps that goes clear into your childhood to find a comparable occurrence. And the problem is solved."

White expanded on this somewhat at a different session.

"We are now discussing diffused attention, I think, in the recall secondary triangle," he began, "and I think we have finished with the active plane and we are ready to go on and have perhaps gone on into the diffused attention of the passive plane.

"We went clear through all three planes of recall with focused attention. Now we are at diffused attention on the passive plane. Here Monas has to get busy. He has a diffused attention and he must get down into the passive plane of the subconscious to get a complementary empirical knowledge to complete his action or solve his problem or write his poem or do something. And it is a voluntary act on the part of Monas with diffused attention, which is broad and not just one focused thing. Diffused attention is the same always. Is that clear?"

<u>Recall, amplified; diffused attention (state No. 17)</u>

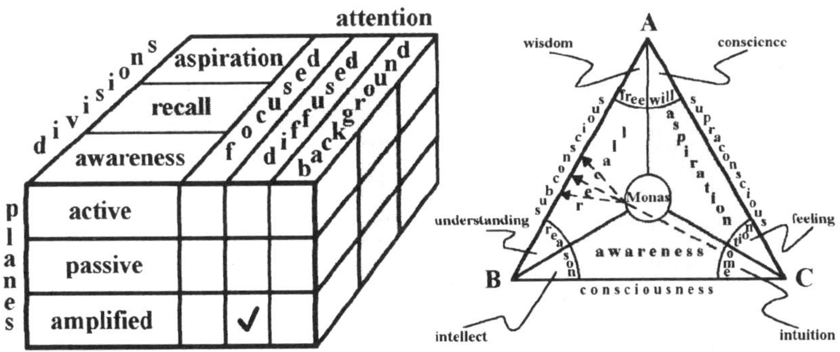

Figure 26

"Now we come to amplified recall with diffused attention, and here again we get into the psychiatric field." White then abruptly dropped the subject but later picked it up again.

"All modern mental therapeutics are based on amplified recall and the use of the three types of attention on the same," he said. "That third plane is all one subject."

From Betty we have the following speech.

"This is a type of subconscious knowledge that may or may not be formulated as a dream," she began. "Under certain stresses a person by the use of diffused attention in the subconscious can recall to his awareness things that he has willed to forget. These matters are usually regretful to him -- something that he has put aside in many cases successfully. But if he has not been completely successful in putting them aside and if they have not been handled by the quality of his supraconscious flowing over the 'A' hinge, they can create a subconscious disturbance that may manifest itself in a restless sleep of unremembered dreams. Here is where the physician can sometimes advantageously step in, and by the use of methods lately developed, and which the doctor can discuss with you, aid the patient in uncovering this subtle and to him unknown and unconnected disturbance."

In Figure 27 Betty is dictating. It is a continuation from the speech given directly above.

"Now the third type of attention, background attention on amplified recall is rarely if ever recognized by the dreamer without specific aid," she continued. "Usually it boils and moils in the subconscious without even formulating itself into the shape of a dream. This happens when individual exper-

Recall, amplified; background attention (state No. 18)

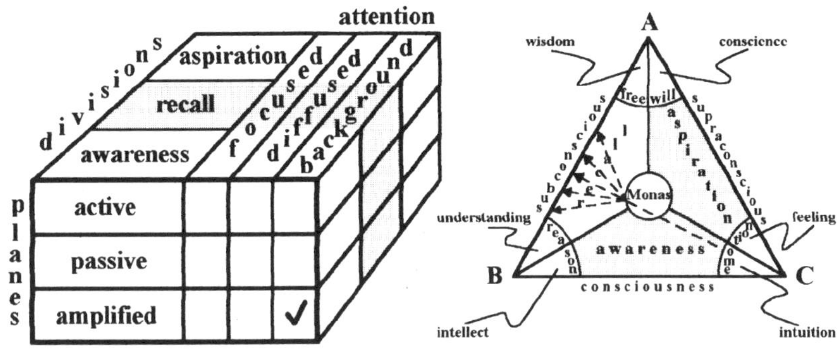

Figure 27

iences are accentuated in the subconscious band by racial or degree experiences from the supraconscious. They can be of two types: a racial knowledge that is below the quality of the individual and so disturbing to him and antagonizing to him, or the opposite, that is, race knowledge awakened in the subconscious so far beyond the qualitative ability of the individual as to upset him.

"Now these things that I have said to you about the three types of attention directed at amplified recall of the subconscious are the barest outline," she continued. "They are suggestive only and are intended to provoke questions and discussion. I wish to say that this is a new and enormous field. It is not your province or ours to go into it too deeply. But it must be recognized and enough must be said for the specialist to be given a new key for analysis. We would like to clear this before we discuss the AOC secondary triangle."

"Why is the word 'amplified' used in this secondary triangle or in any secondary triangle?" asked Emmet. "What is the special significance of the word in this connection?"

"The term 'amplified' means pretty much what it says in your ordinary definition of the word," replied Betty. "Beese gave Ruth an example of an application of it this morning that is pat. The active part of a radio is the input from the antenna to the grid. The passive part of the radio equals the B Battery. The output or audio circuit equals amplification. In other words, amplification is the result of the other two."

"I am not quite satisfied yet," said Emmet. "What is the point of similarity between amplified awareness and amplified recall?"

"Similar in intensity," she replied. "The 'C' hinge is conditioned by two bands that meet -- perception and supraconscious. Suppose we take a concrete example that Beese has been dealing with -- his friend Hooge. It is not possible to get the attention line from the 'C' hinge as deep in the recall secondary triangle as the amplification plane without a tilt.

"Now it is at this hinge, the 'C' hinge, that the closest connection is made with the XYZ triangle. Unbalance of either triangle puts a stress on the other. Hooge started out with a fairly normal dream difficulty, an adolescent dream difficulty. Certain impingements were made on his perception band and carried into his awareness that were of a highly emotional nature. He had had a bad home experience and was unlucky in love -- both dealing directly as far as he was concerned with his sex instinct. His quality was not of the type to will this out. So the background attention of the supraconscious, which is quite directly connected with race experience and racial instinct, got to operating in his amplified subconscious, where all this stuff had naturally gone.

"Now from here you can take up the doctor's diagnosis. All I have done, and what he could not do at the time because we had not then created the mechanism of the triangles, is to tell you the operation of the resulting fact or condition diagramatically."

"It seems to me," said Harwood, "the amplification always come from the outside."

"You mean that amplification is the result of both active and passive attention," said Betty. "Consequently it is a direct impingement from, now get this, the XYZ triangle or the BC line. What does this mean? We are talking, remember of the subconscious. You can get a subconscious reaction from any internal bodily disturbance or in prolonged awareness disturbance.

"What I was going to say was that in no other of the secondary triangles save that of recall is amplification affected in the same way. It is true, however, that the body and its functions do affect all three secondary triangles and their functions. But the one most affected is the AOB secondary triangle, because the attention line operating through it drops from the 'C' hinge, which is the closest connection with the XYZ triangle."

"Is an amplified memory caused by a stimulated emotion?" This from Harwood.

"It could be," Betty replied. "It could also be caused by the type of memory it is, being strengthened or enhanced by direct supraconscious contact over the 'A' hinge."

Betty rarely being present at these sessions, the topic was further elaborated by Stewart Edward White.

"Amplified recall is always influenced or increased by some impingement outside Monas," he began. "Active and passive are controlled entirely by Monas. The third recall, namely, amplified, is partially controlled by Monas but impelled in the first instance by an outside influence or impingement.

"Do you see," he continued, "how this one plane of each of the three secondary triangles would be impinged upon and amplified from the outside, rather than just by Monas himself?"

"Well," said Harwood, "impingement on the BC line --"

"That was shock," interrupted White. "We agree upon that. We gave several examples.

"Now on the subconscious band when you get amplified recall, you must have another type of shock. It can come from the XYZ triangle in the form of a very sharp illness or it can come in the form of an unsatisfied race hunger or in the form of an emotion that is very much uncontrolled by Monas and which is a race or degree emotion, or which originates in the XYZ triangle. That is why in this particular plane of recall you have your psychiatric field. Does that mean anything?"

"A lot to me," replied Harwood.

At this point the machine was turned off for a moment while Ruth was trying to collect herself. Then Harwood started asking a series of questions that he had written out.

"How do active and passive awareness interact to produce amplified awareness?" he said.

"It is not a question of interaction so much as it is one of passing through the three phases of awareness," White replied. "Any awareness that is focused or diffused appears first in the active plane. If it gets consideration it goes into the passive plane where it is given further consideration. That is, it is more than a momentary focus. And then if there is a repeat of the impingement or if the original impingement is very severe, very great, either in shock or extreme happiness or extreme humor or anything of the kind, it goes on into the amplified plane. It is a kind of intensification, an upward intensification of the original impingement."

At this point Harwood professed to be somewhat confused.

"Let's get to a definition," said White. "Take shock because it is the easiest. In a case of shock where you have a resultant amplified awareness, the mind accepts the first shock, then it considers it and gets a realization in the passive plane of awareness of the enormity of the shock, and then it goes back into the active consideration of it and then it passes back into the passive and on to the amplified. That is just a human action you can realize if you figure it out for yourself. First there is a shock that attracts your focused attention in the active field."

"It might be in the amplified field." suggested Harwood.

"No, not at first," replied White.

"It has to get in first," contributed Emmet.

"Let me state my understanding," he continued. "The thing goes in your active as the result of focused attention. The active then passes it into the passive where it gets diffused attention. Now it is a shock and it won't stay put. It tarries a while, taking the normal course in the passive but it refuses to stay there, bobbing back into the focused attention in the active field and there it is again turned over, fussed with and fumed about and ultimately in consequence of all this consideration it has had (I don't know whether it goes again then into the passive, I suppose it does), in any case it floods the whole field and gets into the amplified recall region and then it may be entirely out of hand. That is what happens to people, though I am not sure that my statement of it makes the matter clear."

"Yes it does," replied White. "You go further than I. I did not carry it outside the field of awareness for the first example. But that is exactly what occurs. You see the amplified band in the awareness field can jump. It can flow into the subconscious, as it does, and go immediately into the amplified field of recall without having anything else happen to it in the subconscious."

At this point Emmet said he thought that battle shock might be an illustration of this."

"Yes, I should think it would be this way," said Harwood. "If something happened that brought a condition of battle shock to a person it would go into either the passive or active awareness. That would produce a state of amplified awareness immediately."

"The mind operates this way, ditching all terminology for the moment," replied White. "You have a shock. You are quite aware of it, and instantaneously you think something about it. Then you stop thinking about it. Now that thinking is in the passive plane. You are aware and you are thinking in the passive plane. All of that is done. The active plane does thinking too but it is a momentary thinking. But in the case of shock it goes back and forth and you may get a recurrence of the shock."

"Back and forth," Harwood chimed in. "Then it goes into amplified awareness and focused attention."

"No," White corrected. "Amplified awareness and usually diffused attention. Because you see it is a very high degree of attention. Or the person may become very stunned by the shock. It may go into background attention and when it does go in the background attention, it immediately jumps into amplified recall. It is put from amplified awareness into amplified recall. And that is why with the shock stuff you get this peculiar shock condition. The amplified subconscious is the depths of the subconscious. It is up closest to the 'A' hinge. It is where you get your quickest reaction from the AC line."

<u>Recall, active; background attention (state No. 12)</u>

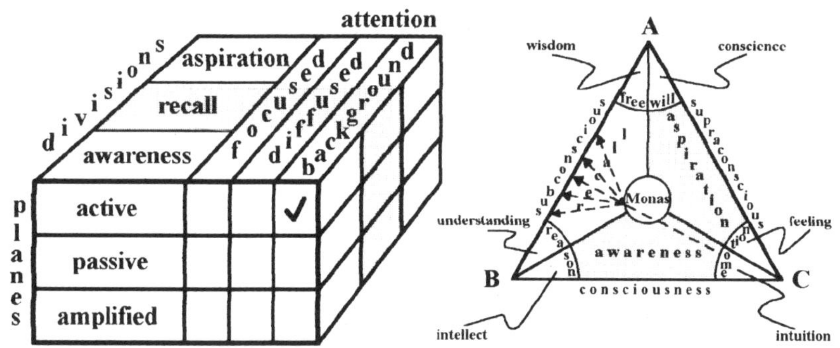

Figure 28

For the programmers we have a couple of tidbits at this point. Harwood was speaking. He wanted some information on imagination.

"Where does imagination reside?" he asked. "In the Betty records it was spoken of as the key to the pattern."

"Imagination resides, understand, resides, in background attention of active recall," said White. It operates in the intellect cone and on the thought line. It has to operate there."

"Good answer," said Harwood. "Now where does the desire wish reside?"

"The desire wish resides in the focused attention of the active aspiration triangle," said White.

"Fine," replied Harwood.

"It operates like all your modern processes through will down in your 'B' hinge," White added.

"Can't it also operate through the instinct and emotion aspects?" asked Harwood.

"Not until you have thought about it," replied White.

We now return to background attention and active recall. White is speaking.

"Now active recall as we told you in the beginning is the recall that is close, that takes very little, in fact, no effort," he began. "And this background that is on the alert is just floating around of itself, very lazy like, half thinking, etc. It is suddenly attracted by an active recall and it comes into the memory and it may be important and it may not be important. But it is there. You are idly sitting in a glider on the porch and you see a lovely sunset over the river and you admire it and you don't think much of anything about it. You are just watching the colors. Suddenly out of active recall into this background of attention comes a memory of a sunset at the hill. That is all it is."

On another occasion he undertook the definition of background attention.

"Background attention must be thoroughly understood of itself before it can be applied to the subconscious or to any of the planes," he said.

"Background attention is the -- it is attention but it is not focused and it is not diffused. It is just attention -- that is all. Here is where you experience it quite definitely: just before you go to sleep. You kind of half know the telephone is ringing and you are just not going to bother doing anything about it."

"I think it is more than that," said Emmet.

"Let me make an amusing picture of it," said Harwood. "Focused attention is a round blob of something that sits just in one spot. In the case of diffused attention, the blob gets spread out over an area thick. In the case of background attention, it is spread over a bigger area and thinner."

"Very good," said White. "You mean diffused attention is fat."

"Take this example," said Emmet. "Focused attention is a beam of light straight and direct. Diffused attention has a cone of light made by, say, a lamp shade. Background attention is just a general light and a dimmer one."

"Like sheet lightning," said White.

"Like any spread out light," said Emmet. "In one case you have a direct beam, as with a flashlight. In another case you have a shaded lamp that diffuses light over a reading area. In the third case you have the whole room illuminated dimmer."

"The first is a searchlight," said White.

"Now we have background attention with active recall," he continued. "And here again you get a musing mood. It is hardly awareness. You have gone back of awareness. You have gone with your background attention into your subconscious and you are kind of just thinking of things that happened recently."

"Reverie," suggested Harwood.

"That is the word," concurred White. "Exactly the word."

"As applied to the subconscious," corrected Emmet. "In the BOC triangle it would be something else again."

"Something more definite," said White. "But here in this triangle, where you have background attention on the subconscious, that is all you have got."

"One is inside and the other is outside," said Harwood. "Otherwise they are the same."

"Yes," concurred White.

"In the one case you are paying attention to things that happen --," began Harwood.

"You are just watching the outside world," White interrupted. "And in the other case you are watching memories of the day that has just gone by. You are just sort of dreaming about it, turning it over in your mind."

"That is very clear," said Harwood.

"Now we take up passive recall with background attention," White continued. "Here you are getting closer to contemplation. You have empirical knowledge in passive recall. And your background attention is not exactly seeking it, but it is connected with it. Background attention is very inactive, very lazy. It is not prodded the way the other attentions are, though Monas does have to operate it."

"I am afraid Monas has to operate everything," said Emmet.

"Yes," White agreed. "But background attention and passive recall are difficult to explain. Well, it is a point of this kind: I can give you only an example I find in the station's mind. It is background attention plus passive recall where you can get out of your own mind and later formulate a poem, put it

Recall, passive; background attention (state No. 15)

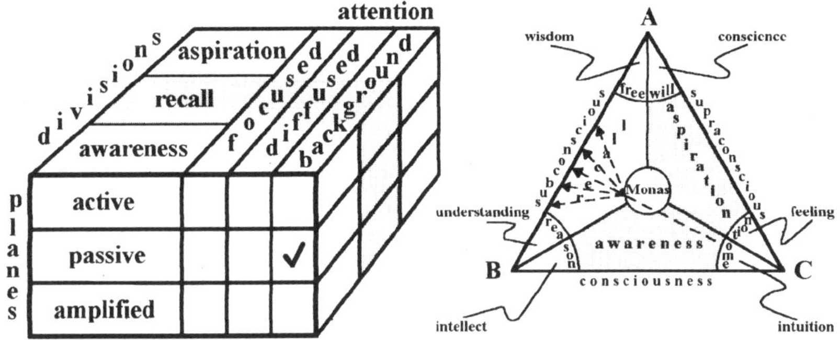

Figure 29

into form like a sonnet. Background attention sort of seeps through your empirical knowledge and finds something worth bringing out or turning over to intellect for actual thought."

"As I see it, it is a reverie state, which is --," began Harwood.

Here White interrupted. "The first was reverie," he said.

"It is hard not to use the same word," complained Harwood. "It is a dreamy state though you are awake."

"But all background attention is more or less a dreamy state," said his brother.

"That's what I mean," continued Harwood. "It is a dreamy state where you are not concerned with your immediate recollection, but which arises slowly out of the past or the deeper layers of your subconscious. In the more active recall you would have things streaming through it, and in passive recall with background attention you just sense it as a sort of influence. Eventually --"

"You have said it," interrupted White. "You sense it as an influence upon yourself, as something you possess, and then you activate it afterward."

"You probably don't even recall it immediately," suggested Emmet.

"No," said White. "It is just a sense of a thing that is there, that you ought to be able to grasp."

"It probably comes upgrade," said Emmet. "Up through the passive into --"

"It might not even come up grade," interrupted Harwood. "It might remain as a coloration only."

"It is a very delicate state of conscious subconscious," said White. "That is a queer way of saying it, but it is really what it is. You see we are so handicapped for words."

"I think the thing that expresses it clearest to me is the difference between an influence you feel in your subconscious and a fact that presents itself as a concrete memory." This from Harwood.

"Yes," said White. "You see in both of your other types of attention you do get concrete definite memories."

"You get a net result," said Emmet.

"Yes, that is good," said White. "In the other two types of attention in the subconscious you get a net result in the passive recall. But in this you don't. You just get the color -- a sort of feeling."

"Background attention might stimulate other types of attention and thus apply them also," suggested Emmet.

"That is what I said," replied White. "Later you apply the other attentions. Background attention just simply gives you the feeling that you can write this poem -- do you see?"

"Or, not to be so artistic about it, it might just give you the feeling that there is something down there that has to do with this thing here," Emmet contributed. "Then you get the feel of it, the touch of it, but you don't do anything about it."

"But you do do something about it ultimately," said White.

"Then you can say, I am going to do something about that. I am going to find out what it is," said Harwood.

"Then you recall the exact memory," said White.

"We might argue this way, correlating it with the first secondary triangle," said Emmet. "Background attention there is easily explained, and things do register. But take the case of the observant man who was referred to the other day. He noted everything in the room and if you ask him ten minutes later he would remember everything in the room. On the other hand, if you asked the average fellow ten minutes later what color the wallpaper was, etc., etc., he would not know. And yet when you get that same background attention applied in the subconscious he probably does know what color the paper was and he gets the feeling of it in the background, and later on he will be able to remember what the color of the paper in the room was. But if you asked him just after he left the room what the color of the paper was, he would not know."

"Precisely," said White. "That is one of the phenomena of this very thing. I am sorry we ourselves could not get it through, but we did get it through you. That is definite and actual. That is the purpose of the background attention on passive recall. Just that."

"Much more than writing poems," said Emmet.

This completes the material on the recall mind.

Chapter 12. The Aspiration Mind

THE aspiration mind is the third part of the mind, the particular contribution of White and the Invisibles to a subject which they said was generally thought to consist of only two parts, the conscious and subconscious minds. It has strong religious connotations and on this basis was at first resisted by both Emmet and Harwood. But White was firm on this point and eventually the other two gave in. There is no record of a similar objection from Ruth; but we know from other sources that both she and Betty were deeply religious anyway.

I will start with material generic to the aspiration secondary triangle -- the aspiration mind. Following this I will present material specific to the nine states of the aspiration mind.

The aspiration mind: an overview

The following material is from a very late session, one of the last in the series. It took place on June 20, 1947, with both Stewart Edward and Betty White present. White is dictating.

"We left off our discussion last evening with trying to tell you about the use of the amplified aspiration in connection with the three types of attention," White began. "Amplified aspiration is the climax, the result of active and passive aspiration. Here it is that you actually contact the source.

"I find in Ruth's mind a quite definite modern example of how this works," she continued. "She gave you a book the other day, Beese, by a man named Emmett Fox who has built up a tremendous following on one point, and this is what he calls scientific prayer. It is a very good psychological method that he has taught people to use. And in about 90 cases out of 100 it works. Ruth is sold on it because it has worked for her.

"Now his method that he teaches in simple language is this. You formulate by means of prayer the thought that you are troubled about or on which you want help, that you want solved. Then you stop thinking about it, and you meditate not upon your problem but upon something that is more aspiring and inspiring to you. If you are fond of the Bible you read verses of scripture. If you are fond of verse you repeat or read verse to yourself and try to understand it, try to get the other person's point of view. But in all cases you drive out of your mind the difficulty concerning which you have formulated your approach to the AC line, which is, so far as you are concerned, the Source. That is, it is the direct connection with the source.

"Now according to Fox you raise your consciousness -- that is what he calls it -- by your meditation not upon your problem but on something greater than your problem, something infinitely better than your problem. And in doing so you permit the inflow through the amplified attention of the solution from the source, the help that you have asked for. He has got -- and that is one reason for his success -- very close to the actual facts of the case though he has never diagrammed the matter. He simply has it in words, simply in his own understanding. He knew how he touched the source and he simply translated it for other people.

"The thing to remember is that the AC band contains all with which you come into the world endowed, plus all the potentiality that is afterward developed. It joins directly on your perception line or band, the conscious band of your world existence. Here is where perception first touches you and the first perceptions that come are very slight. They do not make much of an impression on the awareness mechanism or as you now term it the awareness secondary triangle.

"But you also have to remember that at the 'C' hinge is the arc of emotion, the cone of feeling and cone of intuition. Now as you watch children develop you must have realized that their first use, their first contact with the world, is through those three aspects of their minds -- emotion, feeling and intuition. You don't have to teach a baby to nurse. It blindly seeks sustenance. It instinctively does that. It expresses feeling before it has any real perception. And certainly you have emotion reaction before you have real perception.

"Now the line that runs from the 'C' hinge directly to Monas is instinct, and in all this arc you have man's instinctive, emotional, intuitive, feeling knowledge that somewhere, some place, some how, he is part of a thing that is greater than he and that ought to be able to serve him.

"There are people who use that intuitive knowledge. They get quick reactions. They are not people who in your modern day and age are most admired usually. If they do that they are frequently lacking in understanding of their fellow men. They are primitives in a way.

"So for the modern man to operate his AC line he must use his 'C' hinge secondarily and the hinge from which his attention drops to the AC band primarily, and on that hinge is reason, intellect and understanding.

"There is a choice of prayer. Certainly no intelligent person would ask for that which he knows cannot be accomplished. But you have to use your intellect first, get understanding, deliberately project it into your aspiration triangle, and then loosen your intellect, or rather yourself, from your intellectual processes enough to permit the operation of passive attention on the aspiration center, if you are going to get actual inflow through the amplified aspiration field.

"Because, I told you last night, that amplified aspiration is not wholly at the disposal of Monas. Active aspiration, passive aspiration, yes. Active aspiration and passive aspiration on the part of Monas feed amplified aspiration. But always somewhere from the outside comes an accentuation of amplified consciousness. And in the case of the AC line it comes from the degree of which Monas is a part and out of which Monas came."

The material for Figure 30 starts with conversation between the two White brothers.

"We have yet to trace the various types of attention in the various planes of the AOC triangle." This from Harwood.

"Very well," said White. "We will apply the three types of attention first to the active plane of aspiration. In this triangle the active plane is some type of prayer. It is a formulation of a considered and long thought about and intellectualized and reasoned about wish. It is something that Monas has decided he wants. That is focused active attention." In the model's terms, focused attention on active aspiration.

"Outline a method of approaching the AC line for the intellectually overbalanced person," requested Harwood. "The person who is in the grip of his intellect and cannot get away from it."

Aspiration, active; focused attention (state No. 19)

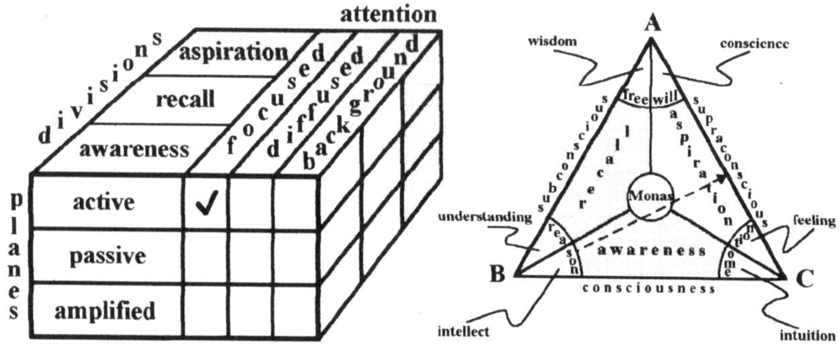

Figure 30

"That method," White replied, "is to all intents and purposes the same method that I have just outlined for approaching the AC line.

"We assume that most people who will read this divulgence have a fairly good intellect," he continued. "The man who is hide-bound intellectually, and self-sufficient intellectually -- or thinks he is -- will probably have to have an emotional shock for him to will his approach to the AC line at all -- if by the AC line you mean help by way of contact with the source.

"It is true that many intellectual people feed from their AC line without realizing the contact. This is done through the 'A' hinge, and they are people of very high talent in some special gift approaching genius. They are psychic and they will beyond peradventure pick up through their inspiration band and the 'A' hinge direct inspiration and direct solution of problems such as invention, a musical score, the plot of a story and what have you.

"I admit that in discussing formerly the amplified aspiration aspect, that I had in my own thought more the peace of mind that man so desperately needs at this time on earth. The route for the hide-bound intellectual is, again, through the focused attention on the active aspiration. You will not get your result through amplified aspiration. You will get it up over the 'A' hinge and down through the inspiration band."

"I was a hide-bound intellectual," confessed Harwood. "So I know what a person of that type is up against. Last night I was talking about one approach. It seemed to me a very good one -- an approach through the medium of feeling or that perception you have just been talking about. It seems to me a person could identify that more concretely, with more conviction, than most anything else."

"There may be people who could," admitted White. "But I doubt it, if they were as hide-bound as you seem to wish this example to be. I think that first you have to have the desire-wish, and the desire-wish is certainly the focused attention on the active aspiration. You aspire to feel, you want to get away from this intellectually hide-bound influence that is not giving you mental satisfaction, certainly not emotional satisfaction. You can jump from one thing to another. There is always a process of building -- a process of evolution even in your thought. So I am of the opinion that you would have to think intellectually back to Monas and then put your aspiration triangle in operation through your focused attention. It might take it some time to work but except as you get down your inspiration line -- now you have said you have had your nose rubbed in this. What is that nose rubbing?"

"I would like to know," declared Harwood. "What is that process by which I started with communication and gradually got to the other thing?"

"Inspiration," said White.

"It came that way?" asked Harwood.

"It came down from the 'A' hinge," insisted White.

"Please trace the route," said Harwood.

"Focused attention on the active aspiration," replied White. "You aspired to something. You are a psychic of a type. You got your aspiration secondary triangle into motion. It began to fluctuate, to operate. It is a part of your mind. And so what came to you is obvious. In addition to being intellectual you had the psychic quality with which you were born. It was a talent with you. It was inspired and it came down the inspiration line. Then it turned into instinct and ran down the instinct band and finally wound up in your feeling cone. Why not?"

"When I do this inspiration thing it comes into the AC line up near 'A', doesn't it?" asked Harwood.

"Yes," replied White.

"Where does it go then?" asked Harwood. "Direct to Monas? How does it get down to the 'B' corner? What is the route?"

"It goes to Monas and from Monas it goes down the instinct line," replied White.

"But I get it in the form of an idea, which is over toward 'B'," complained Harwood.

"Well, what is an emotion?" asked White rhetorically. "Something in your mind. It is an idea that has taken hold in your mind in an out-moving way. You cannot have an emotion without having a thought about. If you recognize an emotion you certainly think about it."

"But my question is," continued Harwood, "when you get an inspiration how does it get down to the 'B' corner? Give me the route."

"Entering the 'A' hinge couldn't it leak down the subconscious to the 'B' hinge and then go up the thought line to Monas?" This was Emmet's contribution.

"Yes," White replied. "It can do that with some people. It can run into the subconscious provided only you have had some type of empirical knowledge dropped into the subconscious that attracts it."

"Suppose there is no empirical knowledge?" asked Harwood.

"Now, listen," said White. "In your case there was, because you had all the knowledge about Betty's work and my work."

"Then it did come through my subconscious?" asked Harwood.

"It might have in your case," replied White, "but I doubt it. I think it came as I told you.

"I told you in detail that it came down the inspiration line or band, to Monas, that there it can be recognized by Monas' instinct," said White. "Or it can go as thought over to the reason arc as an idea, where it can be dealt with by reason and intellect."

"Just what I wanted," said Harwood, evidently pleased.

"The latter would be natural for Beese inasmuch as he is fundamentally intellectual rather than emotional," said Emmet.

"Another thing," said Harwood. "I had a so-called cosmic consciousness experience once -- and a half, I might say -- and that was an emotional experience."

"You must realize that the triangle is a whole," said White, "that there are really no boundaries, that all intellectualizations can leap across the awareness secondary triangle towards your emotional arc. You can get different effects without things going up to Monas and back down."

The experience of cosmic consciousness is a major goal of some mystic disciplines. It is discussed in more detail a bit later in this chapter.

There followed material already given concerning the desire wish, which White said resides in the focused attention of the active aspiration triangle, but operates -- like all modern processes -- through will in the "B" hinge.

Aspiration, active; diffused attention (state No. 20)

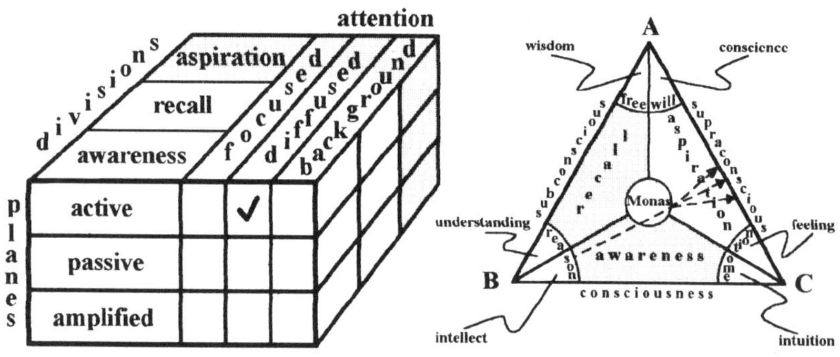

Figure 31

The next several categories were presented in a single lengthy dictation by White. I break them into separate categories here to facilitate the presentation.

"Now we take the diffused active aspiration, which is an attention that is given with the same acuteness that characterizes diffused attention in any other triangle," said White. "And here Monas himself decides to do something about it. He tries to add or draw out of the inspiration band something for himself. In other words, he has aspired, and now he tries himself out in connection with this prayer -- tries to make it active.

"Background attention on active aspiration," continued White, "is not exactly conscience, but a kind of mood -- a sort of frustration too. It is where you find the square pegs in round holes. It

<u>Aspiration, active; background attention</u>

<u>(state No. 21)</u>

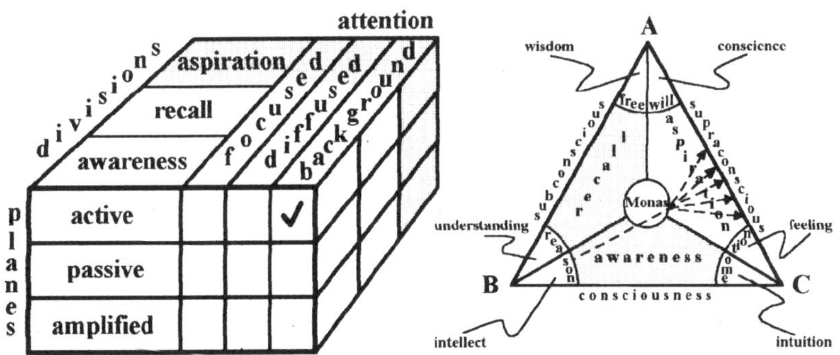

Figure 32

is where you find a man, for instance, who has aspired to be a musician. He does not acquire, that is, he aspires without acquisition. It may not be his own fault, but always in the background of his attention, of his supraconscious, is this wish. And attention is called to this wish, sometimes acutely and sometimes not so acutely. But it is always there and it is the thing he never accomplishes."

"Now we will pass to the passive plane of aspiration with focused attention," continued White with reference to Figure 33. "Here man goes beyond prayer. He has formulated his wish. He knows perfectly well what he wants and gives his focused, meditated thought to it. He reasons about it.

Aspiration, passive; focused attention (state No. 22) plus
Aspiration, passive; diffused attention (state No. 23)

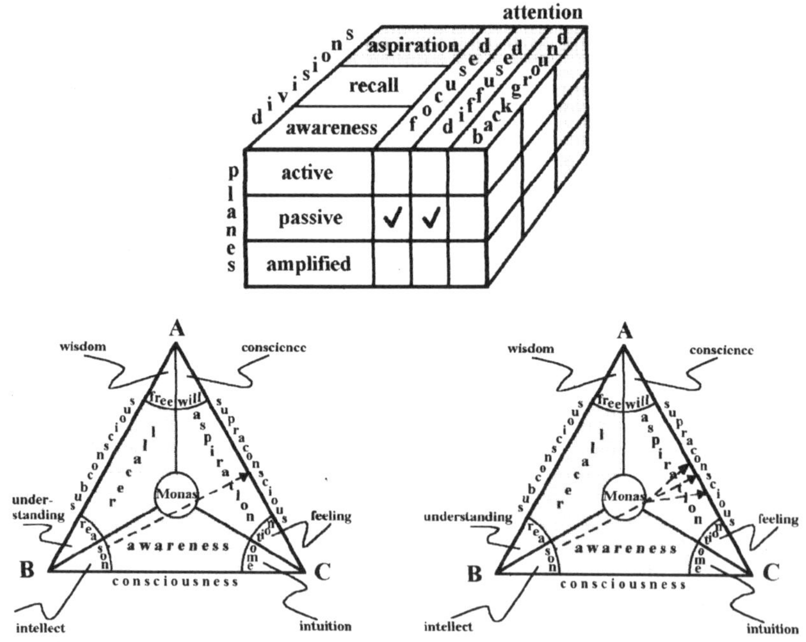

Figure 33

Aspiration, passive; background attention

(state No. 24)

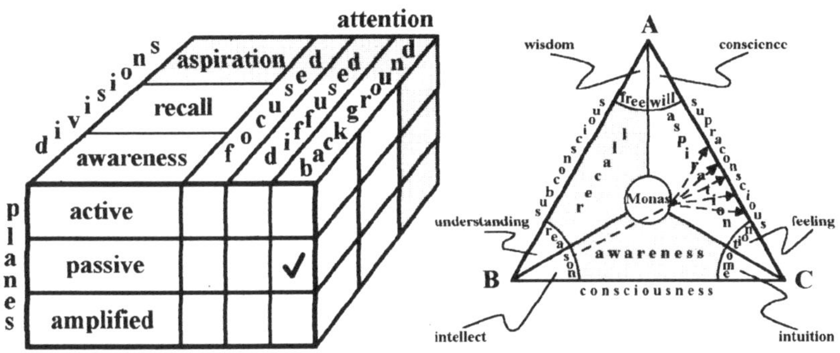

Figure 34

"He intellectualizes over it. He considers it. If he gets as far as diffused attention there, he brings to bear on it a great deal of that which he has placed in his subconscious. All his empirical knowledge. He is now getting very close to his amplified attention. This is true meditation."

"And when you get to the background attention," continued White, "if he has really brought to this meditation all the empirical knowledge he has stored, and has tried to seek, pull out -- and Monas can pull out of all his boundaries -- what is there of his quality, you will have a background attention that lives with him. Now if he has not colored it with dogmatic thinking, it will be something quite comforting to him, because all the time it will be in the background of his general attention on other things. He has thought about it and has meditated on it and is getting very close now to faith, his amplified supraconscious.

The three categories depicted in Figure 35 are presented by White in a single coherent speech.

"Now, amplified supraconscious is very close to

Aspiration, amplified; focused attention (state No. 25) plus Aspiration, amplified; diffused attention (state No. 26) plus Aspiration, amplified; background attention (state No. 27)

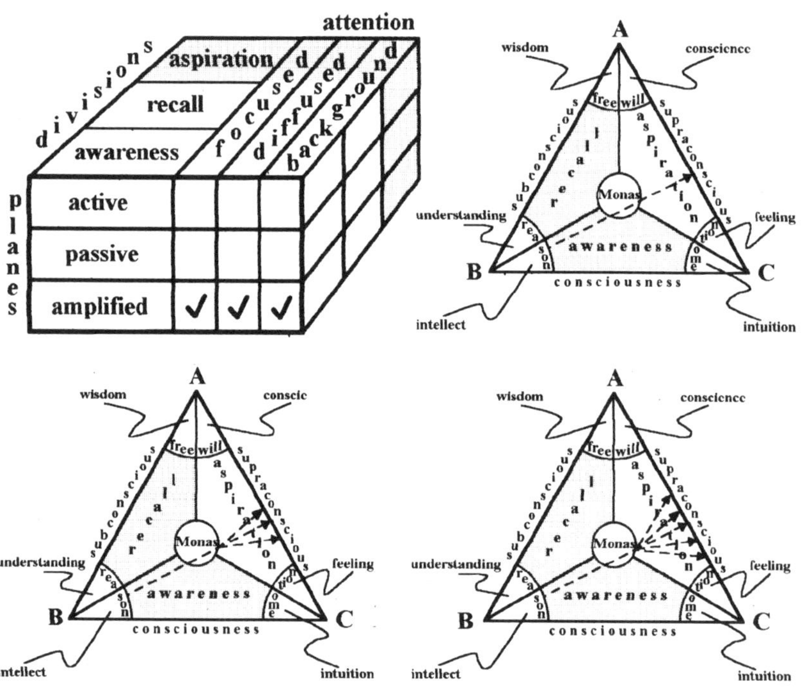

Figure 35

the 'C' hinge," said White, continuing the dictation presented in state No. 24. "You would expect it to be the other way -- up by the 'A' arc. The reason it is close to the 'C' hinge is because it is here that

Monas is emotionally tied to the body he inhabits for gathering of quantity.

"This region is very primitive. It is where all the things that you were educated away from still linger. Here you have it hitched to emotion, which is very close to the XYZ triangle. You have feeling here and intuition and the great line of instinct running up to Monas himself.

"Now we apply Monas' own focused attention to his amplified supraconscious and the thing that Monas wants when he gets to that is faith," White continued. "He wants to know beyond doubt that he is immortal, that he can reach out into this supraconscious of his and not only draw out his own quality but touch his degree for an emergency supply. This is done by the operation of the attention line from the 'B' hinge. And here we have thought and reason and intellect and understanding. And we have to apply that to the amplified supraconscious by means of focused and diffused attention. And when you have faith, you have it in your background attention to live with. You know then that you *are*, that you can *get*. 'Except you become as little children, you cannot enter the kingdom'.

"Now the kingdom is your own faith in your attachment to the whole, your faith that you are a part of the whole, that you can draw on the whole. And you have to become as a little child because it was as such that you came into the world with only your supraconscious, with the potential only of your awareness, your conscious, and of your subconscious. You came in with emotion, with feeling and with intuition. These were your gifts, and you had to develop all the rest out of your own potential."

Summing up the aspiration mind

After this elevated speech even Emmet was cowed.

"The Lord did not make all this reasonable, and I suppose our job is to make it reasonable," said Emmet. "Because it has not been made reasonable is why so many people today are not so much impressed with the Lord. You see he could not make it reasonable in the terms of today."

"No," said White, "but the reason he said you had to become as a little child is because you have to go back and develop that intuitive feeling that is at the 'C' hinge. You have got to get that back, before you are going to have the background attention grounded -- and that is what it means -- in your amplified supraconscious."

"Amplified can be bad as well as good, I suppose," said Emmet. "Can't you get into the psychiatric phase by way of the supraconscious just the same as anywhere else?"

"You will remember I told you that in the diffused attention of the passive phase you had to avoid dogma and emotional hypotheses, and all the rest of it," said White. "That you had to use clear intellect and clear reason -- it is for that that you were given them -- that you had to have understanding.

"I also told you tonight that always in the amplified plane there is a help, an augmentation from outside Monas. Now that applies here. And just as surely as you start to operate that amplified supraconscious with focused attention -- and particularly with diffused attention -- you are going to get that augmentation from the outside. In other words, if you really ask, really knock, it is going to come down your AC line from your degree, or from the outside into your degree. Either way you want to put it. Just exactly as it comes into every other hinge. It works in the same way. The only reason it has not worked in the field of aspiration is because men have forgotten to work it."

"You do not have to ask for functional use at the other hinges," said Emmet. "It just comes along and hits you."

"Well, it used to come along and hit men in this hinge too," said White. "It happens in the other hinges now because you have there used your active and passive planes."

"You can't help it when a bomb hits you on the BC line," observed Emmet.

"That is perfectly true," said White, "but if you use them (active and passive planes) in the aspiration secondary triangle, you darn well cannot help having the result occur there too."

This completes the material on the aspiration mind, and with it the technical description of the model.

Epilogue

A LOT OF WATER has passed under the bridge of Western Civilization since 1940 when Stewart Edward White published, with Ruth Finley's assistance, *The Unobstructed Universe*, and a deal more since 1918 when Margaret Cameron initiated this body of work with her epoch-making book, *The Seven Purposes*. Each of these literary events caused a flurry of excitement and attracted followers both from the general public and from the scientific community.

White reported that scientific work was building progressively toward acceptance of *The Unobstructed Universe*'s unconventional physics. He couldn't have been more wrong. Since his time the positions have hardened, and today's scientist risks his or her career by embracing anything that smacks of the occult.

A similar condition obtains in the field of religion. The findings of Cameron, Finley and Betty White constitute authentic field reports of the deepest possible significance to followers of any faith whatever. Have these reports had an impact on contemporary theologians? None that I can discern.

The scientific community considers these views as medieval superstitions and the natural enemy of science. The religious community follows canons of long ago and finds new material either irrelevant or troublesome. The New Age embraces them of course. But a quarantine sign is up on New Age thought, and mainstream thinkers avoid it like the plague.

You and I know these well-meaning Old Age folk are wrong, of course. I had hoped to point this out in the present volume. But even a book should stick to its last. There is little point to an appendix no one reads.

So be patient. There is a sequel in the works that will address the above concerns. If you are willing to do a bit of heavy mental slogging, we can share these thoughts together, all in good time.

After all, even *fools rush in where angels fear to tread.*

THE END

REFERENCES

Ambulance, The American (1916), *Friends of France* (Houghton Mifflin)

Brackman, Barbara (November/December, 1988), A biographical sketch of Ruth Finley (Quilters Newsletter Magazine)

Cameron, Margaret (1908), *The Cat and The Canary* (Harper)

Cameron, Margaret (1913), *The Golden Rule Dollivers* (Harper)

Cameron, Margaret (1911), *The Pretender Person* (Harper)

Cameron, Margaret (1918), *The Seven Purposes* (Harper & Brothers)

Cameron, Margaret (1919), *Twelve Lessons from The Seven Purposes* (Harper & Brothers)

Chalmers, David J. (1996), *The Conscious Mind* (Oxford University Press)

Chalmers, David J. (1995), 'The Puzzle of Conscious Experience', *Scientific American*, **273** (6) (December), pp. 80-87.

Cobb, John B. Jr. (1975), *Christ in a Pluralistic Age* (The Westminster Press)

Cobb, John B. Jr. and Griffin, David Ray (1976), *Process Theology* (The Westminster Press)

Darby and Joan (1920), *Our Unseen Guest* (Harper & Brothers)

Dennet, Daniel C. (1995), *Darwin's Dangerous Idea,* (Simon & Schuster)

Ebon, Martin (1971), *They Knew the Unknown* (The World Publishing Co.)

Eldredge, Niles and Gould, Stephen Jay (1972), 'Punctuated Equilibria: An Alternative to Phyletic Gradualism', *Models in Paleobiology,* edited by Schopf, Thomas J.M. (Freeman, Cooper & Company)

Finley, Ruth E. (1929), *Old Patchwork Quilts and the Women Who Made Them* ()

Finley, Ruth E. (1992), *Old Patchwork Quilts and the Women Who Made Them* (EPM Publications). This reissue contains a short biography of Ruth Finley written by Barbara Brackman.

Finley, Ruth (1931), *The Lady of Godey's* (J.B. Lippincott)

Ford, Arthur (1958), *Nothing So Strange* (Harper & Brothers)

Freud Sigmund (1969), *Darstellungen der Psychoanalyse* (Fischer Taschenbuch)

Gardner, Martin (1983), *The Whys of a Philosophical Scrivener* (Quill)

Gould, Stephen Jay (1989), *Wonderful Life* (W.W. Norton)

Gould, Stephen Jay (1977), *Ontogeny and Phylogeny* (the Belknap Press of Harvard University Press)

Gould, Stephen Jay (1994), 'The Evolution of Life on the Earth', *Scientific American,* **271** (4)

Holton, Gerald (1993), *Science and Anti-Science* (Harvard University Press)

James, William (1967), *A Pluralistic Universe* (p. Smith)

James, William (1898), *Human Immortality* (Houghton, Mifflin) (Dover 1956)

James, William (1902), *The Varieties of Religious Experience* (Longmans, Green, and Co.)

James, William (1896), *The Will to Believe* (Longman's Green) (Dover 1956)

Jung, C.G. (1965), *Memories, Dreams, Reflections* (Random House's Vintage books)

Kant, Immanuel (1776), *Dreams of a Ghost Seer* ()

Knight, Lovina May (1990), 'Who Was Joan?', *Spiritual Frontiers*, **Vol. XXII**, Spring issue, pp. 78-83.

Kurtz, Paul (1985), *A Skeptic's Handbook of Parapsychology* (Prometheus Books)

Lewis, R.W.B. (1991), *The Jameses* (Farrar, Straus and Giroux)

Lieberman, Philip (1984), *The Biology and Evolution of Language* (Harvard University Press)

Maclean, Norman (1976), *A River Runs Through It* (Simon & Schuster)

Penrose, Roger (1994), *Shadows of the Mind* (Oxford University Press)

Roosevelt, Theodore (1926), *An Autobiography* (Charles Scribner's Sons)

Roosevelt, Theodore (1926), *Literary Essays* (Charles Scribner's Sons)

Scott, Alwyn (1996), 'On Quantum Theories of the Mind', *Journal of Consciousness Studies*, **3** (5/6), pp. 484-491.

Washington, Peter (1995), *Madame Blavatsky's Baboon* (Schocken Books)

White, Stewart Edward (1902), *The Blazed Trail* (McClure, Phillips & Co.)

White, Stewart Edward (1912), The *Land of Footprints* (Doubleday Page & Company)

White, Stewart Edward (1931), *Daniel Boone, Wilderness Scout* (Doubleday, Doran & Company)

White, Stewart Edward (1937), *The Betty Book* (E.P. Dutton)

White, Stewart Edward (1939), *Across the Unknown* (E.P. Dutton)

White, Stewart Edward (1940), *The Unobstructed Universe* (E.P. Dutton)

White, Stewart Edward (1942), *The Road I Know* (E.P. Dutton)

White, Stewart Edward (1946), *The Stars Are Still There* (E.P. Dutton)

White, Stewart Edward (1974), *The Gaelic Manuscripts*, (The Panthean Press)

Whitehead, Alfred North (1960) *Religion in the Making* (Macmillan)

Whitehead, Alfred North (1925), *Science and the Modern World* (Macmillan)

Whitehead, Alfred North (1929), *Process and Reality* (The Macmillan Company)

Whitehead, Alfred North (1960), *Process and Reality* (Harper Torchbook)